# GREAT COOKIES
# YOU CAN BAKE

# GREAT
# COOKIES
## YOU CAN BAKE

## LOIS HILL

GRAMERCY BOOKS
New York • Avenel, New Jersey

This 1992 edition is published by Gramercy Books, distributed by Outlet Book
Company, Inc., a Random House Company, 40 Engelhard Avenue, Avenel, New Jersey
07001.

Printed and bound in the United States of America

Library of Congress Cataloging-in-Publication Data

Hill, Lois.
    Great cookies you can bake / Lois Hill.
        p.      cm.
    ISBN 0-517-69418-2
    1. Cookies.    I. Title.    II. Title: Great cookies you can bake.
TX772.H55    1990
641.8'654—dc20                                                89-29231
                                                                 CIP


8  7  6  5

# CONTENTS

ACKNOWLEDGMENTS

Grateful acknowledgment is given to Phyllis Sternau for the use of
her Gaufrettes Unlimited creations and also to Lucille Santarelli
for her wonderful family recipes. Thanks to Susan Liebegott for her
careful reading of these pages.

# INTRODUCTION

Nothing tastes quite as good as a homemade cookie fresh from the oven. From American classics to international temptations, these recipes will keep your cookie jar filled with delicious treats. Here are 365 great cookie recipes that will add a special spice to every day of the year. There are cookies for all seasons—holiday cookies and party cookies, cookies for midnight snacks and birthday treats, and just plain cookies to bake on a rainy day.

There are bars, brownies, drop cookies, macaroons, meringues, hand-rolled cookies, cookie cutter and pressed cookies, special one-of-a-kind cookies, and sugar-free cookies. The recipes are grouped under their categories, following a natural progression from simple bars to more complex creations, and are alphabetical within each section, except where variation follows theme.

Among this vast assortment of recipes are a few that purists may find a bit off the beaten cookie track. The character of a cookie is naturally defined by its culture—crullers, for instance, are considered cookies in the American South, as are doughnuts in the North. Cream puffs, an elegant afternoon treat with tea or coffee in Europe, have been relegated to the pastry case in the United States. The chess cake, a small relative of the chess pie, takes its cookie origins from the culinary and cookie history of Colonial America. Whatever small liberties have been taken, the selection of cookies presented here reflects a wide variety of cultures and tastes.

Successful cookies require more than just a good recipe and careful measuring. The suggestions that follow will help you make freshly baked cookies that taste just the way you have always imagined they would—absolutely delicious.

- Assemble the ingredients before you begin.
- Always preheat the oven for at least 15 minutes before baking, or until the oven's temperature indicator tells you the desired temperature has been reached. A good technique is to turn the oven on when you begin to assemble the ingredients for baking, except when you're making cookies for which the dough has to be chilled or there are other special instructions. (Be sure to read the recipe through once before beginning, to see if there are any special instructions.)
- Measure all ingredients carefully.

- Always use standard measuring spoons and measuring cups.
- Flour becomes somewhat compressed in the package. One cup of sifted flour is actually less flour than one cup of unsifted flour, so if a recipe calls for sifted flour be sure to sift it.
- For the greatest accuracy, always level the surface of the filled measuring cup or spoon with a flat kitchen knife.
- Dark brown sugar "packs" more densely than refined or light brown sugar. "Firmly packed" means just that; press the sugar firmly into the measuring cup or spoon until it is filled.
- Bake cookies in batches. Two large baking sheets are essential baking equipment. The heavier the weight of the baking sheets, the more evenly the heat will be distributed and the better the cookies will bake. Poor quality baking sheets may cause cookies to bake too quickly and to burn.
- To grease a baking sheet, use about two tablespoons of shortening. Using a paper towel, press the shortening firmly into the bottom and sides of the baking sheet. There are two types of shortening used for greasing: butter or vegetable shortening. Butter is more likely to burn, but many people feel that buttering a baking sheet gives additional flavor to the cookies. Vegetable shortening is safer and certainly more practical for anyone restricting their butter intake.
- There is no need to regrease a baking sheet once it has been greased for the first batch of cookies. Simply wipe off any excess crumbs with a paper towel after the cookies have been removed. Do not wash the baking sheets until all the cookies have been baked.
- Always let the baking sheet cool before placing another batch of unbaked cookies on it. A hot baking sheet will melt the dough prematurely and may alter the texture and the baking time.
- Every oven is different, whether gas or electric. Take the time to learn if your oven runs hot or cold. Then, after a little trial and error, you should be able to adjust the standard baking times given in these recipes to accommodate your oven.
- Remember that heat rises. The top rack of any oven is always hotter. When baking delicate cookies, use only the bottom rack of the oven. When using both racks, always check the cookies on the top rack several minutes before they are supposed to be done. You will find that most cookies brown faster on the top rack. To maintain an even heat, you should make sure that the baking sheets do not touch the walls of the oven.
- Use a wire rack to cool the cookies. If you must use a plate, do not stack the cookies on top of each other, even under a layer of waxed paper. Use a separate plate for each layer of cookies.
- Store cooled cookies in a tightly closed jar or tin, or on a serving plate covered with plastic wrap and layered with sheets of waxed

paper. Most cookies may be frozen in plastic bags after they have been baked and cooled.
- Ingredients hints:

For the best results, always use the whites of jumbo eggs to prepare cookies such as meringues and macaroons.

Solid vegetable shortening, given as an ingredient here, is most commonly sold under the brand name of Crisco®.

Substituting margarine for butter: you may substitute the equivalent amount of margarine for butter in all of these recipes, but the cookies will not taste quite the same as if they had been prepared with butter.

Rose water, an aromatic flavoring, is sold in food specialty shops and Middle Eastern groceries.

Liquors or liqueurs may be substituted or augmented with whatever you have on hand. Bourbon, for instance, could be used instead of Scotch whiskey, or brandy instead of cherry liqueur. Flavoring substitutes, such as brandy flavoring, are often stronger than the original ingredients. One teaspoon of brandy may be replaced with ½ teaspoon of brandy flavoring. You'll need to add ½ teaspoon of water to rebalance the liquid requirements of the recipe when making this substitution, or any substitution using a different amount of liquid than what is called for in the recipe.

Always use cake flour when it is specified in a recipe. Cake flour is made from softer wheat than all-purpose flour, and gives a more crumbly texture to baked goods.

Any flour ages and becomes damp. Particularly for baking pastry sheets and many of the special cookies here, it is recommended that you purchase a fresh package of flour to ensure the best results.
- Appliances:

The days of the strong arm and the wooden spoon are over, although, in a pinch, you can still do things the old-fashioned way. A table-top or hand-held electric mixer is essential equipment in the cookie kitchen. Anyone who has ever spent time beating egg whites by hand will applaud this miracle of culinary technology. A food processor is terrific for creaming butter and beating medium-weight batters. Unless you're beating two or more egg whites, don't try it in the food processor—the liquid volume is not great enough for proper results. Chop the nuts in a food processor and they won't end up all over the floor! Ground nuts may be purchased in food specialty stores or nuts may be ground to order at home. A coffee grinder that has never been used for coffee makes a handy, inexpensive nut grinder.

Whether you're baking florentines and pfeffernusse or recreating the chocolate chip cookies of childhood, *Great Cookies You Can Bake* will fill your cookie jar with sweet, delicious memories.

# *Bars*

The simplest of all cookies, bar cookies—actually a square or rectangular cake that is cut into squares or bars—are almost foolproof to bake. Chewy caramel bars, crunchy granola bars, tempting fresh fruit bars, no-bake bars, three-layer cookies, forgotten cookies, and stained-glass windows are only a few of the delicious recipes that follow. When cutting the bars, to avoid crumbling edges use a sharp knife rinsed frequently in cold water. Although they are actually bar cookies, brownies have been given their own special section by popular demand.

NO. 1

## ALMOND BARS

*Makes about 24 bars*

½ cup unsalted butter
2 eggs plus 2 egg yolks
1½ cups sugar
½ teaspoon almond extract
½ teaspoon grated lemon zest

1 cup sifted flour
½ cup ground almonds
2 egg whites
   Confectioners' sugar

Preheat the oven to 325° F. Thoroughly butter the bottom and sides of a 13 × 9 × 2 inch baking pan.

Melt the butter in a small saucepan over very low heat. Remove from heat and set aside.

In a large mixing bowl, beat the eggs and the egg yolks until foamy. Gradually beat in the sugar, ½ cup at a time, continuing to beat until the batter is light and airy. Mix in the almond extract and the lemon zest. Add the melted butter and mix thoroughly. Stir in the flour all at once. Mix well. Stir in the ground almonds. In a separate bowl, beat the egg whites until they form stiff peaks. Gently fold the egg whites into the batter.

Pour the batter into the baking pan. Smooth with a rubber spatula. Bake for 30 to 35 minutes, or until a toothpick inserted in the center comes out clean. Remove from the oven.

Allow the cake to cool completely, then cut it into 2-inch bars. Remove the bars from the pan with a spatula. Roll each bar in confectioners' sugar and transfer to a serving plate.

NO. **2**                          # APPLE SQUARES

*Makes about 24 bars*

2 eggs
1 cup sugar
1 teaspoon vanilla extract
1 teaspoon grated lemon zest
1 cup sifted flour
2 tablespoons baking powder
½ teaspoon salt

1 teaspoon cinnamon
½ teaspoon allspice
½ teaspoon mace
3 Granny Smith apples,
     peeled, cored, and diced
1 cup walnuts, coarsely
     chopped

Preheat the oven to 375° F. Thoroughly butter the bottom and sides of a 13 × 9 × 2 inch baking pan.

In a large mixing bowl, beat the eggs until foamy. Gradually beat in the sugar, then add the vanilla extract and the lemon zest.

Sift together the flour, baking powder, salt, cinnamon, allspice, and mace. Add the flour mixture to the batter, ⅓ cup at a time. Mix the apples and walnuts together, then stir the mixture into the batter. Pour the batter into the baking pan and smooth the surface with a rubber spatula. Bake for 35 to 40 minutes, or until a toothpick inserted in the center comes out clean. Remove from the oven.

Allow the cake to cool completely, then cut it into 2-inch squares. Remove the squares from the pan with a spatula and transfer to a serving plate.

NO. **3**                # APPLESAUCE WALNUT BARS

*Makes about 24 bars*

½ cup unsalted butter,
     softened
1 cup sugar
2 eggs
1 teaspoon vanilla extract
4 cups sifted flour
2 teaspoons cinnamon

½ teaspoon mace
2 teaspoons baking soda
1 cup unsweetened
     applesauce
1 cup walnuts, coarsely
     chopped

Preheat the oven to 375° F. Thoroughly butter the bottom and sides of a 13 × 9 × 2 inch baking pan.

In a large mixing bowl, cream together the butter and sugar. Beat in the eggs, one at a time. Add the vanilla extract. Sift together the flour, cinnamon, mace, and baking soda. Add the flour mixture to the batter, ½ cup at a time, alternating with the applesauce. Mix the chopped walnuts into the batter.

Pour the batter into the baking pan and smooth the surface with a rubber spatula. Bake for 35 to 40 minutes, or until a toothpick inserted in the center comes out clean. Remove from the oven.

Allow the cake to cool completely, then cut it into 2-inch bars. Remove the bars from the pan with a spatula and transfer to a serving plate.

## NO. 4      APRICOT WALNUT BARS

*Makes about 24 bars*

3 egg whites
¼ teaspoon cream of tartar
1 cup superfine sugar
1 teaspoon vanilla extract
1 cup sifted flour
1 teaspoon baking powder

1½ cups dried apricots, coarsely chopped
1 cup walnuts, coarsely chopped
Confectioners' sugar

Preheat the oven to 350° F. Thoroughly butter the bottom and sides of a 13 × 9 × 2 inch baking pan.

In a large mixing bowl, beat the egg whites with the cream of tartar until the mixture begins to hold soft peaks. Gradually beat in the sugar, a little at a time, until the batter is thick and glossy. Beat in the vanilla extract. Sift the flour with the baking powder. Add the flour mixture to the batter, ½ cup at a time. Gently fold in the chopped apricots and walnuts.

Pour the batter into the baking pan and smooth the surface with a rubber spatula. Bake for about 30 minutes, or until a toothpick inserted in the center comes out clean. Remove from the oven.

Allow the cake to cool completely, then cut it into 2-inch bars. Remove the bars from the pan with a spatula. Roll each bar in confectioners' sugar and arrange on a serving plate.

## NO. 5      ARROWROOT BARS

*Makes about 24 bars*

1 cup unsalted butter, softened
½ cup confectioners' sugar
½ teaspoon almond extract

2 cups arrowroot flour
6 egg whites
½ teaspoon cream of tartar
Confectioners' sugar

Preheat the oven to 350° F. Thoroughly butter the bottom and sides of a 13 × 9 × 2 inch baking pan.

In a large mixing bowl, cream together the butter and sugar. Beat in the almond extract. Gradually mix in the arrowroot flour. In a separate bowl, beat the egg whites and cream of tartar until stiff peaks form. Gently fold the egg whites into the batter.

Pour the batter into the baking pan and smooth the surface with a rubber spatula. Bake for 30 minutes, or until a toothpick inserted in the center comes out clean. Remove from the oven.

Allow the cake to cool completely, then cut it into 2-inch bars. Sprinkle with confectioners' sugar. Remove the bars from the pan with a spatula and transfer to a serving plate.

## NO. 6                                   BLONDIES

*Makes about 24 bars*

½ cup unsalted butter
4 eggs
2 cups sugar
1 teaspoon vanilla extract

1 cup sifted flour
1 cup walnuts, coarsely
   chopped

Preheat the oven to 325° F. Thoroughly butter the bottom and sides of a 13 × 9 × 2 inch baking pan.

Melt the butter in a small saucepan over very low heat. Remove the pan from the heat and set aside.

In a large mixing bowl, beat the eggs until foamy. Gradually beat in the sugar, ½ cup at a time, continuing to beat until the batter is light and airy. Mix in the vanilla extract. Add the melted butter and mix thoroughly. Stir in the flour all at once. Mix well. Stir in the chopped walnuts.

Pour the batter into the baking pan and smooth the surface with a rubber spatula. Bake for 30 minutes, or until a toothpick inserted in the center comes out clean. Remove from the oven.

Allow the cake to cool completely, then cut it into 2-inch bars. Remove the bars from the pan with a spatula and transfer to a serving plate.

## NO. 7                                   BLUEBERRY BARS

*Makes about 20 bars*

6 tablespoons unsalted butter,
   softened
¾ cup dark brown sugar,
   firmly packed
1 egg
1 teaspoon vanilla extract
¾ cup sifted flour
½ teaspoon baking powder
1 teaspoon cinnamon

¼ teaspoon nutmeg
1 teaspoon allspice
¼ teaspoon salt
½ cup walnuts, coarsely
   chopped
2 cups fresh or frozen
   blueberries
Confectioners' sugar

Preheat the oven to 350° F. Thoroughly butter the bottom and sides of an 8 × 8 × 2 inch baking pan.

In a large mixing bowl, cream together the butter and sugar. Beat in the egg and add the vanilla extract. Sift the flour with the baking powder, cinnamon, nutmeg, allspice, and salt. Add the chopped walnuts and blueberries to the batter. Stir in the flour mixture a little at a time.

Pour the batter into the baking pan and smooth the surface with a rubber spatula. Bake for 30 minutes, or until a toothpick inserted in the center comes out clean. Remove from the oven.

Allow the cake to cool completely, then cut it into 2-inch bars. Dust with confectioners' sugar. Remove the bars from the pan with a spatula and transfer to a serving plate.

## NO. 8     BLUEBERRY CHERRY SQUARES

*Makes about 20 bars*

¼ cup unsalted butter,
    softened
1 cup sugar
1 egg
1 teaspoon vanilla extract
½ teaspoon ginger
2 cups sifted flour

2 teaspoons baking powder
1 cup milk
½ cup fresh or frozen
    blueberries
½ cup fresh cherries, halved
    and pitted

Preheat the oven to 350° F. Thoroughly butter the bottom and sides of an 8 × 8 × 2 inch baking pan.

In a large mixing bowl, cream together the butter and sugar. Add the egg and beat in thoroughly. Add the vanilla extract and ginger and mix well. Sift the flour with the baking powder. Add the flour to the sugar mixture, alternating with the milk. Beat until smooth, then stir in the blueberries and cherry halves.

Pour the batter into the baking pan and smooth the surface with a rubber spatula. Bake for 30 minutes, or until a toothpick inserted in the center comes out clean. Remove from the oven.

Allow the cake to cool completely, then cut it into 2-inch squares. Remove the squares from the pan with a spatula and transfer to a serving plate.

## NO. 9     BROWN SUGAR WALNUT SQUARES

*Makes about 20 bars*

1 egg
1 cup dark brown sugar,
    firmly packed
1 teaspoon vanilla extract
1 teaspoon grated orange zest
½ cup sifted flour

¼ teaspoon baking soda
¼ teaspoon salt
1½ cups walnuts, coarsely
    chopped

Preheat the oven to 350° F. Thoroughly butter the bottom and sides of an 8 × 8 × 2 inch baking pan.

In a large mixing bowl, beat the egg until foamy. Gradually beat in the sugar. Continue to beat until the batter thickens. Add the vanilla extract and orange zest. Sift the flour with the baking soda and salt. Stir the flour mixture into the batter. Mix well. Add the chopped walnuts.

Pour the batter into the baking pan and smooth the surface with a rubber spatula. Bake for 20 to 25 minutes, or until a toothpick inserted in the center comes out clean. Remove from the oven.

Allow the cake to cool completely, then cut it into 2-inch squares. Remove the squares from the pan with a spatula and transfer to a serving plate.

NO. **10**                          # CARAMEL BARS
*Makes about 24 bars*

½ cup unsalted butter
4 eggs
2 cups sugar
1 teaspoon vanilla extract

1 cup sifted flour
1 cup walnuts, coarsely
   chopped

## Icing

2 tablespoons heavy cream
½ cup dark brown sugar,
   firmly packed

2 tablespoons unsalted butter
1½ cups confectioners' sugar
2 teaspoons vanilla extract

Preheat the oven to 325° F. Thoroughly butter the bottom and sides of a 13 × 9 × 2 inch baking pan.

Melt the butter in a small saucepan over very low heat. Remove the pan from the heat and set aside.

In a large mixing bowl, beat the eggs until foamy. Gradually add the sugar, ½ cup at a time, continuing to beat until the mixture is light and airy. Mix in the vanilla extract. Add the melted butter and mix thoroughly. Stir in the flour all at once. Add the chopped walnuts and mix well.

Pour the batter into the baking pan and smooth the surface with a rubber spatula. Bake for 30 minutes, or until a toothpick inserted in the center comes out clean. Remove from the oven. Before preparing the icing, allow the bars to cool thoroughly.

To make the icing, combine the cream and the brown sugar in a small saucepan. Bring to a boil over moderate heat, stirring constantly, and continue to boil for 5 minutes. Remove the pan from the heat, and stir in the butter. Pour the confectioners' sugar into a mixing bowl. Add the brown sugar mixture and beat until smooth. Mix in the vanilla extract. Using a spatula, frost the top of the cooled cake. After the icing has hardened, cut the cake into 2-inch bars.

NO. 11                           # CARROT BARS
                                 *Makes about 24 bars*

½ cup margarine, softened
1 cup light brown sugar
2 eggs
1 teaspoon vanilla extract
1 teaspoon grated lemon zest
1 cup grated raw carrots

1 cup walnuts, coarsely
    chopped
1½ cups sifted flour
1½ teaspoons baking powder
1 teaspoon cinnamon
¼ cup orange juice

Preheat the oven to 375° F. Thoroughly grease the bottom and sides of a 13 × 9 × 2 inch baking pan.

In a large mixing bowl, cream together the margarine and the sugar. Beat in the eggs, one at a time, mixing well after each addition. Stir in the vanilla extract and the lemon zest.

Mix the grated carrots and the chopped walnuts into the batter. Sift together the flour, baking powder, and cinnamon. Add the flour mixture, ½ cup at a time, to the batter, alternating with the orange juice.

Pour the batter into the baking pan and smooth the surface with a rubber spatula. Bake for about 25 minutes, or until a toothpick inserted in the center comes out clean. Remove from the oven.

Allow the cake to cool completely, then cut it into 2-inch bars. Remove the bars from the pan with a spatula and transfer to a serving plate.

NO. 12                           # CHEESECAKE BARS
                                 *Makes about 20 bars*

*Crust and Topping*

⅓ cup unsalted butter
⅓ cup light brown sugar
1 cup sifted flour

½ cup blanched almonds,
    finely chopped

*Filling*

8-ounce package cream cheese
¼ cup sugar
1 tablespoon lemon juice

2 tablespoons heavy cream
1 teaspoon vanilla extract

Preheat the oven to 350° F. Thoroughly grease the bottom and sides of an 8 × 8 × 2 inch baking pan.

First make the crust and topping. Melt the butter in a small saucepan over very low heat. In a large mixing bowl, combine the melted butter, sugar, and flour. Add the chopped almonds. Reserving 1 cup for the topping, press the rest of the mixture firmly into the bottom and sides of the baking pan. Bake for 12 minutes. Remove from the oven and set aside. Leave the oven on.

Make the filling. In a small mixing bowl, combine the cream cheese with the sugar, lemon juice, cream, and vanilla extract. Pour this mixture into the baked crust. Sprinkle the remaining almond mixture evenly over the filling. Return the pan to the oven and bake for an additional 25 minutes. Remove from the oven.

Allow the cake to cool completely, then cut it into 2-inch bars. Remove the bars from the pan with a spatula and transfer to a serving plate.

NO. 13

# CHOCOLATE CARAMEL RAISIN BARS

*Makes about 24 bars*

| | |
|---|---|
| ½ cup unsalted butter | 2 cups sugar |
| 4 ounces (4 squares) unsweetened baking chocolate | 1 teaspoon vanilla extract |
| | 1 cup sifted flour |
| | 1 cup raisins |
| 4 eggs | |

## *Icing*

| | |
|---|---|
| 1 tablespoon heavy cream | 2 tablespoons unsalted butter |
| 1 tablespoon strong black coffee | 1½ cups confectioners' sugar |
| ½ cup dark brown sugar, firmly packed | 2 teaspoons vanilla extract |

Preheat the oven to 325° F. Thoroughly butter the bottom and sides of a 13 × 9 × 2 inch baking pan.

Melt the butter and chocolate in a small saucepan over very low heat, stirring constantly. Remove the pan from the heat and set aside.

In a large mixing bowl, beat the eggs until foamy. Gradually add the sugar, ½ cup at a time, continuing to beat until the mixture is light and airy. Mix in the vanilla extract. Add the melted butter and chocolate and mix thoroughly. Stir in the flour all at once. Mix the raisins into the batter.

Pour the batter into the baking pan and smooth the surface with a rubber spatula. Bake for 30 minutes, or until a toothpick inserted in the center comes out clean. Remove from the oven. Before preparing the icing, allow the cake to cool completely.

To make the icing, combine the cream, coffee, and sugar in a small saucepan. Bring to a boil over moderate heat, stirring constantly, and continue to boil for 5 minutes. Turn off the heat, and stir in the butter. Set aside. Pour the confectioners' sugar into a mixing bowl. Stir in the brown sugar mixture and beat until smooth. Mix in the vanilla extract.

Frost the cooled cake. After the icing hardens, cut the cake into 2-inch bars. Remove the bars from the pan with a spatula and transfer to a serving plate.

NO. 14

# CHOCOLATE CHIP TOFFEE BARS

*Makes about 24 bars*

1 cup unsalted butter, softened
1 cup dark brown sugar, firmly packed
1 egg
1 teaspoon vanilla extract
1 teaspoon grated orange zest

2 cups sifted flour
½ teaspoon baking soda
1 cup semi-sweet chocolate morsels
½ cup pecans, coarsely chopped

Preheat the oven to 350° F. Thoroughly butter the bottom and sides of a 13 × 9 × 2 inch baking pan.

In a large mixing bowl, cream together the butter and sugar. Beat in the egg. Add the vanilla extract and orange zest. Sift the flour with the baking soda. Beat the flour into the batter. Stir in the chocolate morsels and the chopped pecans.

Pour the batter into the baking pan and smooth the surface with a rubber spatula. Bake for about 25 minutes, or until a toothpick inserted in the center comes out clean. Remove from the oven.

Allow the cake to cool completely, then cut it into 2-inch bars. Remove the bars from the pan with a spatula and transfer to a serving plate.

NO. 15

# MINT CHOCOLATE CHIP TOFFEE BARS

*Makes about 24 bars*

Follow the recipe for Chocolate Chip Toffee Bars (No. 14), substituting mint chocolate morsels for the semi-sweet chocolate morsels.

NO. **16**       **CHOCOLATE CRISPIES**

*Makes about 24 bars*

4 ounces (4 squares) unsweetened baking chocolate
½ cup unsalted butter
2 eggs
1 cup sugar
1 teaspoon vanilla extract
½ teaspoon cinnamon
½ cup sifted flour
½ cup pecans, finely chopped

Preheat the oven to 400° F. Thoroughly butter the bottom and sides of a 13 × 9 × 2 inch baking pan.

In a small saucepan over very low heat, melt the chocolate with the butter, stirring frequently. Remove the pan from the heat and set aside.

In a large mixing bowl, beat the eggs until foamy. Gradually beat in the sugar and continue to beat until the mixture is light and thick. Beat in the vanilla extract and cinnamon. Add the melted chocolate mixture. Stir in the flour all at once.

Pour the batter into the baking pan and smooth the surface with a rubber spatula. Sprinkle the chopped pecans on top of the batter. Bake for about 10 minutes, or until a toothpick inserted in the center comes out clean. Remove from the oven.

Allow the cake to cool completely, then cut it into 2-inch bars. Remove the bars from the pan with a spatula and transfer to a serving plate.

NO. **17**       **CHOCOLATE GRANOLA BARS**

*Makes about 24 bars*

4 ounces (4 squares) unsweetened baking chocolate
½ cup unsalted butter, softened
1 cup dark brown sugar, firmly packed
½ cup sugar
1 egg
1 teaspoon vanilla extract
1 tablespoon dark molasses
1 cup sifted flour
1 teaspoon baking powder
½ teaspoon salt
1 cup granola cereal
1 cup rolled oats
¾ cup walnuts, coarsely chopped

Preheat the oven to 350° F. Thoroughly butter the bottom and sides of a 13 × 9 × 2 inch baking pan.

Melt the chocolate in the top of a double boiler over simmering water, stirring frequently. Remove the pan from the heat and set aside.

In a large mixing bowl, cream together the butter and sugars. Beat in the egg and mix well. Stir in the melted chocolate. Add the vanilla extract and the molasses. Sift the flour with the baking powder and salt. In a separate bowl, combine the flour mixture with the granola and rolled oats. Work the flour mixture into the batter, 1 cup at a time, mixing well after each addition. Stir in the chopped walnuts.

Turn the batter into the prepared baking pan and smooth the surface with the back of a wooden spoon. Bake for about 15 minutes, or until the top of the cake is firm to the touch and golden brown. Remove from the oven.

Allow the cake to cool completely, then cut it into 2-inch bars. Remove the bars from the pan with a spatula and transfer to a serving plate.

NO. 18                                    **COCONUT APPLE BARS**
*Makes about 24 bars*

2 eggs
1 cup sugar
1 teaspoon vanilla extract
1 teaspoon grated lemon zest
1 cup sifted flour
2 tablespoons baking powder
½ teaspoon salt
1 teaspoon cinnamon

½ teaspoon allspice
½ teaspoon mace
½ cup walnuts, coarsely
   chopped
2 Granny Smith apples,
   peeled, cored, and diced
1 cup unsweetened shredded
   coconut

Preheat the oven to 375° F. Thoroughly butter the bottom and sides of a 13 × 9 × 2 inch baking pan.

In a large mixing bowl, beat the eggs until foamy. Gradually beat in the sugar, then add the vanilla extract and the lemon zest. Sift together the flour, baking powder, salt, cinnamon, allspice, and mace. Add the flour mixture to the batter, ⅓ cup at a time. Mix the chopped walnuts with the diced apples and coconut. Stir the mixture into the batter.

Pour the batter into the baking pan and smooth the surface with a rubber spatula. Bake for 35 to 40 minutes, or until a toothpick inserted in the center comes out clean. Remove from the oven.

Allow the cake to cool completely, then cut it into 2-inch bars. Remove the bars from the pan with a spatula and transfer to a serving plate.

## NO. 19                    COFFEE CARAMEL BARS
*Makes about 24 bars*

½ cup unsalted butter
4 eggs
2 cups sugar
2 teaspoons coffee liqueur

1 cup sifted flour
1 cup walnuts, coarsely
   chopped

### Icing

1 teaspoon instant espresso
   coffee powder
2 teaspoons vanilla extract
2 tablespoons heavy cream

½ cup dark brown sugar,
   firmly packed
2 tablespoons unsalted butter
1½ cups confectioners' sugar

Preheat the oven to 325° F. Thoroughly butter the bottom and sides of a 13 × 9 × 2 inch baking pan.

Melt the butter in a small saucepan over very low heat. Remove the pan from the heat and set aside.

In a large mixing bowl, beat the eggs until foamy. Gradually add the sugar, ½ cup at a time, continuing to beat until the mixture is light and airy. Mix in the coffee liqueur. Add the melted butter and mix thoroughly. Stir in the flour all at once. Add the chopped walnuts and mix well.

Pour the batter into the baking pan and smooth the surface with a rubber spatula. Bake for 30 minutes, or until a toothpick inserted in the center comes out clean. Remove from the oven. Before preparing the icing, allow the bars to cool completely.

Make the icing. In a small saucepan, combine the espresso powder, vanilla extract, cream, and sugar. Bring to a boil, and cook, stirring constantly, until the mixture thickens. Remove the pan from the heat and stir in the butter. Pour the confectioners' sugar into a mixing bowl. Add the brown sugar mixture and beat until smooth. Frost the cooled cake. After the icing hardens, cut the cake into 2-inch bars. Remove the bars from the pan with a spatula and transfer to a serving plate.

## NO. 20                          CRANBERRY BARS
*Makes about 24 bars*

2 eggs
1 cup sugar
1 teaspoon vanilla extract
1 teaspoon grated orange zest
1 cup sifted flour
2 tablespoons baking powder
½ teaspoon salt

2 teaspoons allspice
¼ teaspoon nutmeg
2 cups fresh or frozen
   cranberries, coarsely
   chopped
1 cup walnuts, coarsely
   chopped

Preheat the oven to 375° F. Thoroughly butter the bottom and sides of a 13 × 9 × 2 inch baking pan.

In a large mixing bowl, beat the eggs until foamy. Gradually beat in the sugar, then add the vanilla extract and the orange zest. Sift together the flour, baking powder, salt, allspice, and nutmeg. Add the flour mixture to the batter, ⅓ cup at a time. Stir in the chopped cranberries and walnuts.

Pour the batter into the baking pan and smooth the surface with a rubber spatula. Bake for 35 to 40 minutes, or until a toothpick inserted in the center comes out clean. Remove from the oven.

Allow the cake to cool completely, then cut it into 2-inch bars. Remove the bars from the pan with a spatula and transfer to a serving plate.

## NO. 21     CRUNCHY CORNFLAKE BARS

*Makes about 24 bars*

½ cup unsalted butter, softened

½ cup dark brown sugar, firmly packed

½ cup sugar

1 egg

1 teaspoon vanilla extract

1 tablespoon dark molasses

1 cup sifted flour

1 teaspoon baking powder

½ teaspoon salt

2 cups cornflakes

¾ cup pecans, coarsely chopped

Preheat the oven to 350° F. Thoroughly butter the bottom and sides of a 13 × 9 × 2 inch baking pan.

In a large mixing bowl, cream together the butter and sugars. Beat in the egg and mix well. Add the vanilla extract and the molasses. Sift the flour with the baking powder and salt. Combine the flour mixture with the cornflakes. Work the flour mixture into the batter, 1 cup at a time, mixing gently but well after each addition. Stir in the chopped pecans.

Turn the batter into the prepared baking pan and smooth the surface with the back of a wooden spoon. Bake for about 15 minutes, or until the top of the cake is firm to the touch and golden brown. Remove from the oven.

Allow the cake to cool completely, then cut it into 2-inch bars. Remove the bars from the pan with a spatula and transfer to a serving plate.

NO. **22**                        **CRUNCHY CHOCOLATE
                                    RAISIN BARS**
                                    *Makes about 20 bars*

¼ cup unsalted butter          ½ cup dark brown sugar,
½ cup sifted flour                  firmly packed
½ cup ground walnuts           ¼ teaspoon baking soda

*Topping*

½ cup golden raisins           ½ cup sugar
2 tablespoons Scotch whiskey   1 egg, beaten
2 ounces (2 squares)           1 teaspoon vanilla extract
   unsweetened baking          ¼ cup sifted flour
   chocolate                   ½ teaspoon cinnamon
¼ cup unsalted butter          ½ teaspoon mace

Preheat the oven to 350° F. Lightly grease an 8 × 8 × 2 inch
baking pan with butter or vegetable shortening.

In a small saucepan over very low heat, melt the butter. In a large
mixing bowl, combine the melted butter, flour, walnuts, brown sugar,
and baking soda. Work the mixture until it has the texture of coarse
oatmeal. Press the mixture into the bottom of the baking pan in an
even layer. Bake for 15 minutes. Remove from the oven. Leave the
oven on.

While the cake is baking, make the topping. Soak the raisins in
the Scotch whiskey. In a small saucepan over very low heat, melt
the chocolate with the butter, stirring frequently. Remove the pan
from the heat, and beat the mixture into the white sugar in a small
bowl. Add the egg and vanilla extract. Sift the flour with the cinnamon
and mace. Stir into the sugar mixture. Finally, stir in the raisins and
any remaining Scotch.

Spoon the topping evenly over the cake and smooth the surface
with a rubber spatula. Return to the oven and bake for an additional
15 minutes, or until a knife inserted in the cake comes out clean.
Remove from the oven.

Allow the cake to cool completely, then cut it into 2-inch bars.
Remove the bars from the pan with a spatula and transfer to a serving
plate.

NO. **23**        **CURRANT BARS**

*Makes about 24 bars*

1 cup unsalted butter,
    softened
1 cup sugar
4 eggs

1 cup sifted flour
½ teaspoon baking powder
1 cup dried currants

Preheat the oven to 350° F. Thoroughly butter the bottom and sides of a 13 × 9 × 2 inch baking pan.

In a large mixing bowl, cream together the butter and sugar. Add the eggs one at a time, beating well after each addition. Sift the flour with the baking powder. Beat the flour mixture into the batter, ½ cup at time. Stir until the batter is smooth. Mix in the currants.

Pour the batter into the baking pan and smooth the surface with a rubber spatula. Bake for 30 minutes, or until a toothpick inserted in the center comes out clean. Remove from the oven.

Allow the cake to cool completely, then cut it into 2-inch bars. Remove the bars from the pan with a spatula and transfer to a serving plate.

NO. **24**        **DATE STRIPS**

*Makes about 24 bars*

3 egg whites
¼ teaspoon cream of tartar
1 cup superfine sugar
1 teaspoon vanilla extract
1 cup sifted flour
1 teaspoon baking powder

1½ cups pitted dates, coarsely
    chopped
1 cup walnuts, coarsely
    chopped
Confectioners' sugar

Preheat the oven to 350° F. Thoroughly butter the bottom and sides of a 13 × 9 × 2 inch baking pan.

In a large mixing bowl, beat the egg whites with the cream of tartar until the mixture begins to hold soft peaks. Gradually beat in the sugar, a little at a time, continuing to beat until the mixture is thick and glossy. Beat in the vanilla extract. Sift the flour with the baking powder and fold into the egg white mixture. Gently fold in the chopped dates and walnuts.

Pour the batter into the baking pan and smooth the surface with a rubber spatula. Bake for about 30 minutes, or until a toothpick inserted in the center comes out clean. Remove from the oven.

Allow the cake to cool completely, then cut it into 2-inch bars. Remove the bars from the pan with a spatula, roll them in confectioners' sugar, then arrange them on a serving plate.

NO. **25**

# DOUBLE CHOCOLATE TOFFEE BARS
*Makes about 24 bars*

4 ounces (4 squares) unsweetened baking chocolate
1 cup unsalted butter, softened
1½ cups dark brown sugar, firmly packed
1 egg
1 teaspoon vanilla extract

1 teaspoon grated orange zest
2 cups sifted flour
½ teaspoon baking soda
1 cup milk chocolate morsels
½ cup walnuts, coarsely chopped

Preheat the oven to 350° F. Thoroughly butter the bottom and sides of a 13 × 9 × 2 inch baking pan.

Melt the chocolate in the top of a double boiler over simmering water, stirring frequently. Remove the pan from the heat and set aside.

In a large mixing bowl, cream together the butter and sugar. Beat in the egg. Add the vanilla extract and the orange zest. Stir in the melted chocolate. Sift the flour with the baking soda. Beat the flour into the batter. Stir in the chocolate morsels and the chopped walnuts.

Pour the batter into the baking pan and smooth the surface with a rubber spatula. Bake for about 30 minutes. Remove from the oven.

Allow the cake to cool completely, then cut it into 2-inch bars. Remove the bars from the pan with a spatula and transfer to a serving plate.

NO. **26**

# DUTCH COCONUT SHORTBREAD BARS
*Makes about 24 bars*

½ cup unsalted butter, softened
2 cups sifted flour

½ cup sugar
1 tablespoon water

### Topping

1 cup dark brown sugar, firmly packed
1 cup walnuts, finely chopped
1 cup unsweetened shredded coconut

2 eggs
2 tablespoons flour
½ teaspoon baking powder

Preheat the oven to 325° F. Thoroughly butter the bottom and sides of a 13 × 9 × 2 inch baking pan.

In a large mixing bowl, cut the butter into large pieces. Gradually add the flour and sugar to the butter, using a pastry blender, or two forks, to combine the dry ingredients thoroughly. Add the water and work the mixture into a thick dough. Press the dough firmly into the bottom of the baking pan. Bake for 25 minutes. Remove from the oven, and reduce the oven temperature to 275° F.

Make the topping. In a large mixing bowl, combine the sugar, chopped walnuts, coconut, eggs, flour, and baking powder. Mix thoroughly. Sprinkle the topping evenly onto the browned shortbread base and smooth the surface with a rubber spatula. Bake for about 25 minutes, or until a toothpick inserted in the center comes out clean. Remove from the oven.

Allow the cake to cool completely, then cut it into 2-inch bars. Remove the bars from the pan with a spatula and transfer to a serving plate.

NO. **27**

# FIG BARS

*Makes about 24 bars*

3 egg whites
¼ teaspoon cream of tartar
1 cup superfine sugar
1 teaspoon vanilla extract
1 cup sifted flour
1 teaspoon baking powder

1½ cups dried figs, coarsely chopped
1 cup pecans, coarsely chopped
Confectioners' sugar

Preheat the oven to 350° F. Thoroughly butter the bottom and sides of a 13 × 9 × 2 inch baking pan.

In a large mixing bowl, beat the egg whites with the cream of tartar until the mixture begins to hold soft peaks. Gradually beat in the sugar, a little at a time, until the mixture is thick and glossy. Beat in the vanilla extract. Sift the flour with the baking powder. Fold the flour mixture into the batter. Gently fold in the chopped figs and pecans.

Pour the batter into the baking pan and smooth the surface with a rubber spatula. Bake for about 30 minutes, or until a toothpick inserted in the center comes out clean. Remove from the oven.

Allow the cake to cool completely, then cut it into 2-inch bars. Remove the bars from the pan with a spatula, roll them in confectioners' sugar, and transfer to a serving plate.

NO. **28**                                            # FIVE-LAYER BARS

*Makes about 24 bars*

¼ cup unsalted butter
20 whole graham crackers,
    finely crushed
1 cup unsweetened shredded
    coconut

7½-ounce package butterscotch
    morsels
7½-ounce package semi-sweet
    chocolate morsels
1 cup walnuts, coarsely
    chopped

Preheat the oven to 325° F. Thoroughly butter the bottom and sides of a 13 × 9 × 2 inch baking pan.

In a small saucepan over low heat, melt the butter. Pour the melted butter evenly on the bottom of the baking pan. Sprinkle with a layer of graham cracker crumbs, then add a layer of coconut. Next, make a layer of butterscotch morsels. Add a layer of chocolate morsels. Top with a layer of chopped walnuts. Bake for 30 minutes. Remove from the oven.

Allow the cake to cool completely, then cut it into 2-inch bars. Remove the bars from the pan with a spatula and transfer to a serving plate.

NO. **29**                                            # SIX-LAYER BARS

*Makes about 24 bars*

Follow the recipe for Five-Layer Bars (No. 28), adding an additional layer of 1 cup of milk chocolate morsels before the final layer of walnuts.

NO. **30**                                            # FORGOTTEN COOKIES

*Makes about 24 bars*

These cookies are called "forgotten," because they remain in the oven (with the heat off) overnight.

2 egg whites
½ teaspoon cream of tartar
¼ teaspoon salt
¾ cup sugar

1 teaspoon vanilla extract
½ cup walnuts, finely chopped
½ cup semi-sweet chocolate
    morsels

Preheat the oven to 350° F. Thoroughly butter the bottom and sides of a 13 × 9 × 2 inch baking pan.

In a large mixing bowl, beat together the egg whites, cream of tartar, and salt until the mixture is foamy and begins to hold soft peaks. Gradually beat in the sugar until the mixture is thick and glossy. Beat in the vanilla extract. Gently fold in the chopped walnuts and chocolate morsels.

Pour the batter into the baking pan and smooth the surface with a rubber spatula. Place the baking pan in the oven and *turn off the oven.* Do not open the oven door for at least 12 hours.

The next day, cut the cake into 2-inch bars. Remove the bars from the pan with a spatula and transfer to a serving plate.

NO. 31      **BUTTERSCOTCH FORGOTTEN COOKIES**

*Makes about 24 bars*

Follow the recipe for Forgotten Cookies (No. 30), substituting butterscotch morsels for the semi-sweet chocolate morsels.

NO. 32      **MILK CHOCOLATE FORGOTTEN COOKIES**

*Makes about 24 bars*

Follow the recipe for Forgotten Cookies (No. 30), substituting milk chocolate morsels for the semi-sweet chocolate morsels.

NO. 33      **MINT CHOCOLATE FORGOTTEN COOKIES**

*Makes about 24 bars*

Follow the recipe for Forgotten Cookies (No. 30), substituting mint chocolate morsels for the semi-sweet chocolate morsels.

NO. 34      **GERMAN ALMOND BARS**

*Makes about 24 bars*

½ cup unsalted butter, softened
⅓ cup sugar
3 egg yolks, beaten
1½ cups sifted flour
2 tablespoons milk

3 egg whites
1 cup superfine sugar
1½ cups blanched almonds, finely chopped
2 tablespoons confectioners' sugar

Preheat the oven to 350° F. Thoroughly butter the bottom and sides of a 13 × 9 × 2 inch baking pan.

In a large mixing bowl, cream together the butter and the ⅓ cup of sugar. Beat in the egg yolks. Beat in the flour, ½ cup at a time. Add the milk after the first cup of flour has been mixed in.

Knead the mixture to a smooth dough. If the dough is sticky, add more flour, a little at a time, until it is easier to work. On a floured work surface, roll out the dough to a thickness of ½ inch. Line the bottom of the baking pan with the dough.

In another bowl, beat the egg whites until they hold stiff peaks. Gradually beat in the 1 cup of sugar. Continue beating until the mixture is thick and glossy. Gently fold in the chopped almonds. Pour the batter into the baking pan and smooth the surface with a rubber spatula. Sprinkle with confectioners' sugar. Bake for about 30 minutes, or until a toothpick inserted in the center comes out clean. Remove from the oven.

Allow the cake to cool completely, then cut it into 2-inch bars. Remove the bars from the pan with a spatula and transfer to a serving plate.

## NO. 35     GERMAN CHOCOLATE ALMOND BARS

*Makes about 24 bars*

2 eggs
1 cup dark brown sugar, firmly packed
1 teaspoon vanilla extract
1 ounce (1 square) unsweetened baking chocolate, grated

¼ cup ground almonds
2 cups sifted flour
1 tablespoon baking powder
¼ teaspoon cinnamon

Preheat the oven to 350° F. Thoroughly butter the bottom and sides of a 13 × 9 × 2 inch baking pan.

In a large mixing bowl, beat the eggs until foamy. Gradually beat in the sugar. Continue beating until the mixture is thick. Add the vanilla extract and the grated chocolate. Mix well. Stir in the ground almonds. Sift the flour with the baking powder and cinnamon. Beat the flour mixture into the batter, ½ cup at a time. Mix well after each addition.

Pour the batter into the baking pan and smooth the surface with a rubber spatula. Bake for about 30 minutes, or until a toothpick inserted in the center comes out clean. Remove from the oven.

Allow the cake to cool for 10 minutes, then cut it into 2-inch bars.

Remove the bars from the pan with a spatula and transfer to a serving plate.

NO. 36 — **GRANOLA BARS**

*Makes about 24 bars*

½ cup unsalted butter,
    softened
½ cup dark brown sugar,
    firmly packed
½ cup sugar
1 egg
1 teaspoon vanilla extract
1 tablespoon dark molasses

1 cup sifted flour
1 teaspoon baking powder
½ teaspoon salt
1 cup granola cereal
1 cup rolled oats
¾ cup walnuts, coarsely
    chopped

Preheat the oven to 350° F. Thoroughly butter the bottom and sides of a 13 × 9 × 2 inch baking pan.

In a large mixing bowl, cream together the butter and sugars. Beat in the egg and mix well. Add the vanilla extract and the molasses. Sift the flour with the baking powder and salt in a large bowl. Combine the granola and rolled oats with the flour. Work the flour mixture into the batter, 1 cup at a time, mixing well after each addition. Stir in the chopped walnuts.

Turn the batter into the prepared baking pan and smooth the surface with the back of a wooden spoon. Bake for about 15 minutes, or until the top of the cake is firm to the touch and golden brown. Remove from the oven.

Allow the cake to cool completely, then cut it into 2-inch bars. Remove the bars from the pan with a spatula and transfer to a serving plate.

NO. 37 — **CHOCOLATE CHIP GRANOLA BARS**

*Makes about 24 bars*

Follow the recipe for Granola Bars (No. 36), adding one 7½-ounce package of semi-sweet chocolate morsels to the batter.

NO. 38 — **FRUIT GRANOLA BARS**

*Makes about 24 bars*

Follow the recipe for Granola Bars (No. 36), adding ½ cup of coarsely chopped dried apricots and ½ cup of golden raisins to the batter.

NO. **39**                       **MILK CHOCOLATE CHIP**
                                      **GRANOLA BARS**
                                    *Makes about 24 bars*

Follow the recipe for Granola Bars (No. 36), adding one 7½-ounce
package of milk chocolate morsels to the batter.

NO. **40**            **PEANUT BUTTER CHOCOLATE**
                          **CHIP GRANOLA BARS**
                                    *Makes about 24 bars*

Follow the recipe for Granola Bars (No. 36), adding 1 cup of peanut
butter morsels and one 7½-ounce package of semi-sweet chocolate
morsels to the batter.

NO. **41**                               **FRUIT SQUARES**
                                    *Makes about 24 bars*

½ cup unsalted butter,           2 cups sifted flour
    softened                     ½ teaspoon cinnamon
¾ cup sugar                      ½ teaspoon ground ginger
2 eggs                           ½ cup golden raisins
¼ cup dark molasses              ½ cup dried currants
½ teaspoon baking soda           ½ cup walnuts, coarsely
¼ cup boiling water                  chopped

Preheat the oven to 350° F. Thoroughly butter the bottom and sides
of a 13 × 9 × 2 inch baking pan.

In a large mixing bowl, cream together the butter and sugar. Beat
in the eggs, one at a time. Dissolve the molasses and baking soda in
the boiling water. Beat the molasses mixture into the egg mixture.
Sift the flour with the cinnamon and ginger. Work the flour mixture
into the batter, ½ cup at a time, mixing well after each addition.
Stir in the raisins, currants, and chopped walnuts.

Pour the batter into the baking pan and smooth the surface with
a rubber spatula. Bake for about 30 minutes, or until a toothpick
inserted in the center comes out clean. Remove from the oven.

Allow the cake to cool completely, then cut it into 2-inch squares.
Remove the squares from the pan with a spatula and transfer to a
serving plate.

NO. **42**                    # GINGER RAISIN SQUARES

*Makes about 48 bars*

½ cup unsalted butter
1 cup dark molasses
½ cup buttermilk
½ teaspoon baking soda
½ teaspoon ground cloves

1 tablespoon ground ginger
2 teaspoons grated lemon zest
¾ cup golden raisins
3 cups sifted flour
½ cup confectioners' sugar

Preheat the oven to 400° F. Lightly grease two large baking sheets with butter or vegetable shortening.

Cut the butter into large chunks and place in a medium saucepan. Add the molasses and simmer over low heat, stirring constantly with a wooden spoon, until the butter has melted. Remove the pan from the heat and turn the mixture into a large mixing bowl. Beat in the buttermilk, baking soda, cloves, ginger, and lemon zest. Mix well. Stir in the raisins. Pour the flour into a separate bowl. Pour the batter over the flour.

Knead the mixture to a smooth dough. If the dough is sticky, add more flour, a little at a time, until it is easier to work. Divide the dough in half. On a floured work surface, roll out each half into a rectangle ¼ inch thick. Transfer each rectangle to a baking sheet. Sprinkle with confectioners' sugar. Bake for 12 to 15 minutes, or until a toothpick inserted in the center comes out clean. Remove from the oven.

Cut the cakes into 3-inch squares while still warm. Using a spatula, transfer the squares from the baking sheets to wire racks to cool completely.

NO. **43**                    # GRASSHOPPERS

*Makes about 24 bars*

1⅓ cups unsalted butter,
    softened
2 cups sugar
4 eggs
1 teaspoon vanilla extract
2 tablespoons light corn syrup

1½ cups sifted flour
¾ cup unsweetened baking
    cocoa
½ teaspoon salt
2 cups walnuts, coarsely
    chopped

### Icing

2 cups confectioners' sugar
4 tablespoons unsalted butter,
    softened
2 tablespoons milk

1 teaspoon peppermint
    extract
3 drops green food coloring
4 ounces semi-sweet chocolate

Preheat the oven to 350° F. Thoroughly butter the bottom and sides of a 13 × 9 × 2 inch baking pan.

In a large mixing bowl, cream together the butter and sugar. Beat in the eggs, one at a time. Stir in the vanilla extract and corn syrup and mix well. Sift the flour with the cocoa and salt. Add the flour mixture to the batter, ½ cup at a time, mixing well after each addition. Stir in the chopped walnuts.

Pour the batter into the baking pan and smooth the surface with a rubber spatula. Bake for about 45 minutes, or until a toothpick inserted in the center comes out clean. Remove from the oven. Cool thoroughly.

While the cake is cooling, prepare the icing. In a large mixing bowl, combine the confectioners' sugar, butter, milk, peppermint extract, and food coloring. Beat until the mixture is smooth. Spread evenly over the cooled cake. When the icing is firm to the touch, melt the chocolate in the top of a double boiler over simmering water, stirring frequently. Swirl the melted chocolate over the icing. Let it harden.

When the chocolate icing has set, cut the cake into 2-inch bars. Remove the bars from the pan with a spatula and transfer to a serving plate.

## NO. 44 — LINZERTORTEN

*Makes about 20 bars*

| | |
|---|---|
| ½ cup unsalted butter, softened | 1 egg, beaten |
| ½ cup dark brown sugar, firmly packed | 1½ cups sifted flour |
| ¼ cup sugar | ¾ teaspoon baking powder |
| ⅔ cup ground almonds | ½ teaspoon allspice |
| | ⅛ teaspoon salt |
| | Confectioners' sugar |

### Filling

| | |
|---|---|
| ¾ cup raspberry jam | 1 tablespoon brandy |
| 1 teaspoon grated lemon zest | |

Preheat the oven to 375° F. Thoroughly butter the bottom and sides of an 8 × 8 × 2 inch baking pan.

Cream the butter and sugars together in a large mixing bowl. Beat in the ground almonds and the egg. Mix well. Sift the flour with the baking powder, allspice, and salt. Add the flour mixture to the batter, ½ cup at a time, mixing well after each addition. Divide the dough into two unequal balls, two-thirds and one-third. Press the larger dough ball into the bottom of the baking pan.

Roll out the remaining dough between two sheets of waxed paper to a thickness of ¼ inch. Chill in the refrigerator for 15 minutes, or until firm.

Make the filling. In a small saucepan, combine the raspberry jam, lemon zest, and brandy. Cook over low heat, stirring constantly with a wooden spoon, until the jam is liquid. Remove the pan from the heat. Spread the jam mixture evenly over the dough in the baking pan.

Remove the top sheet of waxed paper from the chilled dough. Cut the dough into strips ½ inch wide. Arrange the strips in a lattice pattern on top of the filling. Bake for about 30 minutes or until the lattice crust is golden brown. Remove from the oven. Dust the top of the cake with confectioners' sugar.

Allow the cake to cool completely, then cut it into 2-inch bars. Remove the bars from the pan with a spatula and transfer to a serving plate.

NO. **45**      # MAPLE WALNUT BARS

*Makes about 24 bars*

½ cup unsalted butter
4 eggs
1 cup sugar
1 cup maple syrup

1 teaspoon vanilla extract
1 cup sifted flour
1 cup walnuts, coarsely
   chopped

Preheat the oven to 325° F. Thoroughly butter the bottom and sides of a 13 × 9 × 2 inch baking pan.

In a small saucepan, melt the butter over very low heat. Remove the pan from the heat and set aside.

In a large mixing bowl, beat the eggs until foamy. Gradually beat in the sugar, ¼ cup at a time, continuing to beat until the mixture is light and airy. Beat in the maple syrup and the vanilla extract. Stir in the melted butter. Add the flour to the batter, ½ cup at a time. Mix in the chopped walnuts.

Pour the batter into the baking pan and smooth the surface with a rubber spatula. Bake for 30 to 35 minutes, or until a toothpick inserted in the center comes out clean. Remove from the oven.

Allow the cake to cool completely, then cut it into 2-inch bars. Remove the bars from the pan with a spatula and transfer to a serving plate.

NO. **46**                          # NECTARINE SQUARES
*Makes about 24 bars*

2 eggs
1 cup sugar
1 teaspoon vanilla extract
1 teaspoon grated lemon zest
1 cup sifted flour
2 tablespoons baking powder
½ teaspoon salt

1 teaspoon cinnamon
½ teaspoon allspice
½ teaspoon mace
1 cup walnuts, coarsely
    chopped
3½ cups sliced ripe nectarines,
    peeled and pitted

Preheat the oven to 375° F. Thoroughly butter the bottom and sides of a 13 × 9 × 2 inch baking pan.

In a large mixing bowl, beat the eggs until foamy. Gradually beat in the sugar, then add the vanilla extract and the lemon zest. Sift together the flour, baking powder, salt, cinnamon, allspice, and mace. Beat the flour mixture into the batter, ⅓ cup at a time. Combine the chopped walnuts with the sliced nectarines, then stir into the batter.

Pour the batter into the baking pan and smooth the surface with a rubber spatula. Bake for 35 to 40 minutes, or until a toothpick inserted in the center comes out clean. Remove from the oven.

Allow the cake to cool completely, then cut it into 2-inch squares. Remove the squares from the pan with a spatula and transfer to a serving plate.

NO. **47**                          # KRISPY TREATS
*Makes about 24 bars*

¼ cup unsalted butter
4 cups miniature
    marshmallows

1 tablespoon vanilla extract
6 cups Kellogg's Rice Krispies®
    cereal

Thoroughly butter the bottom and sides of a 13 × 9 × 2 inch baking pan.

In a large saucepan, melt the butter over very low heat. When the butter has melted, add the marshmallows. Cook, stirring constantly with a wooden spoon, until the marshmallows have completely dissolved. Stir in the vanilla extract. Turn the mixture into a large mixing bowl and combine with the cereal. Mix well. Press the mixture into the baking pan.

Cool completely. Then cut the mixture into 2-inch bars. Remove the bars from the pan with a spatula and transfer to a serving plate.

NO. **48** **CHOCOLATE KRISPY TREATS**
*Makes about 24 bars*

Follow the recipe for Krispy Treats (No. 47), adding one 7½-ounce package of semi-sweet chocolate morsels to the batter along with the marshmallows, and combining 1 cup of walnuts, coarsely chopped, with the cereal.

NO. **49** **PEACH DREAMS**
*Makes about 24 bars*

2 eggs
1 cup sugar
1 teaspoon brandy
1 teaspoon grated orange zest
1 cup sifted flour
2 tablespoons baking powder
½ teaspoon salt

1 teaspoon cinnamon
1 teaspoon allspice
1 cup pecans, coarsely chopped
4 medium peaches, peeled, pitted, and sliced

Preheat the oven to 375° F. Thoroughly butter the bottom and sides of a 13 × 9 × 2 inch baking pan.

In a large mixing bowl, beat the eggs until foamy. Gradually mix in the sugar, then add the brandy and the orange zest. Sift the flour with the baking powder, salt, cinnamon, and allspice. Add the flour mixture to the batter, ⅓ cup at a time. Gently mix the chopped pecans with the sliced peaches, then stir into the batter.

Pour the batter into the baking pan and smooth the surface with a rubber spatula. Bake for 35 to 40 minutes, or until a toothpick inserted in the center comes out clean. Remove from the oven.

Allow the cake to cool completely, then cut it into 2-inch bars. Remove the bars from the pan with a spatula and transfer to a serving plate.

NO. **50** **PEAR SQUARES**
*Makes about 24 bars*

2 eggs
1 cup sugar
1 teaspoon pear brandy
1 teaspoon grated lemon zest
1 cup sifted flour
2 tablespoons baking powder
½ teaspoon salt

2 teaspoons cinnamon
1 cup walnuts, coarsely chopped
4 medium pears, peeled, cored, and sliced
½ cup golden raisins

Preheat the oven to 375° F. Thoroughly butter the bottom and sides of a 13 × 9 × 2 inch baking pan.

In a large mixing bowl, beat the eggs until foamy. Gradually beat in the sugar, then add the brandy and the lemon zest. Sift the flour with the baking powder, salt, and cinnamon. Add the flour mixture to the batter, ⅓ cup at a time. Gently mix the chopped walnuts with the sliced pears and raisins, then stir into the batter.

Pour the batter into the baking pan and smooth the surface with a rubber spatula. Bake for 35 to 40 minutes, or until a toothpick inserted in the center comes out clean. Remove from the oven.

Allow the cake to cool completely, then cut it into 2-inch squares. Remove the squares from the pan with a spatula and transfer to a serving plate.

NO. **51**                                            # PENUCHE

*Makes about 40 bars*

½ cup unsalted butter,          1 teaspoon grated lemon zest
   softened                    1½ cups sifted flour
½ cup light brown sugar       1 teaspoon baking powder
2 egg yolks                          ⅛ teaspoon salt
1 teaspoon vanilla extract

*Topping*

2 egg whites                         ½ cup walnuts, coarsely
1 cup light brown sugar          chopped
½ teaspoon almond extract

Preheat the oven to 350° F. Thoroughly butter the bottom and sides of an 8 × 8 × 2 inch baking pan

In a large mixing bowl, cream together the butter and sugar. Beat in the egg yolks. Mix in the vanilla extract and the lemon zest. Sift the flour with the baking powder and salt. Add the flour mixture to the batter, ½ cup at a time.

Knead the mixture to a smooth dough. If the dough is sticky, add more flour, a little at a time, until it is easier to work. Press the dough into the bottom of the baking pan.

Make the topping. In a separate bowl, beat the egg whites until they hold stiff peaks. Gradually beat in the sugar. Continue beating until the mixture is thick and glossy. Beat in the almond extract.

Pour the topping onto the dough and smooth the surface with a rubber spatula. Sprinkle with the chopped walnuts. Bake for about 25 minutes, or until a toothpick inserted in the center comes out clean. Remove from the oven.

Allow the cake to cool completely, then cut it into 1-inch squares.

Remove the squares from the pan with a spatula and transfer to a serving plate.

## NO. 52     PINEAPPLE NUT BARS

*Makes about 24 bars*

2 eggs
1 cup sugar
1 teaspoon vanilla extract
1 teaspoon grated lemon zest
1 cup sifted flour
2 tablespoons baking powder
½ teaspoon salt

1 cup walnuts, coarsely
   chopped
2 cups canned pineapple
   slices, drained and
   coarsely chopped
Confectioners' sugar

Preheat the oven to 375° F. Thoroughly butter the bottom and sides of a 13 × 9 × 2 inch baking pan.

In a large mixing bowl, beat the eggs until foamy. Gradually mix in the sugar, then add the vanilla extract and the lemon zest. Sift the flour with the baking powder and salt. Add the flour mixture to the batter, ⅓ cup at a time. Combine the chopped walnuts with the pineapple, then stir into the batter.

Pour the batter into the baking pan and smooth the surface with a rubber spatula. Bake for 35 to 40 minutes, or until a toothpick inserted in the center comes out clean. Remove from the oven.

Allow the cake to cool completely, then cut it into 2-inch bars. Remove the bars from the pan with a spatula. Roll each bar in confectioners' sugar and arrange on a serving plate.

## NO. 53     PRUNE WALNUT BARS

*Makes about 20 bars*

⅔ cup pitted prunes
½ cup unsalted butter,
   softened
1¼ cups dark brown sugar,
   firmly packed
1⅓ cups sifted flour

2 eggs
1 teaspoon vanilla extract
½ teaspoon baking powder
⅔ cup walnuts, coarsely
   chopped
Confectioners' sugar

Preheat the oven to 350° F. Thoroughly butter the bottom and sides of an 8 × 8 × 2 inch baking pan.

Place the prunes in a medium saucepan and cover with cold water. Bring to a boil over high heat. Reduce the heat, and simmer for 10 minutes. Drain the prunes and set aside to cool.

In a large mixing bowl, combine the butter, ¼ cup of the brown sugar, and 1 cup of the flour. Blend until the mixture resembles coarse oatmeal. Press into the bottom of the baking pan. Bake for 15 minutes or until the crust begins to brown. Remove from the oven. Do not turn off the oven.

Finely chop the cooled prunes. In a separate bowl, beat the eggs until foamy. Continue beating and gradually add the remaining cup of brown sugar and the vanilla extract. Mix in the remaining ⅓ cup of flour and the baking powder. Stir in the chopped walnuts and the prunes. Spoon the mixture over the baked crust and smooth the surface with a rubber spatula. Return the pan to the oven and bake for an additional 30 minutes. Remove from the oven.

Allow the cake to cool completely, then cut it into 2-inch bars. Remove the bars from the pan with a spatula and transfer to a serving plate. Dust with confectioners' sugar.

## NO. 54      RASPBERRY MERINGUE BARS
*Makes about 24 bars*

| | |
|---|---|
| ½ cup unsalted butter, softened | 1 cup raspberry jam |
| ½ cup plus ⅓ cup sugar | 2 tablespoons cherry brandy |
| 2 egg yolks | 2 egg whites |
| 1 teaspoon vanilla extract | 1 cup walnuts, coarsely chopped |
| 1½ cups sifted flour | |

Preheat the oven to 350° F. Thoroughly butter the bottom and sides of a 13 × 9 × 2 inch baking pan.

In a large mixing bowl, cream together the butter and ½ cup of the sugar. Beat in the egg yolks and mix well. Add the vanilla extract. Gradually add the flour to the batter.

Pour the batter into the baking pan and smooth the surface with a rubber spatula. Bake for 25 minutes and remove from the oven.

In a small saucepan, heat the jam with the brandy until the jam is liquid. Remove the pan from the heat and set aside to cool. Do not turn off the oven. Spread the cooled jam mixture over the cake. Beat the egg whites until foamy. Add ⅓ cup of the sugar, a little at a time, continuing to beat until stiff, glossy peaks form. Gently fold the chopped walnuts into the meringue. Spread the meringue over the jam layer, and return the pan to the oven. Bake for an additional 25 minutes.

Allow the cake to cool completely, then cut it into 2-inch bars. Remove the bars from the pan with a spatula and transfer to a serving plate.

NO. **55**       **RUSSIAN TEA BARS**
*Makes about 24 bars*

| | |
|---|---|
| 2 tablespoons unsalted butter | 2½ cups sifted flour |
| 2 egg yolks | 1 cup milk |
| ¼ cup confectioners' sugar | 1 cup walnuts, coarsely |
| 1 teaspoon vanilla extract |    chopped |
| ½ teaspoon salt | |

Preheat the oven to 350° F. Thoroughly butter the bottom and sides of a 13 × 9 × 2 inch baking pan.

Melt the butter in a small saucepan over very low heat. Remove the pan from the heat and set aside.

In a large mixing bowl, beat the egg yolks until pale and thick. Beat in the melted butter and the confectioners' sugar. Mix well. Add the vanilla extract and the salt. Add the flour to the batter, ½ cup at a time, alternating with the milk. Beat until the batter is smooth. Mix in the chopped walnuts. Pour the batter into the baking pan and smooth the surface with a rubber spatula. Bake for about 30 minutes, or until a toothpick inserted in the center comes out clean. Remove from the oven.

Allow the cake to cool completely, then cut it into 2-inch bars. Remove the bars from the pan with a spatula and transfer to a serving plate.

NO. **56**       **SCOTCH GINGERBREAD BARS**
*Makes about 24 bars*

| | |
|---|---|
| ½ cup unsalted butter | 2 cups sifted flour |
| ½ cup light molasses | ½ teaspoon baking soda |
| ½ cup sugar | 1 teaspoon cinnamon |
| 2 eggs | 1 teaspoon ground ginger |

Preheat the oven to 350° F. Thoroughly butter the bottom and sides of a 13 × 9 × 2 inch baking pan.

Combine the butter, molasses, and sugar in a saucepan. Cook over low heat, stirring constantly with a wooden spoon, until the butter and sugar have melted. Remove the pan from the heat and set aside to cool.

In a large mixing bowl, beat the eggs until foamy. Beat in the cooled butter mixture. Sift the flour with the baking soda, cinnamon, and ginger. Add the flour mixture to the batter, ½ cup at a time, mixing well after each addition.

Pour the batter into the baking pan and smooth the surface with a rubber spatula. Bake for about 30 minutes, or until a toothpick inserted in the center comes out clean. Remove from the oven.

Allow the cake to cool completely, then cut it into 2-inch bars. Remove the bars from the pan with a spatula and transfer to a serving plate.

NO. 57                                        **SESAME BARS**

*Makes about 24 bars*

| | |
|---|---|
| 1½ cups sesame seeds | 1 cup sugar |
| ¾ cup vegetable oil | 2 cups sifted flour |
| 2 eggs | 1 teaspoon baking powder |
| 2 teaspoons vanilla extract | ½ teaspoon baking soda |

Preheat the oven to 350° F. Thoroughly butter the bottom and sides of a 13 × 9 × 2 inch baking pan.

Spread the sesame seeds evenly on a large baking sheet. Toast the seeds in the oven for 10 minutes, stirring once or twice. Remove from the oven and set aside. Do not turn the oven off.

In a large mixing bowl, beat the oil with the eggs and the vanilla extract. Beat in the sugar, ½ cup at a time. Mix well. Sift the flour with the baking powder and baking soda. Add the flour mixture to the batter, ½ cup at a time, mixing well after each addition. Add the toasted sesame seeds and mix well.

Pour the batter into the baking pan and smooth the surface with a rubber spatula. Bake for 15 to 20 minutes, or until a toothpick inserted in the center comes out clean. Remove from the oven.

Allow the cake to cool completely, then cut it into 2-inch bars. Remove the bars from the pan with a spatula and transfer to a serving plate.

NO. 58                            **SESAME PEANUT BARS**

*Makes about 24 bars*

Follow the recipe for Sesame Bars (No. 57), adding 1½ cups of unsalted peanuts to the batter.

NO. 59                            **SOFT GINGER SQUARES**

*Makes about 24 bars*

| | |
|---|---|
| 1 cup unsalted butter, softened | 1½ cups sifted flour |
| ½ cup sugar | ½ teaspoon baking soda |
| 2 eggs, beaten | ¼ teaspoon ground ginger |
| ½ cup dark molasses | ¼ teaspoon salt |
| | Confectioners' sugar |

Preheat the oven to 400° F. Thoroughly butter the bottom and sides of a 13 × 9 × 2 inch baking pan.

In a large mixing bowl, cream together the butter and sugar. Beat in the eggs. Add the molasses and mix well. Sift the flour with the baking soda, ginger, and salt. Stir the flour mixture into the batter, ½ cup at a time, mixing well after each addition.

Knead the mixture to a smooth dough. If the dough is sticky, add more flour, a little at a time, until it is easier to work. On a floured work surface, roll out the dough in a rectangle to fit into the baking pan. Place the dough in the baking pan. Bake for 15 minutes. Remove from the oven.

While the cake is still warm, cut it into 2-inch squares. Remove the squares from the pan with a spatula, roll them in confectioners' sugar, and transfer to a serving plate.

NO. **60**                            **SPICE GRANOLA BARS**

*Makes about 24 bars*

½ cup unsalted butter, softened
½ cup brown sugar, firmly packed
½ cup sugar
1 egg
1 teaspoon vanilla extract
1 teaspoon lemon extract
1 tablespoon dark molasses
1 cup sifted flour

1 teaspoon baking powder
1 teaspoon cinnamon
½ teaspoon ground cloves
½ teaspoon nutmeg
½ teaspoon ground ginger
½ teaspoon salt
1 cup granola cereal
1 cup rolled oats
¾ cup walnuts, coarsely chopped

Preheat the oven to 350° F. Thoroughly butter the bottom and sides of a 13 × 9 × 2 inch baking pan.

In a large mixing bowl, cream together the butter and sugars. Beat in the egg and mix well. Add the vanilla extract and the lemon extract. Stir in the molasses and mix well. Sift the flour with the baking powder, cinnamon, cloves, nutmeg, ginger, and salt. Combine the flour mixture with the granola and rolled oats. Work the flour mixture into the batter, 1 cup at a time, mixing well after each addition. Stir in the chopped walnuts.

Spoon the batter into the baking pan and smooth the surface with a rubber spatula. Bake for about 15 minutes, or until the top of the cake is firm to the touch and golden brown. Remove from the oven.

Allow the cake to cool completely, then cut it into 2-inch bars. Remove the bars from the pan with a spatula and transfer to a serving plate.

NO. **61**                    ## STAINED GLASS WINDOWS
                                       *Makes about 24 bars*

These cookies require no baking, but they must be refrigerated overnight before serving.

11½- ounce package semi-sweet
   chocolate morsels
¼ cup unsalted butter
3 cups multicolored
   miniature marshmallows

1 cup walnuts, coarsely
   chopped
½ cup unsweetened shredded
   coconut

Thoroughly butter the bottom and sides of a 13 × 9 × 2 inch baking pan.

Melt the chocolate morsels and the butter in the top of a double boiler over simmering water, stirring frequently. Remove the pan from the heat and set aside to cool for 5 minutes. Mix the marshmallows into the chocolate mixture. Stir in the chopped walnuts. Sprinkle half the coconut on the bottom of the baking pan. Turn the chocolate mixture into the baking pan and smooth the surface with a rubber spatula. Sprinkle the remaining coconut on top. Cover with waxed paper and press down. Leave the waxed paper in place, and refrigerate overnight.

The next day, cut the cake into 2-inch bars. Remove the bars from the pan with a spatula and transfer to a serving plate.

NO. **62**          ## MINT-FLAVORED STAINED
                    ## GLASS WINDOWS
                                       *Makes about 24 bars*

Follow the recipe for Stained Glass Windows (No. 61), substituting mint chocolate morsels for the semi-sweet chocolate morsels.

NO. **63**              ## STRAWBERRY JAM SQUARES
                                       *Makes about 20 bars*

½ cup unsalted butter,
   softened
1 cup sugar
2 egg yolks
1 teaspoon vanilla extract

2 cups sifted flour
1 cup walnuts, coarsely
   chopped
½ cup strawberry jam
1 teaspoon brandy

Preheat the oven to 325° F. Thoroughly butter the bottom and sides of an 8 × 8 × 2 inch baking pan.

In a large mixing bowl, cream together the butter and sugar. Beat in the egg yolks. Add the vanilla extract and mix well. Beat in the flour, 1 cup at a time. Stir in the chopped walnuts. Turn half of the batter into the baking pan. Smooth the surface with a rubber spatula.

In a small saucepan, combine the strawberry jam with the brandy. Cook over low heat, stirring constantly with a wooden spoon, until the jam is liquid. Cool slightly. Spread the jam over the batter. Pour the remaining batter over the layer of jam and smooth the top. Bake for about 1 hour, or until a toothpick inserted in the center comes out clean. Remove from the oven.

Allow the cake to cool completely, then cut it into 2-inch squares. Remove the squares from the pan with a spatula and transfer to a serving plate.

NO. **64**   **STRAWBERRY SQUARES**

*Makes about 24 bars*

2 eggs
1 cup sugar
1 teaspoon lemon juice
1 teaspoon grated lemon zest
1 cup sifted flour
2 tablespoons baking powder

½ teaspoon salt
2 teaspoons cinnamon
1 cup walnuts, coarsely
   chopped
3 cups sliced fresh or frozen
   strawberries

Preheat the oven to 375° F. Thoroughly butter the bottom and sides of a 13 × 9 × 2 inch baking pan.

In a large mixing bowl, beat the eggs until foamy. Gradually mix in the sugar, then add the lemon juice and lemon zest. Mix well. Sift the flour with the baking powder, salt, and cinnamon. Add the flour mixture to the batter, ⅓ cup at a time. Gently mix the chopped walnuts with the strawberries, then stir into the batter.

Pour the batter into the baking pan and smooth the surface with a rubber spatula. Bake for 35 to 40 minutes, or until a toothpick inserted in the center comes out clean. Remove from the oven.

Allow the cake to cool completely, then cut it into 2-inch squares. Remove the squares from the pan with a spatula and transfer to a serving plate.

NO. **65**               # THREE-LAYER LEMON BARS

*Makes about 24 bars*

½ cup unsalted butter,
   softened
1⅓ cups sifted flour
3 tablespoons sugar
3 eggs

1 cup dark brown sugar,
   firmly packed
¾ cup walnuts, coarsely
   chopped
¾ cup unsweetened shredded
   coconut

*Icing*

2½ cups confectioners' sugar
¼ cup lemon juice

2 tablespoons grated lemon
zest

Preheat the oven to 350° F. Thoroughly butter the bottom and sides of a 13 × 9 × 2 inch baking pan.

In a large mixing bowl, cut the butter into large pieces. Add the flour and the 3 tablespoons of sugar to the butter. Using a pastry blender, or two forks, work the mixture until it resembles coarse oatmeal. Press the dough firmly into the bottom of the baking pan. Bake for 15 minutes. Remove the pan from the oven, but leave the oven on.

While the first layer is baking, beat the eggs in another bowl until foamy. Gradually beat in the dark brown sugar. Add the chopped walnuts and coconut. Pour on top of the baked layer. Return to the oven. Bake for 25 to 30 minutes, or until a toothpick inserted in the center comes out clean. Remove from the oven. Cool thoroughly before icing.

To make the icing, combine the sugar, lemon juice, and lemon zest in a large mixing bowl. Mix until smooth. Spread the icing evenly over the cake and let it set. When the icing has hardened, cut the cake into 2-inch bars. Remove the bars from the pan with a spatula and transfer to a serving plate.

NO. **66**               # THREE-LAYER ORANGE BARS

*Makes about 24 bars*

½ cup unsalted butter,
   softened
1⅓ cups sifted flour
3 tablespoons sugar
3 eggs

1 cup dark brown sugar,
   firmly packed
¾ cup walnuts, coarsely
   chopped
¾ cup unsweetened shredded
   coconut

### Icing

| | |
|---|---|
| 2½ cups confectioners' sugar | 2 tablespoons grated orange |
| ¼ cup orange juice | zest |

Preheat the oven to 350° F. Thoroughly butter the bottom and sides of a 13 × 9 × 2 inch baking pan.

In a large mixing bowl, cut the butter into chunks. Add the flour and the 3 tablespoons of sugar to the butter. Using a pastry blender, or two forks, blend the mixture until it resembles coarse oatmeal. Press the dough firmly into the bottom of the baking pan. Bake for 15 minutes. Remove from the oven, but leave the oven on.

In another bowl, beat the eggs until foamy. Gradually beat in the brown sugar. Add the chopped walnuts and the coconut and mix well. Pour the batter on top of the baked layer. Return the pan to the oven. Bake for 25 to 30 minutes, or until a toothpick inserted in the center comes out clean. Remove from the oven. Cool thoroughly before icing.

Make the icing. In a large mixing bowl, combine the confectioners' sugar, orange juice, and orange zest. Mix until smooth. Spread the icing evenly over the cake and let it set.

When the icing has hardened, cut the cake into 2-inch bars. Remove the bars from the pan with a spatula and transfer to a serving plate.

NO. **67** # VERY GOOD COOKIES

*Makes about 40 bars*

| | |
|---|---|
| ½ cup sugar | 1 cup unsalted butter, |
| 2 hard-boiled egg yolks | softened |
| 2 eggs, separated | 3½ cups sifted flour |

### Topping

| | |
|---|---|
| ¾ cup light brown sugar | 2 teaspoons cinnamon |
| ½ cup blanched almonds, | 1 egg white, beaten |
| finely chopped | |

Preheat the oven to 400° F. Lightly grease two large baking sheets with butter or vegetable shortening.

Combine the sugar and hard-boiled egg yolks in a large mixing bowl. Using a pastry blender, or two forks, work the sugar into the eggs until the mixture is a paste. In a separate bowl, beat the raw egg yolks until foamy. Gradually blend the beaten egg yolks into the paste. In another bowl, beat the egg whites until they hold stiff peaks. Stir the beaten egg whites into the paste. Add the butter and flour alternately, and knead into a smooth dough. Divide the dough in half.

On a floured work surface, roll out each ball of dough into a rectangle, ¼ inch thick. Line each baking sheet with dough.

Make the topping. In a small mixing bowl, combine the brown sugar, chopped almonds, and cinnamon. Brush each sheet of dough with beaten egg white and sprinkle on half of the topping. Bake for 10 minutes. Remove from the oven.

Cool thoroughly, then cut into 2-inch bars. Remove the bars from the pans with a spatula and transfer to a serving plate.

NO. **68**                                    # WALNUT BARS

*Makes about 24 bars*

½ cup unsalted butter,
   softened
⅓ cup sugar
3 egg yolks, beaten
1½ cups sifted flour
2 tablespoons milk

3 egg whites
1 cup superfine sugar
1½ cups walnuts, finely
   chopped
2 tablespoons confectioners'
   sugar

Preheat the oven to 350° F. Thoroughly butter the bottom and sides of a 13 × 9 × 2 inch baking pan.

In a large mixing bowl, cream together the butter and ⅓ cup of the sugar. Beat in the egg yolks and mix well. Beat in the flour, ½ cup at a time. Add the milk after the first cup of flour has been mixed in.

Knead the mixture to a smooth dough. If the dough is sticky, add more flour, a little at a time, until it is easier to work. On a floured work surface, roll out the dough in a rectangle, ½ inch thick. Line the bottom of the baking pan with the dough.

In a separate bowl, beat the egg whites until they hold stiff peaks. Gradually beat in the sugar. Continue beating until the mixture is thick and glossy. Gently fold in the chopped walnuts.

Pour the batter into the baking pan and smooth the surface with a rubber spatula. Sprinkle with confectioners' sugar. Bake for about 30 minutes, or until a toothpick inserted in the center comes out clean. Remove from the oven.

Allow the cake to cool completely, then cut it into 2-inch bars. Remove the bars from the pan with a spatula and transfer to a serving plate.

NO. **69**

# ZUCCHINI BARS
*Makes about 24 bars*

½ cup unsalted butter,
   softened
1 cup light brown sugar
2 eggs
1 teaspoon vanilla extract
1 teaspoon grated lemon zest
1 cup grated raw zucchini

1 cup walnuts, coarsely
   chopped
1½ cups sifted flour
1½ teaspoons baking powder
1 teaspoon cinnamon
¼ cup orange juice

Preheat the oven to 375° F. Thoroughly butter the bottom and sides of a 13 × 9 × 2 inch baking pan.

In a large mixing bowl, cream together the butter and sugar. Add the eggs, one at a time, beating well after each addition. Stir in the vanilla extract and the lemon zest. Add the grated zucchini and the chopped walnuts. Sift together the flour, baking powder, and cinnamon. Add the flour mixture, ½ cup at a time, to the batter, alternating with the orange juice.

Pour the batter into the baking pan and smooth the surface with a rubber spatula. Bake for about 25 minutes, or until a toothpick inserted in the center comes out clean. Remove from the oven.

Allow the cake to cool completely, then cut it into 2-inch bars. Remove the bars from the pan with a spatula and transfer to a serving plate.

# Brownies

From the moment you lick your first brownie bowl there is no return. That deep bowl, coated with rich chocolate batter, is only a prelude to the exquisite sensation of biting into a freshly baked brownie. Brownies are bar cookies, but because they are in a class of their own, this special chapter for brownie lovers presents a comprehensive selection including many variations on the classic brownie theme.

Some people like their brownies chewy, others prefer a more cakelike texture. Use a smaller pan (8 × 8 × 2 inch) for cakelike results and a 13 × 9 × 2 inch pan for the more traditional chewy texture. To make brownies without nuts, simply omit the nuts from the recipe. For those who prefer their brownies with chocolate icing, here's a recipe that will add a special something:

## CHOCOLATE FUDGE ICING

3 ounces (3 squares) unsweetened baking chocolate
⅔ cup sugar
⅓ cup strong coffee
¼ cup heavy cream
⅛ teaspoon salt
1 tablespoon unsalted butter
1 teaspoon vanilla extract

Prepare any brownie recipe and let the cake cool. In a saucepan over low heat, combine the chocolate, sugar, coffee, cream, and salt. Bring to a boil and cook, stirring constantly, until the mixture reaches the soft-ball stage (when a teaspoon of liquid dropped into a glass of water forms a soft ball). Remove the pan from the heat. Stir in the butter and vanilla. Ice the brownie cake. Let the icing harden, then cut the cake into 2-inch bars.

NO. 70

## CLASSIC BROWNIES

*Makes about 24 bars*

4 ounces (4 squares) unsweetened baking chocolate
½ cup unsalted butter
4 eggs
2 cups sugar
2 teaspoons vanilla extract
1 cup sifted flour
1 cup walnuts, coarsely chopped

Preheat the oven to 325° F. Thoroughly butter the bottom and sides of a 13 × 9 × 2 inch baking pan.

In a small saucepan set over very low heat, melt the butter and chocolate together, stirring constantly. Remove the pan from the heat and set aside.

In a large mixing bowl, beat the eggs until foamy. Gradually add the sugar, ½ cup at a time, and continue to beat until the mixture is light and airy. Stir in the vanilla extract. Add the melted chocolate mixture and blend thoroughly. Stir in the flour all at once. Add the chopped walnuts and mix well.

Pour the batter into the baking pan and smooth the surface with a rubber spatula. Bake for 30 minutes, or until a toothpick inserted in the center comes out clean. Remove from the oven.

Allow the cake to cool completely, then cut it into 2-inch bars. Remove the bars from the pan with a spatula and transfer to a serving plate.

## NO. 71     BLACK-AND-WHITE BROWNIES

*Makes about 24 bars*

4 eggs
2 cups sugar
1 teaspoon vanilla extract
1 cup unsalted butter

2 ounces (2 squares) unsweetened baking chocolate
1 cup sifted flour
1 cup walnuts, coarsely chopped

Preheat the oven to 350° F. Thoroughly butter the bottom and sides of a 13 × 9 × 2 inch baking pan.

In a large mixing bowl, beat the eggs until foamy. Gradually add the sugar, ½ cup at a time, and continue to beat until the mixture is light and foamy. Stir in the vanilla extract.

In a small saucepan set over low heat, melt ½ cup of the butter. In a separate saucepan over very low heat, combine the remaining butter with the chocolate. Cook, stirring constantly, until the butter and chocolate are melted. Divide the egg mixture into two bowls. Add the melted butter to one bowl and the butter and chocolate mixture to the other. Beat ½ cup of the flour into each bowl of batter. Stir half the chopped walnuts into each mixture.

Pour the white batter into the baking pan and smooth the surface with a rubber spatula. Carefully pour the chocolate batter on top of the first layer. Bake for 25 to 30 minutes, or until a toothpick inserted in the center comes out clean. Remove from the oven.

Allow the cake to cool completely, then cut it into 2-inch bars. Remove the bars from the pan with a spatula and transfer to a serving plate.

NO. **72**                   # BUTTERSCOTCH BROWNIES
*Makes about 24 bars*

Follow the recipe for Classic Brownies (No. 70), adding 1 cup of
butterscotch morsels with the chopped walnuts.


NO. **73**                   # DOUBLE CHOCOLATE
# BROWNIES
*Makes about 24 bars*

Follow the recipe for Classic Brownies (No. 70), but add 1 cup of
milk chocolate morsels with the chopped walnuts.


NO. **74**                   # MINTY FUDGE BROWNIES
*Makes about 24 bars*

Follow the recipe for Classic Brownies (No. 70), but add 1 cup of
mint chocolate morsels with the chopped walnuts.


NO. **75**                   # PEANUT BUTTER BROWNIES
*Makes about 24 bars*

Follow the recipe for Classic Brownies (No. 70), but add 1 cup of
peanut butter morsels with the chopped walnuts.


NO. **76**                   # TRIPLE NUT BROWNIES
*Makes about 24 bars*

Follow the recipe for Classic Brownies (No. 70), but add 1 cup of
finely chopped hazelnuts and 1 cup of finely chopped almonds with
the chopped walnuts.

NO. 77 COCONUT BROWNIES

*Makes about 24 bars*

4 ounces (4 squares)
    unsweetened baking
    chocolate
½ cup unsalted butter
4 eggs
2 cups sugar

1 teaspoon almond extract
1 cup sifted flour
1 cup blanched almonds,
    finely chopped
¾ cup unsweetened shredded
    coconut

Preheat the oven to 325° F. Thoroughly butter the bottom and sides of a 13 × 9 × 2 inch baking pan.

Melt the chocolate and butter together in a small saucepan over very low heat, stirring constantly. Remove the pan from the heat and set aside.

In a large mixing bowl, beat the eggs until foamy. Gradually beat in the sugar, ½ cup at a time, continuing to beat until the mixture is light and airy. Mix in the almond extract. Add the melted chocolate mixture and mix thoroughly. Stir in the flour all at once. Mix in the chopped almonds and the coconut.

Pour the batter into the baking pan and smooth the surface with a rubber spatula. Bake for 30 minutes, or until a toothpick inserted in the center comes out clean. Remove from the oven.

Allow the cake to cool completely, then cut it into 2-inch bars. Remove the bars from the pan with a spatula and transfer to a serving plate.

NO. 78 MERINGUE-TOPPED BROWNIES

*Makes about 24 bars*

4 ounces (4 squares)
    unsweetened baking
    chocolate
½ cup unsalted butter
4 eggs

2 cups sugar
1 teaspoon vanilla extract
1 cup sifted flour
1 cup walnuts, coarsely
    chopped

*Topping*

2 egg whites
¼ teaspoon cream of tartar

1 cup superfine sugar

Preheat the oven to 325° F. Thoroughly butter the bottom and sides of a 13 × 9 × 2 inch baking pan.

Melt the chocolate and butter together in a small saucepan over very low heat, stirring frequently. Remove the pan from the heat and set aside.

In a large mixing bowl, beat the eggs until they are foamy. Gradually beat in the sugar, ½ cup at a time, continuing to beat until the mixture is light and airy. Mix in the vanilla extract. Add the melted chocolate mixture and blend thoroughly. Add the flour all at once. Stir in the chopped walnuts. Pour the batter into the baking pan and smooth the surface with a rubber spatula.

Prepare the topping. In a large mixing bowl, beat the egg whites with the cream of tartar until they hold stiff peaks. Beat in the sugar, a little at a time, until the meringue is stiff and glossy. Carefully spread the meringue over the batter. Bake for 30 minutes, or until a toothpick inserted in the center of the cake comes out clean. Remove from the oven.

Allow the cake to cool completely, then cut it into 2-inch bars. Remove the bars from the pan with a spatula and transfer to a serving plate.

NO. 79        **MERINGUE-TOPPED COCONUT CHOCOLATE CHIP BROWNIES**
*Makes about 24 bars*

Follow the recipe for Meringue-Topped Brownies (No. 78), sprinkling ¾ cup of unsweetened shredded coconut and one 7½-ounce package of semi-sweet chocolate morsels on top of the batter before laying on the meringue.

NO. 80        **MERINGUE-TOPPED BUTTERSCOTCH BROWNIES**
*Makes about 24 bars*

Follow the recipe for Meringue-Topped Chocolate Chip Brownies (No. 79), substituting butterscotch morsels for the semi-sweet chocolate morsels.

NO. 81        **MERINGUE-TOPPED MINT CHOCOLATE CHIP BROWNIES**
*Makes about 24 bars*

Follow the recipe for Meringue-Topped Chocolate Chip Brownies (No. 79), substituting mint chocolate morsels for the semi-sweet chocolate morsels.

NO. 82

# MOCHA BROWNIES

*Makes about 24 bars*

4 ounces (4 squares)
    unsweetened baking
    chocolate
½ cup unsalted butter
2 tablespoons espresso coffee
    powder

4 eggs
2 cups sugar
1 teaspoon vanilla extract
1 cup sifted flour
1 cup pecans, coarsely
    chopped

Preheat the oven to 325° F. Thoroughly butter the bottom and sides of a 13 × 9 × 2 inch baking pan.

In a small saucepan, melt the chocolate and butter over very low heat, stirring frequently. Dissolve the coffee powder in the mixture. Remove the pan from the heat and set aside.

In a large mixing bowl, beat the eggs until they are foamy. Gradually beat in the sugar, ½ cup at a time, continuing to beat until the mixture is light and airy. Mix in the vanilla extract. Add the melted chocolate mixture and mix thoroughly. Add the flour all at once. Mix well. Stir in the chopped pecans. Pour the batter into the baking pan and smooth the surface with a rubber spatula. Bake for 30 minutes, or until a toothpick inserted in the center comes out clean. Remove from the oven.

Allow the cake to cool completely, then cut it into 2-inch bars. Remove the bars from the pan with a spatula and transfer to a serving plate.

NO. 83

# WHITE CHOCOLATE LEMON BROWNIES

*Makes about 24 bars*

4 ounces white chocolate
    (sweetened)
½ cup unsalted butter
4 eggs
1 cup sugar
1 teaspoon vanilla extract

1 teaspoon grated lemon zest
1 teaspoon grated orange zest
1 cup sifted flour
1 cup walnuts, coarsely
    chopped

Preheat the oven to 325° F. Thoroughly butter the bottom and sides of a 13 × 9 × 2 inch baking pan.

Melt the chocolate and butter in a small saucepan over very low heat, stirring frequently. Remove the pan from the heat and set aside.

In a large mixing bowl, beat the eggs until foamy. Gradually add the sugar, ½ cup at a time. Continue to beat until the mixture is light and airy. Stir in the vanilla extract and lemon and orange zest.

Add the melted chocolate mixture and mix thoroughly. Add the flour all at once. Stir in the chopped walnuts.

Pour the batter into the baking pan and smooth the surface with a rubber spatula. Bake for 30 minutes, or until a toothpick inserted in the center comes out clean. Remove from the oven.

Allow the cake to cool completely, then cut it into 2-inch bars. Remove the bars from the pan with a spatula and transfer to a serving plate.

# Drop Cookies

Whether they're jumbles, chews, rocks, chocolate chips galore, curved almond tiles, cry babies (an old-fashioned molasses cookie often given—or so it's been said—to young children in order to make them smile again), oatmeal cookies, or gumdrop cookies, drop cookies are the most versatile treat around. You determine the size of the cookie (and therefore the yield of the recipe) by how much dough you drop onto the baking sheet. All drop cookie yields are based on one heaping teaspoonful of batter, unless otherwise noted. Some recipes, particularly chocolate chip cookies and oatmeal cookies, lend themselves to oversize, or monster, cookies. Monster cookies may be created from half cups of batter. These will take anywhere from 5 to 10 minutes longer to bake through at the given temperature.

## NO. 84      ALMOND ORANGE DROP COOKIES

*Makes about 36 cookies*

4 egg yolks
½ cup superfine sugar
2 teaspoons grated orange zest

½ teaspoon almond extract
3½ cups blanched almonds, coarsely chopped

Preheat the oven to 325° F. Lightly grease two large baking sheets with butter or vegetable shortening.

In a large mixing bowl, beat the egg yolks until thick. Gradually beat in the sugar. Continue beating until the batter is smooth and thick. Mix in the orange zest and the almond extract. Add the chopped almonds and mix well.

Drop rounded teaspoonfuls of batter onto the baking sheets, about 2 inches apart. Bake for 10 minutes, or until the cookies are dry to the touch. Remove from the oven.

After the cookies have cooled for 2 to 3 minutes, but are still warm to the touch, use a spatula to transfer them to wire racks to cool completely.

NO. **85**                              # ALMOND TILES
*Makes about 24 cookies*

1 cup blanched almonds,            ½ cup sugar
    finely chopped             1 teaspoon almond extract
3 tablespoons flour                1 teaspoon grated lemon zest
1 egg, beaten

Preheat the oven to 375° F. Lightly grease two large baking sheets
with butter or vegetable shortening and dust with flour. Shake off
any loose flour.

In a large mixing bowl, combine the chopped almonds with the
flour, beaten egg, sugar, almond extract, and lemon zest. Blend
thoroughly.

Drop rounded teaspoonfuls of batter onto the baking sheets, about
2 inches apart. Moisten a fork with cold water and flatten the top
of each cookie. Bake for 8 to 10 minutes.

Remove from the oven and immediately transfer each cookie, with
the top down, to a rolling pin or empty wine bottle. Press gently so
a slight curve is formed. Cool slightly (until the shape has set), then
transfer the cookies to a serving plate. If the remaining cookies harden
before you are able to mold them, put them back in the oven for
another few seconds.


NO. **86**                              # ANISE COOKIES
*Makes about 60 cookies*

Before baking, these cookies must stand overnight.

4 eggs                             2 cups sifted flour
2 cups confectioners' sugar        1½ teaspoons baking powder
2 tablespoons ground
    aniseed

Lightly grease two large baking sheets with vegetable shortening.

In a large mixing bowl, beat the eggs until foamy. Gradually add
the sugar, ¼ cup at a time, mixing thoroughly. Add the aniseed. Sift
the flour with the baking powder. Work the flour into the egg mixture.

Drop rounded teaspoonfuls of batter onto the baking sheets, about
2 inches apart. Let the cookies stand uncovered overnight, or for
about 12 hours.

Preheat the oven to 325° F. Bake the cookies for 10 to 12 minutes,
or until they are golden brown.

After the cookies have cooled for 2 to 3 minutes, but are still

warm to the touch, use a spatula to transfer them to wire racks to cool completely.

NO. 87                            **ANISEED CAKES**

*Makes about 48 cookies*

| | |
|---|---|
| 4 eggs | ¼ cup cornstarch |
| 1 cup sugar | 2 tablespoons whole |
| 1¼ cups sifted flour |    aniseed |

Preheat the oven to 350° F. Lightly grease two large baking sheets with butter or vegetable shortening.

Combine the eggs and sugar in the top of a double boiler. Cook over boiling water, beating constantly with a wooden spoon, until the mixture thickens. Remove the top of the double boiler from the heat and continue to beat the mixture until it has cooled.

Sift the flour with the cornstarch. Mix in the aniseed. Gradually add the flour mixture to the egg mixture and blend until smooth.

Drop rounded teaspoonfuls of batter onto the baking sheets, about 2 inches apart. Flatten the top of each cookie with the tines of a fork. Bake for 10 to 15 minutes, or until the cookies are brown around the edges. Remove from the oven.

After the cookies have cooled for 2 to 3 minutes, but are still warm to the touch, use a spatula to transfer them to wire racks to cool completely.

NO. 88                    **APPLESAUCE COOKIES**

*Makes about 50 cookies*

| | |
|---|---|
| ¼ cup unsalted butter, softened | 2 eggs |
| 1 cup light brown sugar | 3 cups pound cake crumbs |
| ½ teaspoon salt | 1¼ cups unsweetened applesauce |
| 1 teaspoon cinnamon | ½ cup walnuts, coarsely chopped |
| 1 teaspoon allspice | 2 cups sifted flour |
| 1½ teaspoons baking soda | |

Preheat the oven to 375° F. Lightly grease two large baking sheets with butter or vegetable shortening.

In a large mixing bowl, cream together the butter and sugar. Mix in the salt, cinnamon, allspice, and baking soda. Add the eggs, one at a time, mixing well after each addition. Stir the cake crumbs into the batter, then add the applesauce. Add the chopped walnuts and mix well. Finally, stir in the flour, ½ cup at a time.

Drop rounded teaspoonfuls of batter onto the baking sheets, about 2 inches apart. Bake for 8 to 10 minutes, or until the cookies are brown around the edges. Remove from the oven.

After the cookies have cooled for 2 to 3 minutes, but are still warm to the touch, use a spatula to transfer them to wire racks to cool completely.

NO. **89**                    # APRICOT FANCIES
*Makes about 50 cookies*

½ cup unsalted butter,
   softened
⅓ cup dark brown sugar,
   firmly packed
1 egg
1 teaspoon vanilla extract
1 teaspoon grated orange zest

1 cup plus 2 tablespoons
   sifted flour
½ teaspoon baking soda
½ teaspoon salt
1 cup dried apricots, coarsely
   chopped
1 cup walnuts, coarsely
   chopped

Preheat the oven to 375° F. Lightly grease two large baking sheets with butter or vegetable shortening.

In a large mixing bowl, cream together the butter and sugar. Beat in the egg, vanilla extract, and orange zest. Sift together the flour, baking soda, and salt. Gradually add the flour mixture to the batter. Stir the apricots and walnuts into the batter. Mix well.

Drop rounded teaspoonfuls of batter onto the baking sheets, about 2 inches apart. Bake for 10 to 12 minutes, or until the cookies are brown. Remove from the oven.

After the cookies have cooled for 2 to 3 minutes, but are still warm to the touch, use a spatula to transfer them to wire racks to cool completely.

NO. **90**              # BANANA DROP COOKIES
*Makes about 36 cookies*

1½ cups sifted flour
1 cup sugar
½ teaspoon baking soda
1 teaspoon salt
½ teaspoon cinnamon
¼ teaspoon ground ginger
¼ teaspoon nutmeg

¾ cup margarine, softened
½ cup walnuts, coarsely
   chopped
1¾ cups quick-cooking oatmeal
1 egg, beaten
1 cup mashed, very ripe
   bananas (2 to 3 bananas)

Preheat the oven to 375° F. Lightly grease two large baking sheets with butter or vegetable shortening.

Sift together the flour, sugar, baking soda, salt, cinnamon, ginger, and nutmeg. Using a pastry blender or two forks, work the margarine into the flour mixture until thoroughly mixed. Mix the chopped walnuts with the oatmeal, then stir into the flour mixture. Beat in the egg and the banana. Mix well.

Drop rounded teaspoonfuls of batter onto the baking sheets, about 2 inches apart. Bake for 12 to 15 minutes, or until the cookies have browned around the edges. Remove from the oven.

After the cookies have cooled for 2 to 3 minutes, but are still warm to the touch, use a spatula to transfer them to wire racks to cool completely.

NO. 91 **BRANDY SNAPS**

*Makes about 24 cookies*

5 tablespoons unsalted butter
⅓ cup sugar
¼ cup dark molasses
1 teaspoon ground ginger

⅛ teaspoon salt
¾ cup sifted flour
1 tablespoon brandy

Preheat the oven to 375° F. Lightly grease two large baking sheets with butter or vegetable shortening.

In a medium saucepan, melt the butter over low heat. Stir in the sugar, molasses, ginger, and salt. Cook, stirring constantly, until the sugar dissolves. Pour the mixture into a large mixing bowl. Beat in the flour and the brandy.

Drop rounded teaspoonfuls of batter onto the baking sheets, about 2 inches apart. Bake for 7 to 8 minutes, or until the cookies have browned around the edges. Remove from the oven.

After the cookies have cooled for 2 to 3 minutes, but are still warm to the touch, use a spatula to transfer them to wire racks to cool completely.

NO. 92            **BUTTERSCOTCH CHOCOLATE CHIP COOKIES**

*Makes about 50 small cookies*

½ cup unsalted butter, softened
⅓ cup dark brown sugar, firmly packed
⅓ cup sugar
1 egg
1 teaspoon vanilla extract
1 cup plus 2 tablespoons sifted flour

½ teaspoon baking soda
½ teaspoon salt
¾ cup walnuts, coarsely chopped
1 cup semi-sweet chocolate morsels
1 cup butterscotch morsels

Preheat the oven to 375° F. Lightly grease two large baking sheets with butter or vegetable shortening.

In a large mixing bowl, cream the butter and the sugars together. Beat in the egg and the vanilla extract. Sift together the flour, baking soda, and salt. Gradually add the flour mixture to the batter. Stir in the chopped walnuts and the chocolate and butterscotch morsels.

Drop rounded teaspoonfuls of batter onto the baking sheets, about 2 inches apart. Bake for 10 to 12 minutes, or until the cookies are golden brown. Remove from the oven.

After the cookies have cooled for 2 to 3 minutes, but are still warm to the touch, use a spatula to transfer them to wire racks to cool completely.

NO. 93            **BUTTERSCOTCH OATMEAL COOKIES**

*Makes about 36 cookies*

1 cup quick-cooking oatmeal
¾ cup sifted flour
1 teaspoon baking powder
¼ teaspoon salt
¼ cup unsweetened shredded coconut

7½-ounce package butterscotch morsels
6 tablespoons unsalted butter
1 teaspoon vanilla extract
1 egg, beaten

Preheat the oven to 350° F. Lightly grease two large baking sheets with butter or vegetable shortening.

Combine the oatmeal, flour, baking powder, salt, and coconut in a large mixing bowl. Set aside. In a small saucepan, over very low heat, melt the butterscotch morsels with the butter. Stir in the vanilla extract and remove the pan from the heat. Stir the beaten egg into the oatmeal mixture, then add the melted butterscotch mixture. Mix well.

Drop rounded teaspoonfuls of batter onto the baking sheets, about 2 inches apart. Bake for 10 minutes, or until the cookies have browned around the edges. Remove from the oven.

After the cookies have cooled for 2 to 3 minutes, but are still warm to the touch, use a spatula to transfer them to wire racks to cool completely.

## NO. 94 BUTTERSCOTCH OATMEAL RAISIN COOKIES

*Makes about 36 cookies*

1 cup quick-cooking oatmeal
¾ cup sifted flour
1 teaspoon baking powder
¼ teaspoon salt
7½-ounce package butterscotch morsels

6 tablespoons unsalted butter
½ teaspoon almond extract
1 egg, beaten
1 cup golden raisins
½ cup walnuts, coarsely chopped

Preheat the oven to 350° F. Lightly grease two large baking sheets with butter or vegetable shortening.

In a large mixing bowl, combine the oatmeal, flour, baking powder, and salt. Set aside.

Combine the butterscotch morsels and the butter in a small saucepan. Cook over very low heat, stirring constantly, until the mixture has completely melted. Stir in the almond extract. Remove the pan from the heat and set aside. Stir the beaten egg into the oatmeal mixture, then add the melted butterscotch. Mix in the raisins and the chopped walnuts.

Drop rounded teaspoonfuls of batter onto the baking sheets, about 2 inches apart. Bake for 10 minutes, or until the cookies have browned around the edges. Remove from the oven.

After the cookies have cooled for 2 to 3 minutes, but are still warm to the touch, use a spatula to transfer them to wire racks to cool completely.

NO. **95**                          **CARAMEL PECAN ROCK**
**COOKIES**

*Makes about 50 cookies*

½ cup milk
½ cup unsalted butter,
   softened
1½ cups dark brown sugar,
   firmly packed

1 egg, beaten
1 teaspoon vanilla extract
2 cups sifted flour
½ teaspoon baking soda
1½ cups pecans, finely chopped

Preheat the oven to 375° F. Lightly grease two large baking sheets with butter or vegetable shortening.

In a small saucepan, heat the milk until it coats the back of a metal spoon. Remove the pan from the heat and set aside.

In a large mixing bowl, cream together the butter and sugar. Beat in the egg. Continue to beat until the batter is light and creamy. Stir in the warm milk and the vanilla extract. Sift the flour with the baking soda and fold into the batter. Add the chopped pecans and mix well.

Drop rounded teaspoonfuls of batter onto the baking sheets, about 2 inches apart. Bake for 15 to 18 minutes, or until the cookies have browned around the edges. Remove from the oven.

After the cookies have cooled for 2 to 3 minutes, but are still warm to the touch, use a spatula to transfer them to wire racks to cool completely.

NO. **96**                          **CARDAMON COOKIES**

*Makes about 30 cookies*

These cookies must stand overnight before baking.

2 eggs
1 cup confectioners' sugar
½ teaspoon grated lemon zest

1 tablespoon ground
   cardamon seed
1 cup sifted flour
¾ teaspoon baking powder

Lightly grease two large baking sheets with vegetable shortening.

In a large mixing bowl, beat the eggs until foamy. Gradually stir in the sugar, ¼ cup at a time, mixing thoroughly. Add the lemon zest and the cardamon. Sift the flour with the baking powder. Slowly work the flour into the egg mixture.

Drop rounded teaspoonfuls of batter onto the baking sheets, about 2 inches apart. Let the cookies stand uncovered overnight, or for about 12 hours.

Preheat the oven to 325° F. Bake the cookies for 10 to 12 minutes, or until they are golden brown.

After the cookies have cooled for 2 to 3 minutes, but are still warm to the touch, use a spatula to transfer them to wire racks to cool completely.

## NO. 97 — CHERRY CENTERS

*Makes about 48 cookies*

| | |
|---|---|
| 1 cup unsalted butter, softened | 2¾ cups sifted flour |
| 1 cup confectioners' sugar | 2 teaspoons baking powder |
| 2 eggs | ¼ teaspoon salt |
| 1 teaspoon vanilla extract | 48 maraschino cherries, drained |
| 2 tablespoons milk | |

Preheat the oven to 375° F. Lightly grease two large baking sheets with butter or vegetable shortening.

In a large mixing bowl, cream together the butter and sugar. Beat in the eggs, one at a time, mixing well after each addition. Beat in the vanilla extract and the milk, continuing to beat until the batter is smooth. Sift the flour with the baking powder and salt. Gradually work the flour into the batter, ½ cup at a time, until it is smooth.

Drop rounded teaspoonfuls of batter onto the baking sheets, about 2 inches apart. Place a cherry in the center of each cookie. Bake for 10 minutes, or until the cookies have browned around the edges. Remove from the oven.

After the cookies have cooled for 2 to 3 minutes, but are still warm to the touch, use a spatula to transfer them to wire racks to cool completely.

## NO. 98 — CHERRY COCONUT CHEWS

*Makes about 50 cookies*

| | |
|---|---|
| ½ cup milk | ½ teaspoon baking soda |
| ½ cup unsalted butter, softened | ½ cup walnuts, coarsely chopped |
| 1½ cups sugar | 1 cup shredded unsweetened coconut |
| 1 egg, beaten | 1 cup drained maraschino cherries, coarsely chopped |
| 1 teaspoon vanilla extract | |
| 1 teaspoon lemon extract | |
| 2 cups sifted flour | |

Preheat the oven to 375° F. Lightly grease two large baking sheets with butter or vegetable shortening.

In a small saucepan over low heat, warm the milk until it coats the back of a metal spoon. Remove the pan from the heat and set aside.

In a large mixing bowl, cream together the butter and sugar. Beat in the egg, continuing to mix until the batter is light and creamy. Mix in the vanilla extract and the lemon extract. Stir in the milk. Sift the flour with the baking soda and fold into the batter. Fold the chopped walnuts, coconut, and cherries into the batter.

Drop rounded teaspoonfuls of batter onto the baking sheets, about 2 inches apart. Bake for 10 to 12 minutes, or until the cookies have browned around the edges. Remove from the oven.

After the cookies have cooled for 2 to 3 minutes, but are still warm to the touch, use a spatula to transfer them to wire racks to cool completely.

NO. 99

# CHOCOLATE BUTTERSCOTCH COOKIES

*Makes about 36 cookies*

| | |
|---|---|
| 1 cup quick-cooking oatmeal | 7½-ounce package butterscotch |
| ¾ cup sifted flour | morsels |
| ½ cup light brown sugar | 2 ounces (2 squares) |
| 1 teaspoon baking powder | unsweetened baking |
| ¼ teaspoon salt | chocolate |
| ¼ cup unsweetened shredded | 6 tablespoons unsalted butter |
| coconut | 1 teaspoon vanilla extract |
| | 1 egg, beaten |

Preheat the oven to 350° F. Lightly grease two large baking sheets with butter or vegetable shortening.

In a large mixing bowl, combine the oatmeal, flour, sugar, baking powder, salt, and coconut. Set aside.

In a small saucepan combine butterscotch morsels, chocolate, and butter. Cook, over very low heat, stirring constantly, until the mixture has melted. Stir in the vanilla extract. Remove the pan from the heat.

Stir the beaten egg into the oatmeal mixture, then add the melted butterscotch mixture. Mix well.

Drop rounded teaspoonfuls of batter onto the baking sheets, about 2 inches apart. Bake for 10 minutes, or until the cookies have browned around the edges. Remove from the oven.

After the cookies have cooled for 2 to 3 minutes, but are still warm to the touch, use a spatula to transfer them to wire racks to cool completely.

NO. **100**                            **CHOCOLATE CHERRY**
                                                    **JUMBLES**
                                        *Makes about 50 cookies*

4 ounces (4 squares)                    2 cups sifted flour
   unsweetened baking     ½ teaspoon baking soda
   chocolate               ½ cup blanched almonds,
½ cup milk                                 coarsely chopped
½ cup unsalted butter,                  1½ cups unsweetened shredded
   softened                  coconut
2 cups sugar                            1 cup drained maraschino
1 egg, beaten                              cherries, coarsely
2 teaspoons chocolate liqueur              chopped

Preheat the oven to 375° F. Lightly grease two large baking sheets with butter or vegetable shortening.

Combine the chocolate with the milk in a small saucepan. Cook over low heat, stirring frequently, until the chocolate has melted. Remove the pan from the heat and set aside.

In a large mixing bowl, cream together the butter and sugar. Beat in the egg. Continue to beat until the mixture is light and creamy. Mix in the chocolate liqueur. Stir in the melted chocolate mixture. Sift the flour with the baking soda. Fold the flour mixture into the batter. Stir in the chopped almonds, coconut, and cherries.

Drop rounded teaspoonfuls of batter onto the baking sheets, about 2 inches apart. Bake for 10 to 12 minutes, or until the cookies have browned around the edges. Remove from the oven.

After the cookies have cooled for 2 to 3 minutes, but are still warm to the touch, use a spatula to transfer them to wire racks to cool completely.

NO. **101**           **CHOCOLATE CHIP COOKIES**
                                *Makes about 50 small cookies*

½ cup unsalted butter,                  ½ teaspoon baking soda
   softened               ½ teaspoon salt
⅓ cup dark brown sugar,                 7½-ounce package semi-sweet
   firmly packed             chocolate morsels
⅓ cup sugar                             ¾ cup walnuts, coarsely
1 egg                                      chopped
1 teaspoon vanilla extract
1 cup plus 2 tablespoons
   sifted flour

Preheat the oven to 375° F. Lightly grease two large baking sheets with butter or vegetable shortening.

In a large mixing bowl, cream together the butter and the sugars. Beat in the egg and the vanilla extract. Mix well. Sift together the flour, baking soda, and salt. Gradually add the flour mixture to the batter. Add the chocolate morsels and the chopped walnuts. Mix well.

Drop rounded teaspoonfuls of batter onto the baking sheets, about 2 inches apart. Bake for 10 to 12 minutes, or until the cookies have browned around the edges. Remove from the oven.

After the cookies have cooled for 2 to 3 minutes, but are still warm to the touch, use a spatula to transfer them to wire racks to cool completely.

## NO. 102        COCONUT CHOCOLATE CHIP COOKIES
*Makes about 50 small cookies*

Follow the recipe for Chocolate Chip Cookies (No. 101), adding ¾ cup of unsweetened shredded coconut to the batter.

## NO. 103        GUMDROP COOKIES
*Makes about 50 small cookies*

Follow the recipe for Chocolate Chip Cookies (No. 101), but add 2 cups of tiny spearmint gumdrops to the batter and omit the chocolate morsels.

## NO. 104        M&M® COOKIES
*Makes about 50 small cookies*

Follow the recipe for Chocolate Chip Cookies (No. 101), substituting 2 cups of plain M&M® candies for the chocolate morsels.

## NO. 105        PEANUT M&M® COOKIES
*Makes about 50 small cookies*

Follow the recipe for Chocolate Chip Cookies (No. 101), substituting 2 cups of Peanut M&M® candies for the chocolate morsels.

NO. **106**

## MILK CHOCOLATE CHIP COOKIES

*Makes about 50 small cookies*

Follow the recipe for Chocolate Chip Cookies (No. 101), substituting milk chocolate morsels for the semi-sweet chocolate morsels.

NO. **107**

## MINT CHOCOLATE CHIP COOKIES

*Makes about 50 small cookies*

Follow the recipe for Chocolate Chip Cookies (No. 101), substituting mint chocolate morsels for the semi-sweet chocolate morsels.

NO. **108**

## CHOCOLATE CHOCOLATE CHIP COOKIES

*Makes about 60 small cookies*

4 ounces (4 squares) unsweetened baking chocolate
¾ cup unsalted butter, softened
½ cup dark brown sugar, firmly packed
½ cup sugar
2 eggs

1 teaspoon vanilla extract
1½ cups sifted flour
1 teaspoon baking soda
½ teaspoon salt
1 cup walnuts, coarsely chopped
7½-ounce package semi-sweet chocolate morsels

Preheat the oven to 375° F. Lightly grease two large baking sheets with butter or vegetable shortening.

Melt the baking chocolate in the top of a double boiler over hot water, stirring constantly. Remove the pan from the heat and set aside.

In a large mixing bowl, cream together the butter and sugars. Beat in the eggs and the vanilla extract. Mix well. Stir in the melted chocolate. Sift together the flour, baking soda, and salt. Gradually add the flour mixture to the batter. Add the chopped walnuts and chocolate morsels to the batter.

Drop rounded teaspoonfuls of batter onto the baking sheets, about 2 inches apart. Bake for 10 to 12 minutes, or until the cookies have browned around the edges. Remove from the oven.

After the cookies have cooled for 2 to 3 minutes, but are still warm to the touch, use a spatula to transfer them to wire racks to cool completely.

NO. **109**           CHOCOLATE BUTTERSCOTCH
                                  CHIP COOKIES
                      *Makes about 60 small cookies*

Follow the recipe for Chocolate Chocolate Chip Cookies (No. 108), substituting butterscotch morsels for the semi-sweet chocolate morsels.

NO. **110**              MINT CHOCOLATE
                 CHOCOLATE CHIP COOKIES
                      *Makes about 60 small cookies*

Follow the recipe for Chocolate Chocolate Chip Cookies (No. 108), substituting mint chocolate morsels for the semi-sweet chocolate morsels.

NO. **111**        CHOCOLATE CINNAMON SOUR
                    CREAM DROP COOKIES
                       *Makes about 48 cookies*

2 ounces (2 squares)          1 teaspoon vanilla extract
    unsweetened baking      2½ cups sifted flour
    chocolate                 1 teaspoon baking soda
¼ cup unsalted butter,        1 tablespoon cinnamon
    softened                  ½ teaspoon nutmeg
1¾ cups light brown sugar     1 cup sour cream
2 eggs, beaten

Preheat the oven to 375° F. Lightly grease two large baking sheets with butter or vegetable shortening.

Melt the chocolate in the top of a double boiler over simmering water, stirring frequently. Remove the pan from the heat and set aside.

In a large mixing bowl, cream together the butter and sugar. Beat in the eggs. Continue to beat until the batter is very light. Add the melted chocolate and the vanilla extract. Mix well. Sift the flour with the baking soda and cinnamon. Mix the nutmeg into the sour cream. Add the flour mixture to the batter, 1 cup at a time, alternating with the sour cream. Mix well.

Drop rounded teaspoonfuls of batter onto the baking sheets, about 2 inches apart. Bake for 12 to 15 minutes, or until the cookies have browned around the edges. Remove from the oven.

After the cookies have cooled for 2 to 3 minutes, but are still warm to the touch, use a spatula to transfer them to wire racks to cool completely.

NO. 112

# CHOCOLATE JUMBLES

*Makes about 50 cookies*

4 ounces (4 squares) unsweetened baking chocolate
½ cup milk
½ cup unsalted butter, softened

2 cups confectioners' sugar
1 egg, beaten
2 teaspoons rum
2 cups sifted flour
½ teaspoon baking soda
1 teaspoon cinnamon

Preheat the oven to 375° F. Lightly grease two large baking sheets with butter or vegetable shortening.

Combine the chocolate with the milk in a small saucepan. Cook over low heat, stirring frequently, until the chocolate has melted. Remove the pan from the heat and set aside.

In a large mixing bowl, cream together the butter and sugar. Beat in the egg. Continue to beat until the mixture is light and creamy. Mix in the rum. Stir in the melted chocolate mixture. Sift the flour with the baking soda and cinnamon. Fold the flour mixture into the batter.

Drop rounded teaspoonfuls of batter onto the baking sheets, about 2 inches apart. Bake for 10 to 12 minutes, or until the cookies have browned around the edges. Remove from the oven.

After the cookies have cooled for 2 to 3 minutes, but are still warm to the touch, use a spatula to transfer them to wire racks to cool completely.

NO. 113

# CHOCOLATE HAZELNUT JUMBLES

*Makes about 50 cookies*

Follow the recipe for Chocolate Jumbles (No. 112), adding 1 cup of hazelnuts, coarsely chopped, to the batter.

NO. 114          **CHOCOLATE MARSHMALLOW DELIGHTS**

*Makes about 30 cookies*

½ cup unsalted butter,
   softened
1 cup sugar
1 egg
1 teaspoon vanilla extract
1 teaspoon grated orange zest
¼ cup heavy cream

1¾ cups sifted cake flour
½ cup unsweetened cocoa
   powder
½ teaspoon baking powder
15 marshmallows, halved
   Walnut halves

Preheat the oven to 350° F. Lightly grease two large baking sheets with butter or vegetable shortening.

In a large mixing bowl, cream together the butter and sugar. Beat in the egg, then add the vanilla extract and the orange zest. Beat in the cream. Sift the flour with the cocoa and baking powder. Stir the flour mixture into the batter, ½ cup at a time, mixing well after each addition.

Drop rounded teaspoonfuls of batter onto the baking sheets, about 2 inches apart. Bake for 8 minutes. Remove from the oven, and leave the oven on. Top each cookie first with a marshmallow half and then with a walnut half. Return to the oven and bake for an additional 2 minutes. Remove from the oven.

After the cookies have cooled for 2 to 3 minutes, but are still warm to the touch, use a spatula to transfer them to wire racks to cool completely.


NO. 115          **CHOCOLATE PECAN COOKIES**

*Makes about 50 cookies*

2 ounces (2 squares)
   unsweetened baking
   chocolate, grated
½ cup milk
½ cup unsalted butter,
   softened

1½ cups light brown sugar
1 egg, beaten
2 cups sifted flour
½ teaspoon baking soda
1¼ cups pecans, finely chopped

Preheat the oven to 375° F. Lightly grease two large baking sheets with butter or vegetable shortening.

Combine the chocolate and the milk in the top of a double boiler over simmering water. Stir until the chocolate has melted. Remove the pan from the heat and set aside.

In a large mixing bowl, cream together the butter and sugar. Beat in the egg, continuing to beat until the batter is light and creamy.

Stir in the melted chocolate mixture. Sift the flour with the baking soda and fold into the batter. Add the chopped pecans to the batter and mix well.

Drop rounded teaspoonfuls of batter onto the baking sheets, about 2 inches apart. Bake for 15 to 18 minutes, or until the cookies have browned around the edges. Remove from the oven.

After the cookies have cooled for 2 to 3 minutes, but are still warm to the touch, use a spatula to transfer them to wire racks to cool completely.

## NO. 116     CHOCOLATE RAISIN POPPY SEED COOKIES

*Makes about 24 cookies*

¼ cup milk
½ cup poppy seeds
2 ounces (2 squares) unsweetened baking chocolate
¼ cup unsalted butter, softened
½ cup sugar
1 egg yolk

1 teaspoon lemon zest
1 teaspoon vanilla extract
¾ cup sifted flour
½ teaspoon baking powder
½ teaspoon cinnamon
⅛ teaspoon ground cloves
¼ cup raisins, coarsely chopped

Preheat the oven to 350° F. Lightly grease two large baking sheets with butter or vegetable shortening.

In a small saucepan, heat the milk until it coats the back of a metal spoon. Remove from the heat. Stir the poppy seeds into the hot milk and let them soak.

Melt the chocolate in the top of a double boiler over simmering water, stirring frequently. Remove the pan from the heat and set aside.

In a large mixing bowl, cream together the butter and sugar. Beat in the egg yolk, lemon zest, and vanilla extract. Mix well. Stir in the melted chocolate. Sift the flour with the baking powder, cinnamon, and cloves. Gradually add the flour mixture to the batter, ⅓ cup at a time. Add the chopped raisins to the batter. Stir in the poppy seed mixture and mix well.

Drop rounded teaspoonfuls of batter onto the baking sheets, about 2 inches apart. Bake for about 20 minutes, or until the cookies have browned around the edges. Remove from the oven.

After the cookies have cooled for 2 to 3 minutes, but are still warm to the touch, use a spatula to transfer them to wire racks to cool completely.

NO. **117**            **CHOCOLATE WALNUT ROCK**
**COOKIES**

*Makes about 50 cookies*

4 ounces (4 squares)
    unsweetened baking
    chocolate
½ cup milk
½ cup unsalted butter,
    softened
2 cups sugar

1 egg, beaten
1 teaspoon vanilla extract
2 cups sifted flour
½ teaspoon baking soda
1½ cups walnuts, coarsely
    chopped

Preheat the oven to 375° F. Lightly grease two large baking sheets with butter or vegetable shortening.

Melt the chocolate in the top of a double boiler over simmering water, stirring frequently. Remove from the heat and set aside.

In a small saucepan over moderate heat, warm the milk until it coats the back of a metal spoon. Remove from the heat and set aside.

In a large mixing bowl, cream together the butter and sugar. Beat in the egg. Continue to mix until the batter is light and creamy. Mix in the melted chocolate and the vanilla extract. Stir in the warm milk. Sift the flour with the baking soda and fold into the batter. Stir in the chopped walnuts and mix well.

Drop rounded teaspoonfuls of batter onto the baking sheets, about 2 inches apart. Bake for 15 to 18 minutes, or until the cookies have browned around the edges. Remove from the oven.

After the cookies have cooled for 2 to 3 minutes, but are still warm to the touch, use a spatula to transfer them to wire racks to cool completely.

NO. **118**            **COCONUT DROP COOKIES**

*Makes about 36 cookies*

½ cup unsalted butter,
    softened
1 cup sugar
1 egg

1 cup unsweetened shredded
    coconut
½ teaspoon almond extract
1 cup sifted flour
1 teaspoon baking powder

Preheat the oven to 400° F. Lightly grease two large baking sheets with butter or vegetable shortening.

In a large mixing bowl, cream together the butter and sugar. Beat in the egg, then add the coconut and almond extract. Mix well. Sift the flour with the baking powder and add the mixture to the batter, ½ cup at a time.

Drop rounded teaspoonfuls of batter onto the baking sheets, about 2 inches apart. Bake for 10 to 15 minutes, or until the cookies have browned around the edges. Remove from the oven.

After the cookies have cooled for 2 to 3 minutes, but are still warm to the touch, use a spatula to transfer them to wire racks to cool completely.

NO. **119**

# COCONUT WAFERS

*Makes about 40 cookies*

¼ cup unsalted butter, softened
1 cup sugar
3 eggs, separated
¼ teaspoon baking soda
2 teaspoons hot water

1 teaspoon rose water
2 cups sifted flour
½ cup buttermilk
1 cup unsweetened shredded coconut

Preheat the oven to 400° F. Lightly grease two large baking sheets with butter or vegetable shortening.

In a large mixing bowl, cream together the butter and sugar. Beat in the egg yolks, one at a time, mixing thoroughly after each addition. Dissolve the baking soda in the hot water. Add the rose water to the baking soda mixture. Add the flour to the batter, ½ cup at a time, alternating with the buttermilk, the soda mixture, and the coconut. In another bowl, beat the egg whites until stiff. Gently fold the beaten egg whites into the batter.

Drop rounded teaspoonfuls of batter onto the baking sheets, about 2 inches apart. Bake for 10 to 12 minutes, or until the cookies have browned around the edges. Remove from the oven.

Immediately loosen the cookies from the baking sheet with a spatula and transfer to wire racks to cool completely. (The cookies will break if allowed to cool on the baking sheets.)

NO. **120**

# CULPEPPER OATMEAL COOKIES

*Makes about 50 cookies*

½ cup unsalted butter, softened
½ cup sugar
1 egg, separated
½ teaspoon baking soda
2 teaspoons hot water

1 tablespoon milk
½ teaspoon vanilla extract
1½ cups raisins
1 cup sifted flour
1 cup rolled oats

Preheat the oven to 450° F. Lightly grease two large baking sheets with butter or vegetable shortening.

In a large mixing bowl, cream together the butter and sugar. Beat in the egg yolk and mix well. Dissolve the baking soda in the hot water. Add the soda mixture, milk, and vanilla extract and beat until the mixture is creamy. In a separate bowl, beat the egg white until stiff peaks form. Gently fold the beaten egg white into the batter. Add the raisins. In another bowl, combine the flour with the oats. Quickly stir the flour mixture into the batter.

Drop rounded teaspoonfuls of batter onto the baking sheets, about 2 inches apart. Flatten each cookie with the bottom of a glass. Bake for about 10 minutes, or until the cookies have browned around the edges. Remove from the oven.

After the cookies have cooled for 2 to 3 minutes, but are still warm to the touch, use a spatula to transfer them to wire racks to cool completely.

NO. 121                        **CURRANT COOKIES**

*Makes about 36 cookies*

2 cups sifted flour
1½ teaspoons baking powder
½ teaspoon salt
½ cup dried currants
¼ cup dark brown sugar,
    firmly packed

1 teaspoon grated lemon zest
2 tablespoons unsalted butter,
    softened
1 cup milk

Preheat the oven to 400° F. Lightly grease two large baking sheets with butter or vegetable shortening.

Sift the flour with the baking powder and salt into a large mixing bowl. Add the currants, brown sugar, and lemon zest. Mix well. Cut the butter into chunks and add to the mixture. Using a pastry blender or two forks, work the mixture to the texture of coarse oatmeal. Add the milk, mixing quickly and lightly.

Drop rounded teaspoonfuls of batter onto the baking sheets, about 2 inches apart. Bake for 12 to 15 minutes, or until the cookies have browned around the edges. Remove from the oven.

After the cookies have cooled for 2 to 3 minutes, but are still warm to the touch, use a spatula to transfer them to wire racks to cool completely.

NO. **122**

# CRY BABIES

*Makes about 48 cookies*

½ cup unsalted butter
½ cup dark brown sugar,
    firmly packed
½ cup dark molasses
2 eggs, beaten
1 teaspoon vanilla extract
1 teaspoon grated lemon zest

2 cups sifted flour
¼ teaspoon salt
½ teaspoon cinnamon
½ teaspoon nutmeg
1 teaspoon baking soda
½ cup boiling water

Preheat the oven to 375° F. Lightly grease two large baking sheets with butter or vegetable shortening.

Melt the butter in a small saucepan over very low heat. Pour the melted butter into a large mixing bowl and combine with the sugar. Beat in the molasses. Stir in the beaten eggs. Add the vanilla extract and lemon zest. Sift the flour with the salt, cinnamon, and nutmeg. Dissolve the baking soda in the boiling water. Add the flour mixture to the batter, ⅓ cup at a time, alternating with the soda mixture. Beat until the batter is smooth.

Drop rounded teaspoonfuls of batter onto the baking sheets about 2 inches apart. Bake for 12 to 15 minutes, or until the cookies are firm to the touch. Remove from the oven.

After the cookies have cooled for 2 to 3 minutes, but are still warm to the touch, use a spatula to transfer them to wire racks to cool completely.

NO. **123**

# DATE DROPS

*Makes about 30 cookies*

½ cup unsalted butter,
    softened
1 cup sugar
2 eggs, beaten
1 teaspoon baking soda
4 tablespoons water
1½ cups sifted flour
1 teaspoon baking powder

1 teaspoon cinnamon
½ teaspoon ground cloves
¼ teaspoon salt
1 cup pecans, coarsely
    chopped
4 cups pitted dates, coarsely
    chopped

Preheat the oven to 425° F. Lightly grease two large baking sheets with butter or vegetable shortening.

In a large mixing bowl, cream together the butter and sugar. Beat in the eggs, and mix well. Dissolve the baking soda in the water. Sift the flour with the baking powder, cinnamon, cloves, and salt. Add the flour mixture to the batter, ½ cup at a time, alternating with the baking soda mixture. Mix well after each addition. When the batter is smooth, stir in the chopped pecans and dates.

Drop rounded teaspoonfuls of batter onto the baking sheets, about 2 inches apart. Bake for 8 to 10 minutes, or until the cookies have browned around the edges. Remove from the oven.

After the cookies have cooled for 2 to 3 minutes, but are still warm to the touch, use a spatula to transfer them to wire racks to cool completely.

NO. **124**                        # DROP TEA CAKES

*Makes about 36 cookies*

| | |
|---|---|
| 4 eggs | 1½ cups sifted flour |
| 1 teaspoon grated lemon zest | ¼ teaspoon salt |
| 1 teaspoon vanilla extract | 1 cup superfine sugar |

Preheat the oven to 325° F. Lightly grease two large baking sheets with butter or vegetable shortening.

In a large mixing bowl, beat the eggs until foamy. Mix in the lemon zest and the vanilla extract. Sift the flour with the salt. Add the flour to the egg mixture, ½ cup at a time, alternating with the sugar. Mix until the batter is smooth.

Drop rounded teaspoonfuls of batter onto the baking sheets, about 2 inches apart. Bake for 10 to 15 minutes, or until the cookies have browned around the edges. Remove from the oven.

After the cookies have cooled for 2 to 3 minutes, but are still warm to the touch, use a spatula to transfer them to wire racks to cool completely.

NO. **125**                        # DUTCH SPONGE COOKIES

*Makes about 36 cookies*

| | |
|---|---|
| 4 egg yolks | ½ teaspoon ground cloves |
| 2 cups sifted confectioners' sugar | 1 teaspoon cinnamon |
| 2 cups sifted flour | Confectioners' sugar |

Preheat the oven to 325° F. Lightly grease two large baking sheets with butter or vegetable shortening.

In a large mixing bowl, beat the egg yolks until foamy and thick. Beat in the sugar, ¼ cup at a time. Continue to beat until the batter is light and very thick. Sift the flour with the cloves and cinnamon, then sift the mixture once more. Gently fold into the batter; do not beat.

Drop rounded teaspoonfuls of batter onto the baking sheets, about 2 inches apart. Bake for about 15 minutes, or until the cookies are golden brown and firm to the touch. Remove from the oven.

After the cookies have cooled for 2 to 3 minutes, but are still warm to the touch, use a spatula to transfer them to wire racks to cool completely. When the cookies are cool, dust them with confectioners' sugar.

NO. **126**                    **FANCY JUMBLES**

*Makes about 50 cookies*

½ cup milk
½ cup unsalted butter, softened
2 cups sugar
1 egg, beaten
2 teaspoons rum

2 cups sifted flour
½ teaspoon baking soda
½ teaspoon mace
½ teaspoon cinnamon
1 cup coarsely chopped citron

Preheat the oven to 375° F. Lightly grease two large baking sheets with butter or vegetable shortening.

In a small saucepan, heat the milk until it coats the back of a metal spoon. Remove the pan from the heat and set aside.

In a large mixing bowl, cream together the butter and sugar. Add the egg. Continue to beat until the batter is light and creamy. Mix in the rum. Stir in the milk. Sift the flour with the baking soda, mace, and cinnamon. Fold the flour mixture into the batter and mix until smooth. Stir in the chopped citron.

Drop rounded teaspoonfuls of batter onto the baking sheets, about 2 inches apart. Bake for 10 to 12 minutes, or until the cookies have browned around the edges. Remove from the oven.

After the cookies have cooled for 2 to 3 minutes, but are still warm to the touch, use a spatula to transfer them to wire racks to cool completely.

NO. **127**                    **FRUIT DROP COOKIES**

*Makes about 36 cookies*

2 eggs
1 cup light brown sugar
1 cup coarsely chopped citron
½ cup walnuts, coarsely chopped
1½ cups sifted flour

½ teaspoon baking soda
1 teaspoon cream of tartar
¼ teaspoon nutmeg
½ teaspoon ground cloves
1 teaspoon cinnamon

Preheat the oven to 400° F. Lightly grease two large baking sheets with butter or vegetable shortening.

In a large mixing bowl, beat the eggs until they are thick and foamy. Beat in the sugar. Add the chopped citron and walnuts and mix well. Sift the flour with the baking soda, cream of tartar, nutmeg, cloves, and cinnamon. Quickly fold the flour mixture into the batter.

Drop rounded teaspoonfuls of batter onto the baking sheets, about 2 inches apart. Bake for 10 to 15 minutes, or until the cookies have browned around the edges. Remove from the oven.

After the cookies have cooled for 2 to 3 minutes, but are still warm to the touch, use a spatula to transfer them to wire racks to cool completely.

NO. **128**                    **FRUIT OATMEAL COOKIES**

*Makes about 48 cookies*

⅓ cup unsalted butter, softened
½ cup sugar
1 egg
2 tablespoons dark molasses
1 cup sifted flour
½ teaspoon baking soda
½ teaspoon salt

½ teaspoon cinnamon
1 cup rolled oats
½ cup walnuts, coarsely chopped
½ cup raisins
½ cup coarsely chopped dried apricots

Preheat the oven to 400° F. Lightly grease two large baking sheets with butter or vegetable shortening.

In a large mixing bowl, cream together the butter and sugar. Beat in the egg and mix well. Stir in the molasses. Sift the flour with the baking soda, salt, and cinnamon. Add half the flour to the butter mixture and stir until thoroughly blended. Mix in the oats, then gently stir in the remaining flour. Add the walnuts, raisins, and apricots. Mix well.

Drop rounded teaspoonfuls of batter onto the baking sheets, about 2 inches apart. Bake for 10 to 12 minutes, or until the cookies have browned around the edges. Remove from the oven.

After the cookies have cooled for 2 to 3 minutes, but are still warm to the touch, use a spatula to transfer them to wire racks to cool completely.

## NO. 129     FRUIT AND WALNUT COOKIES

*Makes about 36 cookies*

½ cup unsalted butter,
    softened
½ cup dark brown sugar,
    firmly packed
¼ cup superfine sugar
2 eggs, beaten
½ teaspoon baking soda

2 teaspoons hot water
1½ cups sifted flour
1 teaspoon cinnamon
¼ teaspoon salt
2 cups walnuts, coarsely
    chopped
1 cup raisins

Preheat the oven to 400° F. Lightly grease two large baking sheets with butter or vegetable shortening.

In a large mixing bowl, cream together the butter and sugars. Beat in the eggs. Dissolve the baking soda in the hot water. Sift the flour with the cinnamon and salt. Add the flour to the batter, ½ cup at a time. Add the baking soda mixture after the first cup of flour has been mixed in. Stir in the chopped walnuts and the raisins.

Drop rounded teaspoonfuls of batter onto the baking sheets, about 2 inches apart. Bake for about 15 minutes, or until the cookies have browned around the edges. Remove from the oven.

After the cookies have cooled for 2 to 3 minutes, but are still warm to the touch, use a spatula to transfer them to wire racks to cool completely.

## NO. 130     GINGER SNAPS

*Makes about 36 cookies*

½ cup unsalted butter,
    softened
2 cups sugar
¼ cup dark molasses
2 eggs

1 cup sifted flour
2 teaspoons baking soda
1 teaspoon ground ginger
½ teaspoon ground cloves
¼ teaspoon salt

Preheat the oven to 350° F. Lightly grease two large baking sheets with butter or vegetable shortening.

In a large mixing bowl, cream together the butter and sugar. Stir in the molasses. Beat in the eggs, one at a time. Sift the flour with the baking soda, ginger, cloves, and salt. Add the flour mixture to the batter, ⅓ cup at a time, mixing well after each addition. Beat until the batter is smooth.

Drop rounded teaspoonfuls of batter onto the baking sheets, about 2 inches apart. Bake for 8 to 10 minutes, or until the cookies have browned around the edges. Remove from the oven.

After the cookies have cooled for 2 to 3 minutes, but are still

warm to the touch, use a spatula to transfer them to wire racks to cool completely.

NO. 131                 # HAZELNUT COCONUT DROP
                                                  # COOKIES

*Makes about 36 cookies*

½ cup unsalted butter,
   softened
1 cup sugar
1 egg
¾ cup unsweetened shredded
   coconut

½ teaspoon almond extract
1 cup sifted flour
1 teaspoon baking powder
½ cup hazelnuts, finely
   chopped

Preheat the oven to 400° F. Lightly grease two large baking sheets with butter or vegetable shortening.

In a large mixing bowl, cream together the butter and sugar. Beat in the egg, then add the coconut and almond extract. Mix well. Sift the flour with the baking powder and add the mixture to the batter, ½ cup at a time. Stir in the chopped hazelnuts.

Drop rounded teaspoonfuls of batter onto the baking sheets, about 2 inches apart. Bake for 10 to 15 minutes, or until the cookies have browned around the edges. Remove from the oven.

After the cookies have cooled for 2 to 3 minutes, but are still warm to the touch, use a spatula to transfer them to wire racks to cool completely.

NO. 132                                 # JACKSON JUMBLES

*Makes about 50 cookies*

½ cup unsalted butter,
   softened
2 cups sugar
1 egg, beaten
2 teaspoons brandy

2 teaspoons grated lemon zest
½ teaspoon baking soda
½ cup sour cream
2 cups sifted flour

Preheat the oven to 375° F. Lightly grease two large baking sheets with butter or vegetable shortening.

In a large mixing bowl, cream together the butter and sugar. Beat in the egg. Continue to beat until the batter is light and creamy. Mix in the brandy and lemon zest. In another bowl, mix together the baking soda and sour cream. Fold the flour into the batter, ½ cup at a time, alternating with the sour cream mixture.

Drop rounded teaspoonfuls of batter onto the baking sheets, about

2 inches apart. Bake for 10 to 12 minutes, or until the cookies have browned around the edges. Remove from the oven.

After the cookies have cooled for 2 to 3 minutes, but are still warm to the touch, use a spatula to transfer them to wire racks to cool completely.

NO. **133**

# JAM COOKIES

*Makes about 36 cookies*

½ cup unsalted butter, softened
⅔ cup sugar
1 egg
1 tablespoon heavy cream
1 teaspoon vanilla extract

1 teaspoon grated orange zest
¼ cup apricot jam
2 cups sifted flour
1 teaspoon baking powder
⅛ teaspoon salt

Preheat the oven to 375° F. Lightly grease two large baking sheets with butter or vegetable shortening.

In a large mixing bowl, cream together the butter and sugar. Beat in the egg. Add the cream, vanilla extract, orange zest, and apricot jam. Mix well. Sift the flour with the baking powder and salt. Beat the flour mixture into the batter, ½ cup at a time.

Drop rounded teaspoonfuls of batter onto the baking sheets, about 2 inches apart. Bake for 10 to 12 minutes, or until the cookies have browned around the edges. Remove from the oven.

After the cookies have cooled for 2 to 3 minutes, but are still warm to the touch, use a spatula to transfer them to wire racks to cool completely.

NO. **134**

# LACE COOKIES

*Makes about 36 cookies*

⅓ cup unsalted butter
½ cup sifted flour
¼ teaspoon baking powder
⅛ teaspoon salt
½ cup sugar

½ cup rolled oats
2 tablespoons light corn syrup
2 tablespoons heavy cream
1 teaspoon vanilla extract

Preheat the oven to 350° F. Lightly grease two large baking sheets with butter or vegetable shortening.

Melt the butter in a small saucepan over very low heat. Remove the pan from the heat and set aside.

Sift the flour with the baking powder, salt, and sugar. In a large mixing bowl, combine the oats and the flour mixture. In another bowl, combine the melted butter, corn syrup, cream, and vanilla extract. Pour into the flour mixture. Mix well, but do not beat.

Drop rounded teaspoonfuls of batter onto the baking sheets, about 4 inches apart. (These cookies really spread as they bake.) Bake for about 8 minutes, or until the cookies are light brown. Remove from the oven.

After the cookies have cooled for about 30 seconds, remove them from the baking sheets with a spatula and transfer to wire racks to cool completely. (If these cookies cool longer than 30 seconds, they will stick to the baking sheets.)

NO. **135**                        **LEMON JUMBLES**

*Makes about 50 cookies*

½ cup milk
½ cup unsalted butter,
   softened
2 cups sugar
1 egg, beaten
2 teaspoons lemon juice

3 teaspoons grated lemon zest
2 cups sifted flour
½ teaspoon baking soda
1 cup coarsely chopped
   citron

Preheat the oven to 375° F. Lightly grease two large baking sheets with butter or vegetable shortening.

In a small saucepan, heat the milk until it coats the back of a metal spoon. Remove the pan from the heat and set aside.

In a large mixing bowl, cream together the butter and sugar. Beat in the egg. Continue to beat until the batter is light and creamy. Mix in the lemon juice and the lemon zest. Stir in the warm milk. Sift the flour with the baking soda. Fold the flour mixture into the batter and mix until smooth. Stir in the chopped citron.

Drop rounded teaspoonfuls of batter onto the baking sheets, about 2 inches apart. Bake for 10 to 12 minutes, or until the cookies have browned around the edges. Remove from the oven.

After the cookies have cooled for 2 to 3 minutes, but are still warm to the touch, use a spatula to transfer them to wire racks to cool completely.

NO. **136**                     **LEMON DROP COOKIES**

*Makes about 36 cookies*

2 eggs
1 cup light brown sugar
2 teaspoons grated lemon zest
1 teaspoon lemon juice

1½ cups sifted flour
½ teaspoon baking soda
1 teaspoon cream of tartar

Preheat the oven to 400° F. Lightly grease two large baking sheets with butter or vegetable shortening.

In a large mixing bowl, beat the eggs until they are thick and foamy. Beat in the sugar. Add the lemon zest and lemon juice. Mix well. Sift the flour with the baking soda and cream of tartar. Quickly fold the flour mixture into the batter.

Drop rounded teaspoonfuls of batter onto the baking sheets, about 2 inches apart. Bake for 10 to 15 minutes, or until the cookies have browned around the edges. Remove from the oven.

After the cookies have cooled for 2 to 3 minutes, but are still warm to the touch, use a spatula to transfer them to wire racks to cool completely.

## NO. 137    MACADAMIA NUT CHOCOLATE CHIP COOKIES

*Makes about 50 small cookies*

½ cup unsalted butter, softened

⅓ cup dark brown sugar, firmly packed

⅓ cup sugar

1 egg

1 teaspoon vanilla extract

1 cup plus 2 tablespoons sifted flour

½ teaspoon baking soda

½ teaspoon salt

1 cup macadamia nuts, finely chopped

7½-ounce package semi-sweet chocolate morsels

Preheat the oven to 375° F. Lightly grease two large baking sheets with butter or vegetable shortening.

Cream the butter and sugars together in a large mixing bowl. Beat in the egg and vanilla extract. Mix well. Sift together the flour, baking soda, and salt. Gradually add the flour mixture to the batter. Stir in the chopped macadamia nuts and chocolate morsels.

Drop rounded teaspoonfuls of batter onto the baking sheets, about 2 inches apart. Bake for 10 to 12 minutes, or until the cookies are golden brown. Remove from the oven.

After the cookies have cooled for 2 to 3 minutes, but are still warm to the touch, use a spatula to transfer them to wire racks to cool completely.

## NO. 138     MAPLE OATMEAL COOKIES

*Makes about 48 cookies*

⅓ cup unsalted butter, softened
1 egg
¾ cup maple syrup
1 cup sifted flour
½ teaspoon baking soda
½ teaspoon salt
½ teaspoon cinnamon
1 cup rolled oats
½ cup walnuts, coarsely chopped

Preheat the oven to 400° F. Lightly grease two large baking sheets with butter or vegetable shortening.

In a large mixing bowl, cream the butter until it is smooth. Beat in the egg. Stir in the maple syrup and mix well. Sift the flour with the baking soda, salt, and cinnamon. Add half of the flour mixture to the butter mixture. Blend well. Mix in the oats. Fold in the remaining flour. Stir in the chopped walnuts.

Drop rounded teaspoonfuls of batter onto the baking sheets, about 2 inches apart. Bake for 10 to 12 minutes, or until the cookies have browned around the edges. Remove from the oven.

After the cookies have cooled for 2 to 3 minutes, but are still warm to the touch, use a spatula to transfer them to wire racks to cool completely.

## NO. 139     MOCHA CHOCOLATE CHUNK COOKIES

*Makes about 50 small cookies*

½ cup unsalted butter, softened
⅓ cup dark brown sugar, firmly packed
⅓ cup sugar
1 egg
1 teaspoon espresso coffee powder
1 tablespoon hot water
1 cup plus 3 tablespoons sifted flour
½ teaspoon baking soda
½ teaspoon salt
1 cup hazelnuts, finely chopped
8 ounces coffee-flavored chocolate, coarsely chopped

Preheat the oven to 375° F. Lightly grease two large baking sheets with butter or vegetable shortening.

In a large mixing bowl, cream the butter and sugars together. Beat in the egg. Dissolve the coffee powder in the hot water and add the mixture to the batter. Sift together the flour, baking soda, and salt. Gradually beat the flour mixture into the batter. Stir in the chopped hazelnuts and chocolate chunks.

Drop rounded teaspoonfuls of batter onto the baking sheets, about 2 inches apart. Bake for 10 to 12 minutes, or until the cookies are brown. Remove from the oven.

After the cookies have cooled for 2 to 3 minutes, but are still warm to the touch, use a spatula to transfer them to wire racks to cool completely.

NO. **140**      # MOLASSES DROP COOKIES
*Makes about 48 cookies*

| | |
|---|---|
| ½ cup unsalted butter, softened | ½ teaspoon baking soda |
| ½ cup sugar | ½ cup hot water |
| 2 eggs | 3 cups sifted flour |
| ½ cup dark molasses | ¼ teaspoon salt |
| | ½ teaspoon ground ginger |

Preheat the oven to 400° F. Lightly grease two large baking sheets with butter or vegetable shortening.

In a large mixing bowl, cream together the butter and sugar. Beat in the eggs, one at a time. Add the molasses and beat until the batter is light and thick. Dissolve the baking soda in the hot water. Sift the flour with the salt and ginger. Add the flour mixture to the batter, 1 cup at a time, alternating with the baking soda mixture. Mix until the batter is smooth.

Drop rounded teaspoonfuls of batter onto the baking sheets, about 2 inches apart. Bake for 10 to 12 minutes, or until the cookies have browned around the edges. Remove from the oven.

After the cookies have cooled for 2 to 3 minutes, but are still warm to the touch, use a spatula to transfer them to wire racks to cool completely.

NO. **141**      # OAT BRAN COOKIES
*Makes about 48 cookies*

| | |
|---|---|
| ⅓ cup unsalted margarine, softened | ½ teaspoon baking soda |
| ½ cup sugar | ½ teaspoon cinnamon |
| 1 egg | 1 cup oat bran |
| 2 tablespoons dark molasses | ½ cup walnuts, coarsely chopped |
| 1 cup sifted flour | |

Preheat the oven to 400° F. Lightly grease two large baking sheets with butter or vegetable shortening.

In a large mixing bowl, cream together the margarine and sugar.

Beat in the egg and mix well. Stir in the molasses. Sift the flour with the baking soda and cinnamon. Add half the flour to the butter mixture and stir until thoroughly blended. Mix in the oat bran, then lightly stir in the remaining flour. Add the chopped walnuts and mix well.

Drop rounded teaspoonfuls of batter onto the baking sheets, about 2 inches apart. Bake for 10 to 12 minutes, or until the cookies have browned around the edges. Remove from the oven.

After the cookies have cooled for 2 to 3 minutes, but are still warm to the touch, use a spatula to transfer them to wire racks to cool completely.

## NO. 142        OATMEAL COOKIES

*Makes about 48 cookies*

⅓ cup unsalted butter, softened  
½ cup sugar  
1 egg  
2 tablespoons dark molasses  
1 cup sifted flour  

½ teaspoon baking soda  
½ teaspoon salt  
½ teaspoon cinnamon  
1 cup rolled oats  
½ cup walnuts, coarsely chopped  

Preheat the oven to 400° F. Lightly grease two large baking sheets with butter or vegetable shortening.

In a large mixing bowl, cream together the butter and sugar. Beat in the egg and mix well. Stir in the molasses. Sift the flour with the baking soda, salt, and cinnamon. Add half the flour to the butter mixture and stir until thoroughly blended. Mix in the oatmeal, then gently stir in the remaining flour. Add the chopped walnuts and mix well.

Drop rounded teaspoonfuls of batter onto the baking sheets, about 2 inches apart. Bake for 10 to 12 minutes, or until the cookies have browned around the edges. Remove from the oven.

After the cookies have cooled for 2 to 3 minutes, but are still warm to the touch, use a spatula to transfer them to wire racks to cool completely.

## NO. 143        OATMEAL APRICOT COOKIES

*Makes about 48 cookies*

Follow the recipe for Oatmeal Cookies (No. 142), adding 1 cup of coarsely chopped dried apricots to the batter.

NO. **144** **OATMEAL CHERRY COOKIES**

*Makes about 36 cookies*

⅓ cup unsalted butter,
  softened
½ cup sugar
1 egg
2 teaspoons grated lemon zest
2 tablespoons dark molasses
1 cup sifted flour
½ teaspoon baking soda

½ teaspoon salt
1 cup rolled oats
½ cup walnuts, coarsely
  chopped
1 cup drained maraschino
  cherries, coarsely
  chopped

Preheat the oven to 400° F. Lightly grease two large baking sheets with butter or vegetable shortening.

In a large mixing bowl, cream together the butter and sugar. Beat in the egg and mix well. Stir in the lemon zest and the molasses. Sift the flour with the baking soda and salt. Add half of the flour to the butter mixture and stir until thoroughly blended. Mix in the oats, then lightly stir in the remaining flour. Add the chopped walnuts and cherries. Mix well.

Drop rounded teaspoonfuls of batter onto the baking sheets, about 2 inches apart. Bake for 10 to 12 minutes, or until the cookies have browned around the edges. Remove from the oven.

After the cookies have cooled for 2 to 3 minutes, but are still warm to the touch, use a spatula to transfer them to wire racks to cool completely.

NO. **145** **CHOCOLATE CHIP OATMEAL CHERRY COOKIES**

*Makes about 48 cookies*

Follow the recipe for Oatmeal Cherry Cookies (No. 144), adding one 7½-ounce package of semi-sweet chocolate morsels to the batter.

NO. **146** **CHOCOLATE CHIP APRICOT OATMEAL COOKIES**

*Makes about 48 cookies*

Follow the recipe for Oatmeal Cookies (No. 142), adding one 7½-ounce package of semi-sweet chocolate morsels and 1 cup of coarsely chopped dried apricots to the batter.

NO. 147                    # MILK CHOCOLATE CHIP
                             OATMEAL COOKIES
*Makes about 48 cookies*

Follow the recipe for Oatmeal Cookies (No. 142), adding one 7½-ounce package of milk chocolate morsels to the batter.


NO. 148                    # MINT CHOCOLATE CHIP
                             OATMEAL COOKIES
*Makes about 48 cookies*

Follow the recipe for Oatmeal Cookies (No. 142), adding one 7½-ounce package of mint chocolate morsels to the batter.


NO. 149                    # OLD-FASHIONED OAT CAKES
*Makes about 48 cookies*

1 cup unsalted butter,
  softened
2 cups sugar
2 eggs
2 cups sifted flour
1 teaspoon baking soda

½ teaspoon ground cloves
1 teaspoon cinnamon
1 teaspoon ground ginger
2 cups rolled oats
1 cup buttermilk

Preheat the oven to 375° F. Lightly grease two large baking sheets with butter or vegetable shortening.

In a large mixing bowl, cream together the butter and sugar. Beat in the eggs, one at a time. Mix well. Sift the flour with the baking soda, cloves, cinnamon, and ginger. Combine the flour mixture with the oats. Add the flour mixture to the batter, 1 cup at a time, alternating with the buttermilk. Mix until the batter is smooth.

Drop rounded teaspoonfuls of batter onto the baking sheets, about 2 inches apart. Bake for 12 to 15 minutes, or until the cookies have browned around the edges. Remove from the oven.

After the cookies have cooled for 2 to 3 minutes, but are still warm to the touch, use a spatula to transfer them to wire racks to cool completely.

NO. **150** ORANGE CHOCOLATE CHUNK COOKIES

*Makes about 50 small cookies*

½ cup unsalted butter, softened

⅓ cup dark brown sugar, firmly packed

⅓ cup sugar

1 egg

2 teaspoons orange juice

2 teaspoons grated orange zest

1 cup plus 2 tablespoons sifted flour

½ teaspoon baking soda

½ teaspoon salt

1 cup walnuts, coarsely chopped

8 ounces orange-flavored chocolate, coarsely chopped

Preheat the oven to 375° F. Lightly grease two large baking sheets with butter or vegetable shortening.

In a large mixing bowl, cream the butter and sugars together. Beat in the egg. Mix the orange juice and the orange zest into the batter. Sift together the flour, baking soda, and salt. Gradually add the flour mixture to the batter. Stir in the chopped walnuts and chocolate.

Drop rounded teaspoonfuls of batter onto the baking sheets, about 2 inches apart. Bake for 10 to 12 minutes, or until the cookies are lightly browned. Remove from the oven.

After the cookies have cooled for 2 to 3 minutes, but are still warm to the touch, use a spatula to transfer them to wire racks to cool completely.

NO. **151** ORANGE DROP COOKIES

*Makes about 36 cookies*

2 eggs

1 cup light brown sugar

2 teaspoons grated orange zest

1 teaspoon orange juice

1½ cups sifted flour

½ teaspoon baking soda

1 teaspoon cream of tartar

Preheat the oven to 400° F. Lightly grease two large baking sheets with butter or vegetable shortening.

In a large mixing bowl, beat the eggs until they are thick and foamy. Beat in the sugar. Add the orange zest and orange juice. Mix well. Sift the flour with the baking soda and cream of tartar. Quickly fold the flour mixture into the batter.

Drop rounded teaspoonfuls of batter onto the baking sheets, about 2 inches apart. Bake for 10 to 15 minutes, or until the cookies have browned around the edges. Remove from the oven.

After the cookies have cooled for 2 to 3 minutes, but are still

warm to the touch, use a spatula to transfer them to wire racks to cool completely.

NO. **152**                    # ORANGE-FROSTED PUMPKIN
# COOKIES

*Makes about 48 cookies*

1 cup unsalted butter,
   softened
1 cup sugar
1 egg
1 cup canned pureed
   pumpkin
1 teaspoon vanilla extract
2 cups sifted flour
1 teaspoon baking powder

1 teaspoon baking soda
1 teaspoon cinnamon
¼ teaspoon nutmeg
¼ teaspoon ground cloves
1 cup pitted dates, coarsely
   chopped
½ cup walnuts, coarsely
   chopped

*Icing*

⅓ cup unsalted butter,
   softened
2 cups confectioners' sugar

2 to 3 tablespoons orange
   juice

Preheat the oven to 350° F. Lightly grease two large baking sheets with butter or vegetable shortening.

In a large mixing bowl, cream together the butter and sugar. Beat in the egg. Mix well. Beat in the pumpkin and the vanilla extract. Sift the flour with the baking powder, baking soda, cinnamon, nutmeg, and cloves. Add the flour mixture to the batter, ½ cup at a time, mixing well after each addition. Stir in the chopped dates and walnuts.

Drop rounded teaspoonfuls of batter onto the baking sheets, about 2 inches apart. Bake for 12 to 15 minutes, or until the cookies have browned around the edges. Remove from the oven.

After the cookies have cooled for 2 to 3 minutes, but are still warm to the touch, use a spatula to transfer them to wire racks to cool completely.

When the cookies are completely cool, prepare the icing. In a large mixing bowl, combine the butter, confectioners' sugar, and orange juice. Beat until the icing is smooth. If the mixture seems too stiff to spread, add a little more orange juice. Frost the top of each cookie. After the icing hardens, transfer the cookies to a serving plate.

NO. **153** ORANGE JUMBLES

*Makes about 50 cookies*

½ cup milk
½ cup unsalted butter,
    softened
2 cups sugar
1 egg, beaten
2 teaspoons orange juice

3 teaspoons grated orange
    zest
2 cups sifted flour
½ teaspoon baking soda
1 cup coarsely chopped citron

Preheat the oven to 375° F. Lightly grease two large baking sheets with butter or vegetable shortening.

In a small saucepan, heat the milk until it coats the back of a metal spoon. Remove the pan from the heat and set aside.

In a large mixing bowl, cream together the butter and sugar. Beat in the egg, continuing to mix until the batter is light and creamy. Mix in the orange juice and the orange zest. Stir in the warm milk. Sift the flour with the baking soda. Fold the flour mixture into the batter and mix until smooth. Stir in the chopped citron.

Drop rounded teaspoonfuls of batter onto the baking sheets, about 2 inches apart. Bake for 10 to 12 minutes, or until the cookies have browned around the edges. Remove from the oven.

After the cookies have cooled for 2 to 3 minutes, but are still warm to the touch, use a spatula to transfer them to wire racks to cool completely.

NO. **154** PEANUT BUTTER COOKIES

*Makes about 48 cookies*

1 cup unsalted butter,
    softened
1 cup sugar
1 cup dark brown sugar,
    firmly packed
2 eggs, beaten

1 teaspoon vanilla extract
1 cup peanut butter
2 cups sifted flour
1 teaspoon baking soda
¼ teaspoon salt

Preheat the oven to 350° F. Lightly grease two large baking sheets with butter or vegetable shortening.

In a large mixing bowl, cream together the butter and sugars. Add the beaten eggs and mix thoroughly. Stir in the vanilla extract. Beat in the peanut butter. Sift the flour with the baking soda and salt. Stir the flour mixture into the batter. Mix well.

Drop rounded teaspoonfuls of batter onto the baking sheets, about 2 inches apart. Bake for about 12 minutes, or until the cookies have browned around the edges. Remove from the oven.

After the cookies have cooled for 2 to 3 minutes, but are still warm to the touch, use a spatula to transfer them to wire racks to cool completely.

## NO. 155     PEANUT BUTTER MILK CHOCOLATE CHIP COOKIES

*Makes about 48 cookies*

Follow the recipe for Peanut Butter Cookies (No. 154), adding one 7½-ounce package of milk chocolate morsels to the batter.

## NO. 156     PEANUT WAFERS

*Makes about 36 cookies*

2 tablespoons unsalted butter, softened
2 tablespoons milk
1 cup sugar
1 egg

1 cup sifted flour
½ teaspoon baking soda
1 cup unsalted blanched peanuts, coarsely chopped

Preheat the oven to 400° F. Lightly grease two large baking sheets with butter or vegetable shortening.

In a large mixing bowl, combine the butter, milk, sugar, and egg. Beat until thoroughly blended. Sift the flour with the baking soda. Beat the flour mixture into the batter, ½ cup at a time. Mix until the batter is smooth. Stir in the chopped peanuts.

Drop rounded teaspoonfuls of batter onto the baking sheets, about 2 inches apart. Bake for 8 minutes, then reduce the oven temperature to 350° F and continue to bake for an additional 5 minutes. Remove from the oven.

After the cookies have cooled for 2 to 3 minutes, but are still warm to the touch, use a spatula to transfer them to wire racks to cool completely.

NO. **157**

# PEPPERMINT CRUNCH COOKIES

*Makes about 50 small cookies*

½ cup unsalted butter, softened

⅓ cup dark brown sugar, firmly packed

⅓ cup sugar

1 egg

½ teaspoon peppermint extract

1 cup plus 2 tablespoons sifted flour

½ teaspoon baking soda

½ teaspoon salt

1 cup walnuts, coarsely chopped

1½ cups coarsely crushed peppermint candy canes

Preheat the oven to 375° F. Lightly grease two large baking sheets with butter or vegetable shortening.

In a large mixing bowl, cream together the butter and sugars. Beat in the egg and peppermint extract. Sift together the flour, baking soda, and salt. Gradually add the flour mixture to the batter. Stir in the chopped walnuts and candy canes.

Drop rounded teaspoonfuls of batter onto the baking sheets, about 2 inches apart. Bake for 10 to 12 minutes, or until the cookies are brown. Remove from the oven.

After the cookies have cooled for 2 to 3 minutes, but are still warm to the touch, use a spatula to transfer them to wire racks to cool completely.

NO. **158**

# PISTACHIO COOKIES

*Makes about 48 cookies*

1 cup unsalted butter, softened

2 cups confectioners' sugar

3 eggs

1 teaspoon vanilla extract

1 teaspoon baking soda

2 tablespoons hot water

3 cups sifted flour

¼ teaspoon salt

1 cup unsalted pistachio nuts, finely chopped

Preheat the oven to 400° F. Lightly grease two large baking sheets with butter or vegetable shortening.

In a large mixing bowl, cream together the butter and sugar. Beat in the eggs, one at a time. Add the vanilla extract. Mix well. Dissolve the baking soda in the hot water. Sift the flour with the salt. Add the flour mixture to the batter, 1 cup at a time. Add the baking soda mixture after the first cup of flour. Stir in the chopped pistachio nuts and mix well.

Place rounded teaspoonfuls of batter onto the baking sheets, about

2 inches apart. Bake for 10 to 15 minutes, or until the cookies have browned around the edges. Remove from the oven.

After the cookies have cooled for 2 to 3 minutes, but are still warm to the touch, use a spatula to transfer them to wire racks to cool completely.

NO. **159**                    **POPPY SEED COOKIES**

*Makes about 24 cookies*

¼ cup milk
½ cup poppy seeds
¼ cup unsalted butter,
   softened
½ cup sugar
1 egg yolk

1 teaspoon grated orange zest
1 teaspoon vanilla extract
¾ cup sifted flour
½ teaspoon baking powder
½ teaspoon cinnamon
⅛ teaspoon ground cloves

Preheat the oven to 350° F. Lightly grease two large baking sheets with butter or vegetable shortening.

In a small saucepan, heat the milk until it coats the back of a metal spoon. Remove the pan from the heat, then stir in the poppy seeds and set aside.

In a large mixing bowl, cream together the butter and sugar. Beat in the egg yolk, orange zest, and vanilla extract. Mix well. Sift the flour with the baking powder, cinnamon, and cloves. Gradually add the flour mixture to the batter, ⅓ cup at a time. Stir in the poppy seed mixture and mix well.

Drop rounded teaspoonfuls of batter onto the baking sheets, about 2 inches apart. Bake for about 20 minutes, or until the cookies have browned around the edges. Remove from the oven.

After the cookies have cooled for 2 to 3 minutes, but are still warm to the touch, use a spatula to transfer them to wire racks to cool completely.

NO. **160**                    **POTATO CHIP COOKIES**

*Makes about 36 cookies*

1 cup unsalted butter,
   softened
½ cup sugar
1 teaspoon vanilla extract
1 teaspoon grated lemon zest

½ cup crushed potato chips
½ cup walnuts, coarsely
   chopped
2 cups sifted flour
Confectioners' sugar

Preheat the oven to 350° F. Lightly grease two large baking sheets with butter or vegetable shortening.

In a large mixing bowl, cream together the butter and sugar. Beat in the vanilla extract and the lemon zest. Stir in the potato chips and chopped walnuts. Mix in the flour, ½ cup at a time.

Drop rounded teaspoonfuls of batter onto the baking sheets, about 2 inches apart. Dust each cookie with confectioners' sugar. Bake for 10 to 12 minutes, or until the cookies have browned around the edges. Remove from the oven.

After the cookies have cooled for 2 to 3 minutes, but are still warm to the touch, use a spatula to transfer them to wire racks to cool completely.

NO. **161**            **PLUM COOKIES**

*Makes about 72 cookies*

¾ cup unsalted butter,
    softened
¾ cup light brown sugar
3 eggs, beaten
4 cups sifted flour

2 teaspoons baking soda
½ teaspoon mace
½ teaspoon allspice
2 cups coarsely chopped,
    peeled, ripe sweet plums

Preheat the oven to 350° F. Lightly grease two large baking sheets with butter or vegetable shortening.

In a large mixing bowl, cream together the butter and sugar. Beat in the eggs and mix well. Sift the flour with the baking soda, mace, and allspice. Add the flour mixture to the batter, 1 cup at a time. Stir in the plums.

Drop rounded teaspoonfuls of batter onto the baking sheets, about 2 inches apart. Bake for about 15 minutes, or until the cookies have browned around the edges. Remove from the oven.

After the cookies have cooled for 2 to 3 minutes, but are still warm to the touch, use a spatula to transfer them to wire racks to cool completely.

NO. **162**            **RAISIN DROP COOKIES**

*Makes about 48 cookies*

2 tablespoons unsalted butter
2 eggs
1 cup sugar
1 teaspoon vanilla extract

2 cups sifted flour
2 teaspoons baking powder
¼ teaspoon nutmeg
1 cup raisins

Preheat the oven to 400° F. Lightly grease two large baking sheets with butter or vegetable shortening.

Melt the butter in a small saucepan over very low heat. Remove the pan from the heat and set aside.

In a large mixing bowl, beat the eggs until foamy. Gradually beat in the sugar. Continue to beat until the mixture is thick and light. Beat in the vanilla extract. Stir in the melted butter. Sift the flour with the baking powder and nutmeg. Add the flour mixture to the batter, ½ cup at a time. Stir in the raisins.

Drop rounded teaspoonfuls of batter onto the baking sheets, about 2 inches apart. Bake for 12 to 15 minutes, or until the cookies have browned around the edges. Remove from the oven.

After the cookies have cooled for 2 to 3 minutes, but are still warm to the touch, use a spatula to transfer them to wire racks to cool completely.

## NO. 163     RAISIN SPICE CHOCOLATE CHUNK COOKIES

*Makes about 50 small cookies*

½ cup unsalted butter, softened
⅓ cup dark brown sugar, firmly packed
⅓ cup sugar
1 egg
2 teaspoons orange juice
2 teaspoons grated lemon zest
1 cup plus 2 tablespoons sifted flour

½ teaspoon baking soda
½ teaspoon salt
1 teaspoon cinnamon
1 teaspoon allspice
¼ teaspoon ground cloves
8 ounces semi-sweet chocolate, coarsely chopped
1 cup golden raisins

Preheat the oven to 375° F. Lightly grease two large baking sheets with butter or vegetable shortening.

In a large mixing bowl, cream together the butter and sugars. Beat in the egg. Add the orange juice and lemon zest. Sift together the flour, baking soda, salt, cinnamon, allspice, and cloves. Gradually add the flour mixture to the batter. Stir the chocolate chunks and raisins into the batter.

Drop rounded teaspoonfuls of batter onto the baking sheets, about 2 inches apart. Bake for 10 to 12 minutes, or until the cookies are brown. Remove from the oven.

After the cookies have cooled for 2 to 3 minutes, but are still warm to the touch, use a spatula to transfer them to wire racks to cool completely.

NO. **164**        **RAISIN SPICE DROP COOKIES**

*Makes about 48 cookies*

| | |
|---|---|
| 1 cup unsalted butter, softened | 1 teaspoon mace |
| 2 cups dark brown sugar, firmly packed | 1 teaspoon ground cloves |
| | 2 teaspoons cinnamon |
| 3 eggs | 1 teaspoon cream of tartar |
| 2½ cups sifted flour | 1 cup walnuts, coarsely chopped |
| 1 teaspoon baking soda | 2 cups raisins |

Preheat the oven to 400° F. Lightly grease two large baking sheets with butter or vegetable shortening.

In a large mixing bowl, cream together the butter and sugar. Beat in the eggs, one at a time. Mix well. Sift the flour with the baking soda, mace, cloves, cinnamon, and cream of tartar. Add the flour mixture, chopped walnuts, and raisins to the batter all at once. Stir until all the flour has been absorbed.

Drop rounded teaspoonfuls of batter onto the baking sheets, about 2 inches apart. Bake for 12 to 15 minutes, or until the cookies have browned around the edges. Remove from the oven.

After the cookies have cooled for 2 to 3 minutes, but are still warm to the touch, use a spatula to transfer them to wire racks to cool completely.

NO. **165**        **RASPBERRY CHEWS**

*Makes about 50 cookies*

| | |
|---|---|
| 4 ounces (4 squares) unsweetened baking chocolate | 2 cups sifted flour |
| | ½ teaspoon baking soda |
| ½ cup milk | ½ cup walnuts, coarsely chopped |
| ½ cup unsalted butter, softened | 1½ cups unsweetened shredded coconut |
| 2 cups sugar | 1 cup fresh or frozen raspberries |
| 1 egg, beaten | |
| 2 teaspoons brandy | |

Preheat the oven to 375° F. Lightly grease two large baking sheets with butter or vegetable shortening.

Combine the chocolate and the milk in a small saucepan. Cook over very low heat, stirring frequently, until the chocolate has melted. Remove the pan from the heat and set aside.

In a large mixing bowl, cream together the butter and sugar. Beat in the egg. Continue to beat until the batter is light and creamy.

Mix in the brandy. Stir in the melted chocolate mixture. Sift the flour with the baking soda and fold into the batter. Fold in the chopped walnuts, coconut, and raspberries.

Drop rounded teaspoonfuls of batter onto the baking sheets, about 2 inches apart. Bake for 10 to 12 minutes, or until the cookies have browned around the edges. Remove from the oven.

After the cookies have cooled for 2 to 3 minutes, but are still warm to the touch, use a spatula to transfer them to wire racks to cool completely.

## NO. 166    RASPBERRY MACADAMIA NUT CHOCOLATE CHUNK COOKIES
*Makes about 50 small cookies*

½ cup unsalted butter, softened
⅓ cup dark brown sugar, firmly packed
⅓ cup sugar
1 egg
1 teaspoon vanilla extract
2 teaspoons grated lemon zest
¼ cup raspberry jam

1½ cups sifted flour
1 teaspoon baking soda
½ teaspoon salt
8 ounces semi-sweet chocolate, coarsely chopped
1 cup macadamia nuts, coarsely chopped

Preheat the oven to 375° F. Lightly grease two large baking sheets with butter or vegetable shortening.

In a large mixing bowl, cream together the butter and sugars. Beat in the egg. Add the vanilla extract and the lemon zest. Mix in the raspberry jam. Sift together the flour, baking soda, and salt. Gradually add the flour mixture to the batter. Stir in the chocolate chunks and chopped macadamia nuts.

Drop rounded teaspoonfuls of batter onto the baking sheets, about 2 inches apart. Bake for 10 to 12 minutes, or until the cookies are brown. Remove from the oven.

After the cookies have cooled for 2 to 3 minutes, but are still warm to the touch, use a spatula to transfer them to wire racks to cool completely.

## NO. 167    SANDIES
*Makes about 36 cookies*

2 eggs plus 1 egg yolk
1 cup sugar

½ teaspoon almond extract
2 cups sifted flour

Preheat the oven to 325° F. Lightly grease two large baking sheets with butter or vegetable shortening.

In a large mixing bowl, beat the eggs and the egg yolk until foamy. Gradually beat in the sugar, a little at a time. Continue to beat for 5 minutes. Beat in the almond extract. Very gently fold in all the flour, mixing as little as possible to keep the air in the batter.

Drop rounded teaspoonfuls of batter onto the baking sheets, about 2 inches apart. Bake for about 10 minutes, or until the cookies have browned around the edges. Remove from the oven.

After the cookies have cooled for 2 to 3 minutes, but are still warm to the touch, use a spatula to transfer them to wire racks to cool completely.

NO. **168** PECAN SANDIES

*Makes about 36 cookies*

Follow the recipe for Sandies (No. 167), adding 1 cup of pecans, finely chopped, to the batter.

NO. **169** SHERRY DROP COOKIES

*Makes about 72 cookies*

| | |
|---|---|
| 1½ cups unsalted butter, softened | 3⅓ cups sifted flour |
| 1¾ cups confectioners' sugar | ½ cup dry sherry |
| 2 teaspoons grated lemon zest | 1 cup walnuts, coarsely chopped |

Preheat the oven to 350° F. Lightly grease two large baking sheets with butter or vegetable shortening.

In a large mixing bowl, cream together the butter and sugar. Beat in the lemon zest. Add the flour to the batter, 1 cup at a time, alternating with the sherry. Mix in the chopped walnuts.

Drop rounded teaspoonfuls of batter onto the baking sheets, about 2 inches apart. Bake for 20 to 25 minutes, or until the cookies have browned around the edges. Remove from the oven.

After the cookies have cooled for 2 to 3 minutes, but are still warm to the touch, use a spatula to transfer them to wire racks to cool completely.

NO. **170**               **SOFT OATMEAL COOKIES**
                              *Makes about 48 cookies*

¼ cup unsalted butter,          ½ teaspoon nutmeg
   softened                      ½ teaspoon salt
1 cup light brown sugar          ¾ cup buttermilk
2 eggs                          1¾ cups rolled oats
2 cups sifted flour              2 cups golden raisins
½ teaspoon baking soda

Preheat the oven to 400° F. Lightly grease two large baking sheets
with butter or vegetable shortening.

   In a large mixing bowl, cream together the butter and sugar. Beat
in the eggs, one at a time. Mix well. Sift the flour with the baking
soda, nutmeg, and salt. Add half of the flour mixture to the batter
and mix well. Beat in the buttermilk. Stir in the rolled oats, then
add the remaining flour. Mix well and add the raisins.

   Drop rounded teaspoonfuls of batter onto the baking sheets, about
2 inches apart. Bake for about 15 minutes, or until the cookies have
browned around the edges. Remove from the oven.

   After the cookies have cooled for 2 to 3 minutes, but are still
warm to the touch, use a spatula to transfer them to wire racks to
cool completely.

NO. **171**         **SOUR CREAM DROP COOKIES**
                              *Makes about 48 cookies*

¼ cup unsalted butter,          2½ cups sifted flour
   softened                      1 teaspoon baking soda
1½ cups sugar                    ½ teaspoon nutmeg
2 eggs, beaten                   1 cup sour cream
1 teaspoon lemon extract

Preheat the oven to 375° F. Lightly grease two large baking sheets
with butter or vegetable shortening.

   In a large mixing bowl, cream together the butter and sugar. Beat
in the eggs. Continue to beat until the batter is very light. Add the
lemon extract and mix well. Sift the flour with the baking soda. Mix
the nutmeg into the sour cream. Add the flour mixture to the batter,
1 cup at a time, alternating with the sour cream. Mix well.

   Drop rounded teaspoonfuls of batter onto the baking sheets, about
2 inches apart. Bake for 12 to 15 minutes, or until the cookies have
browned around the edges. Remove from the oven.

   After the cookies have cooled for 2 to 3 minutes, but are still
warm to the touch, use a spatula to transfer them to wire racks to
cool completely.

NO. **172** **SURPRISE COOKIES I**
*Makes about 25 large cookies*

½ cup unsalted butter,
    softened
⅓ cup dark brown sugar,
    firmly packed
⅓ cup sugar
1 egg
1 teaspoon vanilla extract

1 cup plus 2 tablespoons
    sifted flour
½ teaspoon baking soda
½ teaspoon salt
25 miniature peanut butter
    cups

Preheat the oven to 375° F. Lightly grease two large baking sheets with butter or vegetable shortening.

In a large mixing bowl, cream together the butter and sugars. Beat in the egg and the vanilla extract. Sift together the flour, baking soda, and salt. Gradually add the flour mixture to the batter. Mix well.

Drop rounded teaspoonfuls of batter onto the baking sheets, about 2 inches apart. Place 1 peanut butter cup in the center of each cookie and top with more batter, completely covering up the peanut butter cup. Bake for 10 to 12 minutes, or until the cookies are brown. Remove from the oven.

After the cookies have cooled for 2 to 3 minutes, but are still warm to the touch, use a spatula to transfer them to wire racks to cool completely.

NO. **173** **SURPRISE COOKIES II**
*Makes about 25 large cookies*

Follow the recipe for Surprise Cookies I (No. 172), substituting chocolate-covered thin mints for the peanut butter cups.

NO. **174** **WALNUT BROWN SUGAR COOKIES**
*Makes about 48 cookies*

1 cup unsalted butter,
    softened
2 cups dark brown sugar,
    firmly packed
3 eggs
1 teaspoon vanilla extract

1 teaspoon baking soda
2 tablespoons hot water
3 cups sifted flour
¼ teaspoon salt
1 cup walnuts, finely chopped

Preheat the oven to 400° F. Lightly grease two large baking sheets with butter or vegetable shortening.

In a large mixing bowl, cream together the butter and sugar. Beat in the eggs, one at a time. Mix well. Add the vanilla extract. Dissolve the baking soda in the hot water. Sift the flour with the salt. Add the flour mixture to the batter, 1 cup at a time. Add the baking soda mixture after beating in the first cup of flour. Stir in the chopped walnuts and mix well.

Drop rounded teaspoonfuls of batter onto the baking sheets, about 2 inches apart. Bake for 10 to 15 minutes, or until the cookies have browned around the edges. Remove from the oven.

After the cookies have cooled for 2 to 3 minutes, but are still warm to the touch, use a spatula to transfer them to wire racks to cool completely.

NO. **175**                    **WALNUT COOKIES**

*Makes about 36 cookies*

4 egg yolks                        ½ teaspoon vanilla extract
½ cup superfine sugar              3½ cups ground walnuts
2 teaspoons grated lemon zest

Preheat the oven to 325° F. Lightly grease two large baking sheets with butter or vegetable shortening.

In a large mixing bowl, beat the egg yolks until foamy. Gradually beat in the sugar until the batter is thick and light. Mix in the lemon zest and the vanilla extract. Stir in the ground walnuts.

Drop rounded teaspoonfuls of batter onto the baking sheets, about 2 inches apart. Bake for about 10 minutes, or until the cookies are dry to the touch. Remove from the oven.

After the cookies have cooled for 2 to 3 minutes, but are still warm to the touch, use a spatula to transfer them to wire racks to cool completely.

NO. **176**                    **WALNUT WAFERS**

*Makes about 36 cookies*

2 tablespoons unsalted butter,     1 cup sifted flour
    softened                       ½ teaspoon baking soda
2 tablespoons milk                 1 cup walnuts, coarsely
1 cup sugar                            chopped
1 egg

Preheat the oven to 400° F. Lightly grease two large baking sheets with butter or vegetable shortening.

In a large mixing bowl, combine the butter, milk, sugar, and egg. Beat until thoroughly blended. Sift the flour with the baking soda. Beat the flour mixture into the batter, ½ cup at a time. Mix until the batter is smooth. Stir in the chopped walnuts.

Drop rounded teaspoonfuls of batter onto the baking sheets, about 2 inches apart. Bake for 8 minutes, then reduce the oven temperature to 350° F and continue to bake for an additional 5 minutes. Remove from the oven.

After the cookies have cooled for 2 to 3 minutes, but are still warm to the touch, use a spatula to transfer them to wire racks to cool completely.

## NO. 177    WHITE CHOCOLATE CHUNK ALMOND COOKIES

*Makes about 50 cookies*

½ cup unsalted butter, softened
⅓ cup dark brown sugar, firmly packed
⅓ cup sugar
1 egg
½ teaspoon almond extract

1 cup plus 2 tablespoons sifted flour
½ teaspoon baking soda
½ teaspoon salt
½ cup blanched almonds, coarsely chopped
8 ounces white chocolate, coarsely chopped

Preheat the oven to 375° F. Lightly grease two large baking sheets with butter or vegetable shortening.

In a large mixing bowl, cream together the butter and sugars. Beat in the egg and the almond extract. Sift together the flour, baking soda, and salt. Gradually add the flour mixture to the batter. Stir the chopped almonds and chocolate into the cookie batter.

Drop rounded teaspoonfuls of batter onto the baking sheets, about 2 inches apart. Bake for 10 to 12 minutes, or until the cookies are lightly browned. Remove from the oven.

After the cookies have cooled for 2 to 3 minutes, but are still warm to the touch, use a spatula to transfer them to wire racks to cool completely.

NO. **178**              **WHITE CHOCOLATE CHUNK**
                        **MACADAMIA NUT COOKIES**
                        *Makes about 50 small cookies*

½ cup unsalted butter,          1 cup plus 2 tablespoons
   softened                            sifted flour
⅓ cup dark brown sugar,         1 teaspoon baking soda
   firmly packed                   ½ teaspoon salt
⅓ cup sugar                     8 ounces white chocolate,
1 egg                              coarsely chopped
1 teaspoon almond extract       1 cup macadamia nuts,
2 teaspoons grated lemon zest      coarsely chopped

Preheat the oven to 375° F. Lightly grease two large baking sheets with butter or vegetable shortening.

In a large mixing bowl, cream together the butter and sugars. Beat in the egg and mix well. Stir in the almond extract and the lemon zest. Sift together the flour, baking soda, and salt. Gradually add the flour mixture to the batter. Stir the chocolate chunks and chopped macadamia nuts into the batter.

Drop rounded teaspoonfuls of batter onto the baking sheets, about 2 inches apart. Bake for 10 to 12 minutes, or until the cookies are brown. Remove from the oven.

After the cookies have cooled for 2 to 3 minutes, but are still warm to the touch, use a spatula to transfer them to wire racks to cool completely.

# Macaroons

Pleasingly plump and definitely chewy, a macaroon consists mainly of egg whites, sugar, and coconut. Therefore, it's easy to create delicious and unusual variations on a classic macaroon—and many different and delectable variations exist. We attribute this popularity to the special texture and flavor of a good macaroon—you just can't get enough of them! For the best results, it's a good idea to use the whites of jumbo eggs in these macaroon recipes.

NO. **179**

## ALMOND MACAROONS

*Makes about 36 macaroons*

4 egg whites
1½ cups sugar
1 teaspoon vanilla extract
½ teaspoon cinnamon

1½ cups blanched almonds, coarsely chopped
1 cup unsweetened shredded coconut
Blanched almond halves

Preheat the oven to 325° F. Lightly grease two large baking sheets with butter or vegetable shortening.

In a large mixing bowl, beat the egg whites until they hold stiff peaks. Gradually beat in the sugar. Continue beating until the mixture is glossy and stiff. Beat in the vanilla extract and the cinnamon. Gently fold the chopped almonds and coconut into the meringue.

Drop rounded teaspoonfuls of batter onto the baking sheets, about 2 inches apart. Place an almond half on top of each cookie. Bake for about 20 minutes, or until the cookies are lightly browned. Remove from the oven.

After the cookies have cooled for 2 to 3 minutes, but are still warm to the touch, use a spatula to transfer them to wire racks to cool completely.

NO. **180**

## CHOCOLATE MACAROONS

*Makes about 36 macaroons*

4 egg whites
1½ cups sugar
1 teaspoon vanilla extract
½ teaspoon cinnamon
1½ cups blanched almonds, coarsely chopped

4 ounces semi-sweet chocolate, grated
1 cup unsweetened shredded coconut
Blanched almond halves

Preheat the oven to 325° F. Lightly grease two large baking sheets with butter or vegetable shortening.

In a large mixing bowl, beat the egg whites until they hold stiff peaks. Gradually beat in the sugar. Continue to beat until the mixture is thick and glossy. Beat in the vanilla extract and the cinnamon. Gently fold the chopped almonds, grated chocolate, and coconut into the meringue.

Drop rounded teaspoonfuls of batter onto the baking sheets, about 2 inches apart. Place an almond half on top of each cookie. Bake for about 20 minutes, or until the cookies are lightly browned. Remove from the oven.

After the cookies have cooled for 2 to 3 minutes, but are still warm to the touch, use a spatula to transfer them to wire racks to cool completely.

NO. 181                          COCONUT MACAROONS

*Makes about 12 macaroons*

1 egg white
¼ teaspoon cream of tartar
⅓ cup sweetened condensed milk

1½ cups unsweetened shredded coconut
1 teaspoon vanilla extract

Preheat the oven to 300° F. Lightly grease a large baking sheet with butter or vegetable shortening.

In a small mixing bowl, beat the egg white with the cream of tartar until stiff peaks form. In another bowl, combine the condensed milk with the coconut. Stir in the vanilla extract. Gently fold the beaten egg white into the coconut mixture.

Drop rounded teaspoonfuls of batter onto the baking sheet, about 2 inches apart. Bake for 12 to 15 minutes, or until the cookies are golden brown. Remove from the oven.

After the cookies have cooled for 2 to 3 minutes, but are still warm to the touch, use a spatula to transfer them to wire racks to cool completely.

NO. 182                          CREOLE COCONUT
                                       MACAROONS

*Makes about 30 macaroons*

3 egg whites
½ teaspoon cream of tartar
1 cup sugar
2 teaspoons cornstarch

⅛ teaspoon salt
3 cups unsweetened shredded coconut
1 teaspoon vanilla extract

Preheat the oven to 400° F. Lightly grease two large baking sheets with butter or vegetable shortening.

In a small mixing bowl, beat the egg whites with the cream of tartar until stiff peaks form. Sift the sugar with the cornstarch and salt. Gradually beat the sugar mixture into the beaten egg whites. Gently fold in the coconut and vanilla extract.

Drop rounded teaspoonfuls of batter onto the baking sheets, about 2 inches apart. Bake for 10 to 15 minutes, or until the cookies are golden brown. Remove from the oven.

After the cookies have cooled for 2 to 3 minutes, but are still warm to the touch, use a spatula to transfer them to wire racks to cool completely.

## NO. 183 — HAZELNUT MACAROONS

*Makes about 36 macaroons*

| | |
|---|---|
| 4 egg whites | 1½ cups hazelnuts, finely chopped |
| 1½ cups sugar | |
| 1 teaspoon vanilla extract | 1 cup unsweetened shredded coconut |
| ½ teaspoon cinnamon | |
| | Whole hazelnuts |

Preheat the oven to 325° F. Lightly grease two large baking sheets with butter or vegetable shortening.

In a large mixing bowl, beat the egg whites until they hold stiff peaks. Gradually beat in the sugar. Continue beating until the mixture is glossy and stiff. Beat in the vanilla extract and cinnamon. Gently fold the chopped hazelnuts and the coconut into the meringue.

Drop rounded teaspoonfuls of batter onto the baking sheets, about 2 inches apart. Place a hazelnut in the center of each cookie. Bake for about 20 minutes, or until the cookies are lightly browned. Remove from the oven.

After the cookies have cooled for 2 to 3 minutes, but are still warm to the touch, use a spatula to transfer them to wire racks to cool completely.

## NO. 184 — LEMON COCONUT MACAROONS

*Makes about 36 macaroons*

| | |
|---|---|
| 4 egg whites | ½ teaspoon grated lemon zest |
| ½ teaspoon cream of tartar | 1 cup unsweetened shredded coconut |
| 2 cups confectioners' sugar | |
| ¼ teaspoon lemon extract | |

Preheat the oven to 300° F. Lightly grease two large baking sheets with butter or vegetable shortening.

In a large mixing bowl, beat the egg whites until foamy. Continue to beat, adding the cream of tartar and the confectioners' sugar, ½ cup at a time. When the mixture is glossy and holds stiff peaks, mix in the lemon extract, lemon zest, and coconut.

Drop rounded teaspoonfuls of meringue onto the baking sheets, about 2 inches apart. Bake for about 15 minutes, or until the cookies are golden brown. Remove from the oven.

After the cookies have cooled for 2 to 3 minutes, but are still warm to the touch, use a spatula to transfer them to wire racks to cool completely.

NO. **185**                    # ORANGE MACAROONS
                               *Makes about 36 macaroons*

4 egg whites
1½ cups sugar
1 teaspoon rum
2 teaspoons grated orange
   zest

1 cup finely chopped candied
   orange peel
1 cup unsweetened shredded
   coconut

Preheat the oven to 325° F. Lightly grease two large baking sheets with butter or vegetable shortening.

In a large mixing bowl, beat the egg whites until they hold stiff peaks. Gradually beat in the sugar. Continue beating until the mixture is glossy and stiff. Beat in the rum and the orange zest. Gently fold the orange peel and coconut into the meringue.

Drop rounded teaspoonfuls of batter onto the baking sheets, about 2 inches apart. Bake for about 20 minutes, or until the cookies are lightly browned. Remove from the oven.

After the cookies have cooled for 2 to 3 minutes, but are still warm to the touch, use a spatula to transfer them to wire racks to cool completely.

NO. **186**                    # PEANUT MACAROONS
                               *Makes about 36 macaroons*

4 egg whites
1½ cups sugar
1 teaspoon vanilla extract
½ teaspoon cinnamon

1½ cups unsalted peanuts,
   coarsely chopped
1 cup unsweetened shredded
   coconut
Whole peanuts

Preheat the oven to 325° F. Lightly grease two large baking sheets with butter or vegetable shortening.

In a large mixing bowl, beat the egg whites until they hold stiff peaks. Gradually beat in the sugar. Continue beating until the batter becomes glossy and stiff. Beat in the vanilla extract and cinnamon. Gently fold the chopped peanuts and coconut into the egg-white mixture.

Drop rounded teaspoonfuls of batter onto the baking sheets, about 2 inches apart. Place a whole peanut on top of each cookie. Bake for about 20 minutes, or until the cookies are lightly browned. Remove from the oven.

After the cookies have cooled for 2 to 3 minutes, but are still warm to the touch, use a spatula to transfer them to wire racks to cool completely.

## NO. 187     PECAN MACAROONS

*Makes about 12 macaroons*

1 egg white
⅛ teaspoon cream of tartar
1 cup brown sugar, firmly
    packed
¼ teaspoon salt

¼ teaspoon lemon extract
1 cup pecans, coarsely
    chopped
½ cup unsweetened shredded
    coconut

Preheat the oven to 275° F. Lightly grease a large baking sheet with butter or vegetable shortening.

In a large mixing bowl, beat the egg white with the cream of tartar until the mixture forms stiff peaks. Gradually beat in the sugar. Continue beating until the mixture is thick and glossy. Beat in the salt and the lemon extract. Gently fold in the chopped pecans and the coconut.

Drop rounded teaspoonfuls of batter onto the baking sheet, about 2 inches apart. Bake for about 30 minutes, or until the cookies have browned around the edges. Remove from the oven.

After the cookies have cooled for 2 to 3 minutes, but are still warm to the touch, use a spatula to transfer them to wire racks to cool completely.

## NO. 188     ROSE WATER MACAROONS

*Makes about 36 macaroons*

4 egg whites
1½ cups sugar
1 teaspoon rose water

1 cup blanched almonds,
    finely chopped
1 cup unsweetened shredded
    coconut
Blanched almond halves

Preheat the oven to 325° F. Lightly grease two large baking sheets with butter or vegetable shortening.

In a large mixing bowl, beat the egg whites until they hold stiff peaks. Gradually beat in the sugar. Continue beating until the batter is glossy and stiff. Beat in the rose water. Gently fold the chopped almonds and coconut into the meringue.

Drop rounded teaspoonfuls of meringue onto the baking sheets, about 2 inches apart. Place an almond half on top of each cookie. Bake for about 20 minutes, or until the cookies are lightly browned. Remove from the oven.

After the cookies have cooled for 2 to 3 minutes, but are still warm to the touch, use a spatula to transfer them to wire racks to cool completely.

NO. **189**                          # WALNUT MACAROONS
                                     *Makes about 12 macaroons*

1 egg white
⅛ teaspoon cream of tartar
1 cup dark brown sugar,
    firmly packed
¼ teaspoon salt

¼ teaspoon lemon extract
1 cup walnuts, coarsely
    chopped
1 cup unsweetened shredded
    coconut

Preheat the oven to 275° F. Lightly grease a large baking sheet with butter or vegetable shortening.

In a large mixing bowl, beat the egg white with the cream of tartar until stiff peaks form. Gradually beat in the sugar. Continue beating until the mixture is thick and glossy. Beat in the salt and lemon extract. Gently fold in the chopped walnuts and the coconut.

Drop rounded teaspoonfuls of batter onto the baking sheet, about 2 inches apart. Bake for about 30 minutes, or until the cookies are golden brown. Remove from the oven.

After the cookies have cooled for 2 to 3 minutes, but are still warm to the touch, use a spatula to transfer them to wire racks to cool completely.

# Meringues

The most delicate of cookies, meringues seem to be made of spun sugar and air, but actually they're made with heavily beaten egg whites and sugar and baked in a very slow oven. Anyone making a meringue should be aware of the critical stage to be reached in beating the egg whites—before which nothing must be added to the egg whites, except cream of tartar. Do *not* add any sugar or flavoring to the egg whites— either before or during beating—until they can hold extremely stiff peaks; otherwise the meringue will not stiffen properly. Note that the whites from jumbo eggs are recommended for all meringue recipes. If you must use the whites of small eggs, add an additional egg white or two to the recipe. Meringue batter should be refrigerated in between baking batches of cookies, otherwise it may separate.

NO. **190**

## ALMOND MERINGUES
*Makes about 24 meringues*

2 tablespoons Amaretto
  liqueur
2 tablespoons apricot liqueur
1 tablespoon grated orange
  zest
¾ cup ground almonds

2 egg whites
¼ teaspoon cream of tartar
½ cup superfine sugar
1 teaspoon almond extract
  Blanched almond halves

Preheat the oven to 325° F. Lightly grease two large baking sheets with butter or vegetable shortening.

In a small bowl, combine the liqueurs, orange zest, and ground almonds. Mix thoroughly. In a separate bowl, whip the egg whites until foamy. Beat in the cream of tartar. When the mixture forms stiff peaks, beat in the sugar, a few tablespoons at a time. Continue beating until the mixture is stiff and glossy. Beat in the almond extract. Gently fold in the almond mixture, a little at a time.

Drop rounded teaspoonfuls of meringue onto the baking sheets, about 2 inches apart. Place an almond half on top of each cookie. Bake for 15 to 20 minutes, or until the cookies are dry to the touch. Remove from the oven.

After the cookies have cooled for 2 to 3 minutes, but are still warm to the touch, use a spatula to transfer them to wire racks to cool completely.

NO. **191**                    **BROWN SUGAR KISSES**
                                   *Makes about 24 meringues*

1 egg white                        1 teaspoon vanilla extract
¼ teaspoon cream of tartar         ¼ teaspoon salt
1 cup dark brown sugar,            1½ cups blanched filberts,
   firmly packed                      coarsely chopped

Preheat the oven to 325° F. Lightly grease two large baking sheets
with butter or vegetable shortening.

In a large mixing bowl, beat the egg white with the cream of tartar
until the mixture holds stiff peaks. Gradually beat in the sugar, ¼
cup at a time. Continue beating until the meringue is stiff and glossy.
Add the vanilla extract and the salt. Mix well. Gently fold the chopped
filberts into the mixture.

Drop rounded teaspoonfuls of meringue onto the baking sheets,
about 2 inches apart. Bake for 15 minutes, or until the kisses are
puffy and have set. Remove from the oven. The tops will fall and
crinkle up.

After the cookies have cooled for 2 to 3 minutes, but are still
warm to the touch, use a spatula to transfer them to wire racks to
cool completely.

NO. **192**                    **CASHEW MERINGUES**
                                   *Makes about 24 meringues*

2 egg whites                       ½ teaspoon vanilla extract
¼ teaspoon cream of tartar         ½ cup unsalted cashew nuts,
½ cup superfine sugar                 finely chopped

Preheat the oven to 275° F. Lightly grease two large baking sheets
with butter or vegetable shortening.

In a large mixing bowl, beat the egg whites with the cream of
tartar until the mixture holds stiff peaks. Gradually beat in the sugar.
Continue to beat until the meringue is stiff and glossy. Beat in the
vanilla extract. Gently fold in the chopped cashew nuts.

Drop rounded teaspoonfuls of meringue onto the baking sheets,
about 2 inches apart. Bake for about 20 minutes, or until the cookies
are golden brown. Remove from the oven.

After the cookies have cooled for 2 to 3 minutes, but are still
warm to the touch, use a spatula to transfer them to wire racks to
cool completely.

NO. **193**                          **CHOCOLATE MERINGUES**

*Makes about 12 meringues*

To make these elegant cookies, a pastry bag and some care in handling
are required.

| | |
|---|---|
| 2 **egg whites** | ¼ **teaspoon almond extract** |
| ¼ **teaspoon cream of tartar** | 4 **ounces semi-sweet chocolate** |
| ½ **cup sugar** | |

Preheat the oven to 200° F. Line two large baking sheets with baking
parchment. Using a 1½-inch round cookie cutter as a guide, draw
24 circles on the parchment (12 on each baking sheet).

In a large mixing bowl, beat the egg whites with the cream of
tartar until the mixture holds stiff peaks. Gradually add the sugar, a
little at a time, and continue to beat until the mixture is stiff and
glossy. Beat in the almond extract.

Fit a pastry bag with a smooth tip and fill, reserving one quarter
of the meringue. Pipe meringue bases on 12 circles. Smooth the
surface of each base with a rubber spatula. Change to a pastry bag
with a fluted, decorated tip, and using the rest of the meringue, pipe
out a ring of rosettes around each remaining circle.

Place both baking sheets in the oven. Remove the rings after 25
minutes. Carefully loosen from the parchment with the tip of a sharp
knife, and use a spatula to transfer them to wire cooling racks.
Continue to bake the bases for an additional 15 minutes, or until
they are dry to the touch. Remove from the parchment as with the
rings and cool on a wire rack.

Melt the chocolate in the top of a double boiler over simmering
water, stirring frequently. Remove the pan from the heat and set
aside to cool. Using a spatula, spread each meringue base with a
layer of chocolate. Top with a meringue ring. Transfer to a serving
plate.

NO. **194**                          **CINNAMON WALNUT
MERINGUES**

*Makes about 36 meringues*

| | |
|---|---|
| 4 **egg whites** | 2 **teaspoons cinnamon** |
| ½ **teaspoon cream of tartar** | 2 **cups walnuts, coarsely** |
| 2 **cups confectioners' sugar** | **chopped** |

Preheat the oven to 300° F. Lightly grease two large baking sheets
with butter or vegetable shortening.

In a large mixing bowl, beat the egg whites until they hold stiff peaks. Continuing to beat, add the cream of tartar and the confectioners' sugar, ½ cup at a time. When the meringue is glossy stiff, beat in the cinnamon. Fold in the chopped walnuts.

Drop rounded teaspoonfuls of meringue onto the baking sheets, about 2 inches apart. Bake for about 15 minutes, or until the cookies are golden brown. Remove from the oven.

After the cookies have cooled for 2 to 3 minutes, but are still warm to the touch, use a spatula to transfer them to wire racks to cool completely.

**CREAM MERINGUES**

*Makes about 24 meringues*

NO. **195**

**Meringues**
- 2 egg whites
- 1 cup sugar
- ¼ cup water

**Filling**
- 1 cup heavy cream
- 1 tablespoon sugar
- 1 teaspoon vanilla extract

Preheat the oven to 250° F. Lightly grease two large baking sheets with butter or vegetable shortening.

In the top of a double boiler over boiling water, combine the egg whites, sugar, and water. Reduce the heat to a simmer, and cook, stirring constantly, until the mixture has thickened. Place the top of the double boiler over a bowl of cold water. Continue to stir until the mixture has cooled completely.

Drop rounded teaspoonfuls of meringue onto the baking sheets, about 2 inches apart. Bake for about 45 minutes, or until the cookies are golden brown. Remove from the oven.

Using the back of a spoon, immediately crush in the tops of half of the meringues. Allow them to cool for 2 to 3 minutes, then gently remove from the baking sheets with a spatula and transfer them to wire racks to cool completely.

Make the filling. In a mixing bowl, whip the cream until it begins to form stiff peaks. Beat in the sugar and the vanilla extract. The whipped cream should now hold its shape. Fill each crushed bottom meringue with a spoonful of whipped cream, then press on an uncrushed meringue. Continue to fill the meringues until all the ingredients have been used. Transfer to a serving plate, cover, and refrigerate until ready to serve.

NO. **196**        # DATE NUT MERINGUES

*Makes about 24 meringues*

2 egg whites
¼ teaspoon cream of tartar
½ cup superfine sugar
1 teaspoon vanilla extract
1 teaspoon apricot liqueur

2 teaspoons grated orange zest
½ cup pecans, finely chopped
½ cup pitted dates, finely chopped

Preheat the oven to 275° F. Lightly grease two large baking sheets with butter or vegetable shortening.

In a large mixing bowl, beat the egg whites and the cream of tartar until the mixture forms stiff peaks. Beat in the sugar, a few tablespoons at a time. Continue beating until the mixture is stiff and glossy. Beat in the vanilla extract, apricot liqueur, and orange zest. Gently fold in the chopped pecans and dates.

Drop rounded teaspoonfuls of meringue onto the baking sheets, about 2 inches apart. Bake for 15 to 20 minutes, or until the meringues are dry to the touch. Remove from the oven.

After the cookies have cooled for 2 to 3 minutes, but are still warm to the touch, use a spatula to transfer them to wire racks to cool completely.

NO. **197**        # ORANGE DIMPLES

*Makes about 50 meringues*

6 egg whites
1 cup superfine sugar
1 teaspoon orange extract

2 tablespoons finely chopped candied orange peel
½ cup ground almonds

Preheat the oven to 225° F. Lightly grease two large baking sheets with butter or vegetable shortening.

In a large mixing bowl, beat the egg whites until stiff peaks form. Gradually beat in ⅔ cup of the sugar, a little at a time. Continue beating until the mixture is stiff and glossy. Beat in the remaining sugar and the orange extract. Gently fold in the chopped orange peel and ground almonds.

Drop ½ teaspoons of meringue onto the baking sheets, 1 inch apart. Bake for 50 minutes. Turn the oven off and, leaving the oven door open, allow the kisses to rest for an additional 5 minutes before removing from the oven.

After the cookies have cooled for 2 to 3 minutes, but are still warm to the touch, use a spatula to transfer them to wire racks to cool completely.

NO. **198**                        **TINY ALMOND KISSES**

*Makes about 50 meringues*

6 egg whites
1 cup sugar
1 teaspoon vanilla extract
1 cup blanched almonds, finely chopped

Preheat the oven to 225° F. Lightly grease two large baking sheets
with butter or vegetable shortening.

In a large mixing bowl, beat the egg whites until stiff peaks form.
Gradually beat in ⅔ cup of the sugar, a little at a time. Continue
beating until the mixture is stiff and glossy. Beat in the remaining
sugar and the vanilla extract. Gently fold the chopped almonds into
the meringue.

Drop ½ teaspoons of meringue onto the baking sheets, 1 inch apart.
Bake for 50 minutes. Turn the oven off and, leaving the oven door
open, allow the kisses to rest for an additional 5 minutes before
removing from the oven.

After the cookies have cooled for 2 to 3 minutes, but are still
warm to the touch, use a spatula to transfer them to wire racks to
cool completely.


NO. **199**                        **TINY COCOA KISSES**

*Makes about 24 meringues*

2 egg whites
1¼ cups sugar
2 tablespoons unsweetened
   baking cocoa

½ teaspoon cinnamon
1 cup blanched almonds,
   finely chopped

Preheat the oven to 225° F. Lightly grease two large baking sheets
with butter or vegetable shortening.

In a large mixing bowl, beat the egg whites until stiff peaks form.
Gradually beat in ¾ cup of the sugar, a little at a time. Continue
beating until the mixture is stiff and glossy. Beat in the remaining
sugar, the cocoa, and the cinnamon. Gently fold the chopped almonds
into the meringue.

Drop ½ teaspoonfuls of meringue onto the baking sheets, 1 inch
apart. Bake for 50 minutes. Turn the oven off, and leaving the oven
door open, allow the kisses to rest for an additional 5 minutes. Remove
from oven.

After the cookies have cooled for 2 to 3 minutes, but are still
warm to the touch, use a spatula to transfer them to wire racks to
cool completely.

NO. **200**

# TINY COCONUT KISSES

*Makes about 50 meringues*

6 egg whites
1 cup sugar
1 teaspoon vanilla extract

1 cup unsweetened shredded
   coconut

Preheat the oven to 225° F. Lightly grease two large baking sheets with butter or vegetable shortening.

In a large mixing bowl, beat the egg whites until stiff peaks form. Gradually beat in ⅔ cup of the sugar, a little at a time. Continue to beat until the mixture is stiff and glossy. Beat in the remaining sugar and the vanilla extract. Gently fold the coconut into the meringue.

Drop ½ teaspoons of meringue onto the baking sheets, 1 inch apart. Bake for 50 minutes. Turn the oven off, and leaving the oven door open, allow the kisses to rest for an additional 5 minutes before removing from the oven.

After the meringues have cooled for 2 to 3 minutes, but are still warm to the touch, use a spatula to transfer them to wire racks to cool completely.


NO. **201**

# TINY HAZELNUT KISSES

*Makes about 50 meringues*

6 egg whites
1 cup sugar
½ teaspoon almond extract

1 cup blanched hazelnuts,
   finely chopped

Preheat the oven to 225° F. Lightly grease two large baking sheets with butter or vegetable shortening.

In a large mixing bowl, beat the egg whites until stiff peaks form. Gradually beat in ⅔ cup of the sugar, a little at a time. Continue beating until the mixture is stiff and glossy. Beat in the remaining sugar and the almond extract. Gently fold the chopped hazelnuts into the meringue.

Drop ½ teaspoons of the meringue onto the baking sheets, 1 inch apart. Bake for 50 minutes. Turn the oven off and, leaving the oven door open, allow the kisses to rest for an additional 5 minutes before removing from the oven.

After the cookies have cooled for 2 to 3 minutes, but are still warm to the touch, gently remove them from the baking sheets with a spatula and transfer to wire racks to cool completely.

# Hand-Rolled Cookies

Hand-rolled cookies are shaped by hand into balls, crescents, twists, or whatever shape is desired. Balls of cookie dough are often pressed flat (or are slightly flattened) with the bottom of a glass. Tie a piece of cheesecloth over the bottom of the glass and the cookies will not stick to it. When flattening a cookie with the tines of a fork, first dip the fork in flour.

NO. **202**                      **AMARETTO FANTASIES**

*Makes about 36 cookies*

1 cup unsalted butter,
  softened
½ cup sugar
3 tablespoons Amaretto
1 teaspoon vanilla extract
1 teaspoon grated lemon zest

2¼ cups sifted flour
¼ teaspoon salt
½ cup blanched almonds,
  finely chopped
Colored sugar

In a large mixing bowl, cream together the butter and sugar. Beat the liqueur, vanilla extract, and lemon zest. Sift the flour with the salt. Add the flour to the batter, ¼ cup at a time. Add the chopped almonds and mix well. Divide the dough in half, wrap each half in waxed paper, and chill in the refrigerator for about 30 minutes.

Preheat the oven to 350° F. Lightly grease two large baking sheets with butter or vegetable shortening.

Form the chilled dough into 36 pieces. Roll each piece into a ball, then roll each ball in colored sugar. Arrange the balls on the baking sheets, leaving 2-inch spaces between each cookie. Flatten the cookies with the bottom of a glass. Bake for 10 to 15 minutes, or until the cookies are brown around the edges. Remove from the oven.

After the cookies have cooled for 2 to 3 minutes, but are still warm to the touch, use a spatula to transfer them to wire racks to cool completely.

NO. **203**                      **APRICOT ALMOND COOKIES**

*Makes about 36 cookies*

1 cup unsalted butter
1 cup sugar
¼ teaspoon almond extract
3 cups sifted flour
¼ cup ground almonds

3 eggs
1 tablespoon water
½ cup finely chopped dried
  apricots

Preheat the oven to 400° F. Lightly grease two large baking sheets with butter or vegetable shortening.

In a large mixing bowl, cream together the butter, sugar, and almond extract. In another bowl, combine the sifted flour with the ground almonds and mix well. In a small bowl, using a rotary beater, beat the eggs and water together for 3 to 5 minutes, or until the mixture is foamy.

Add the flour mixture, 1 cup at a time, to the butter mixture, alternating with the beaten eggs. Mix well after each addition. Stir in the chopped apricots. Knead to a smooth dough. If the dough is too sticky, add more flour, a little at a time, until it is easier to work.

Pull off small pieces of dough and roll between the palms of the hands into 1-inch balls. Place the balls on the baking sheets 1 inch apart. Bake for 18 to 20 minutes, or until the cookies are golden brown. Remove from the oven.

After the cookies have cooled for 2 to 3 minutes, but are still warm to the touch, use a spatula to transfer them to wire racks to cool completely.

## NO. 204 BELFASTS

*Makes about 36 cookies*

| | |
|---|---|
| 1 cup dried currants | ½ cup unsalted butter, softened |
| 1½ cups sifted whole wheat flour | |
| 1½ cups sifted all-purpose flour | 1 cup sugar |
| ½ teaspoon salt | 1 egg, beaten |
| ¼ teaspoon baking soda | ¾ cup buttermilk |

Preheat the oven to 350° F. Lightly grease two large baking sheets with butter or vegetable shortening.

Combine the currants with the whole wheat flour. Sift together the all-purpose flour, salt, and baking soda. In a large mixing bowl, cream together the butter and sugar. Beat in the egg. Add the buttermilk alternately with the flour mixture and mix thoroughly. Stir in the currant mixture.

On a floured work surface, knead the mixture to a smooth dough. If the dough is sticky, add more flour, a little at a time, until it is easier to work. From the dough make 36 thin flat cakes. Place them 1 inch apart on the baking sheets. Bake for 15 to 18 minutes, or until the cookies have browned around the edges. Remove from the oven.

After the cookies have cooled for 2 to 3 minutes, but are still warm to the touch, use a spatula to transfer them to wire racks to cool completely.

NO. **205**                              # BERLIN CAKES
*Makes about 40 cookies*

½ cup sugar                              3½ cups sifted flour
2 hard-boiled egg yolks                  1 egg white, beaten
2 egg yolks, beaten                      Sugar
1 cup unsalted butter,
   softened

Preheat the oven to 400° F. Lightly grease two large baking sheets
with butter or vegetable shortening.

In a large mixing bowl, combine the sugar and hard-boiled egg
yolks. Using the back of a fork, work the sugar and the eggs into a
paste. Gradually blend the beaten egg yolks into the paste. Add the
butter and flour alternately, and knead into a smooth dough in the
mixing bowl.

Pull off pieces of dough and form into little rings on the baking
sheets. Brush the rings with beaten egg white, then sprinkle with
sugar. Bake for 10 minutes, or until the cookies have browned around
the edges. Remove from the oven.

After the cookies have cooled for 2 to 3 minutes, but are still
warm to the touch, use a spatula to transfer them to wire racks to
cool completely.


NO. **206**                              # BUTTER RINGS
*Makes about 48 cookies*

6 hard-boiled egg yolks                  2 cups sifted flour
¼ cup sugar                              1 egg white, beaten
1 cup unsalted butter,                   Cinnamon and coarse sugar
   softened                                 crystals
½ teaspoon almond extract

Preheat the oven to 350° F. Lightly grease two large baking sheets
with butter or vegetable shortening.

Press the egg yolks through a food mill or puree to a fine consistency
in a food processor or blender. Turn into a large mixing bowl. Add
the sugar, a little at a time. Cut the butter into chunks, and using a
pastry blender or the back of a fork, work the butter into the egg-
yolk mixture. Stir in the almond extract. Gradually add the flour to
the batter and knead slightly. The dough should not be too sticky.
If necessary, add more flour, a little at a time, until the dough is
easy to work.

Pinch off a small ball of dough and form into a roll between the
palms of the hands. Shape into a ring and place on the baking sheet.

Repeat until all the dough is used. Just before baking, brush the cookies with beaten egg white and sprinkle with cinnamon and coarse sugar crystals. Bake for 10 to 15 minutes, or until the cookies have browned around the edges. Remove from the oven.

After the cookies have cooled for 2 to 3 minutes, but are still warm to the touch, use a spatula to transfer them to wire racks to cool completely.

## NO. 207 CHINESE ALMOND COOKIES

*Makes about 48 cookies*

2¾ cups sifted flour
1 cup sugar
½ teaspoon salt
½ teaspoon baking soda

1 cup unsalted butter, softened
1 egg, beaten
1 teaspoon almond extract
Whole blanched almonds

Preheat the oven to 325° F. Lightly grease two large baking sheets with butter or vegetable shortening.

In a large mixing bowl, sift together the flour, sugar, salt, and baking soda. Cut the butter into large chunks. Add the butter to the flour mixture. Using a pastry blender or two forks, work the butter into the dough until the texture resembles that of coarse oatmeal. Mix in the beaten egg and the almond extract.

Pinch off small pieces of dough and form into round balls between the palms of the hands. Transfer to the baking sheets, leaving a 2-inch interval between each cookie. When all the dough has been used, flatten the cookies with the bottom of a glass. Place one whole almond on top of each cookie. Bake for 15 to 18 minutes, or until the cookies have browned around the edges. Remove from the oven.

After the cookies have cooled for 2 to 3 minutes, but are still warm to the touch, use a spatula to transfer them to wire racks to cool completely.

## NO. 208 COCONUT BALLS

*Makes about 36 cookies*

3 cups unsweetened shredded coconut

1 cup sugar
1 egg white

Preheat the oven to 350° F. Lightly grease two large baking sheets with butter or vegetable shortening.

In the top of a double boiler over boiling water, combine the coconut, sugar, and egg white. Mix thoroughly, and cook over medium heat, stirring constantly, for about 12 minutes or until the mixture thickens. Turn the cooked mixture out onto a marble slab. Let cool.

Shape the coconut mixture into 1-inch balls and arrange them on the baking sheets. Bake for 10 to 12 minutes, or until the cookies are light brown. Remove from the oven.

After the cookies have cooled for 2 to 3 minutes, but are still warm to the touch, use a spatula to transfer them to wire racks to cool completely.

## NO. 209       CREAM CHEESE COOKIES

*Makes about 24 cookies*

1½ cups unsalted butter, softened
8- ounce package cream cheese
1 cup sugar
2 eggs
2 tablespoons orange juice
1½ teaspoons grated orange zest
1½ cups sifted flour
1½ teaspoons baking powder
½ cup apricot jam
2 tablespoons apricot brandy
Confectioners' sugar

Preheat the oven to 350° F. Lightly grease two large baking sheets with butter or vegetable shortening.

In a large mixing bowl, cream together the butter, cream cheese, and sugar. Beat in the eggs, one at a time. Beat in the orange juice and orange zest. Sift the flour with the baking powder. Gradually add the flour to the batter. Divide the dough in two equal parts, wrap each half in waxed paper, and chill in the refrigerator for 30 minutes.

From the chilled batter, make 24 2-inch balls. Place them on the baking sheets, leaving at least 2 inches between each ball. Partially flatten each ball with the bottom of a glass. Use a finger to make an indentation in the center of each cookie.

In a small saucepan, heat the jam and brandy together until the jam melts. Cool slightly, then spoon a little jam into each indentation. Bake for 15 minutes, or until the cookies are brown around the edges. Remove from the oven.

After the cookies have cooled for 2 to 3 minutes, but are still warm to the touch, use a spatula to transfer them to wire racks to cool completely. When thoroughly cool, dust the cookies with confectioners' sugar.

NO. **210**

# CHOCOLATE CHIP CREAM CHEESE COOKIES

*Makes about 24 cookies*

1½ cups unsalted butter, softened
8- ounce package cream cheese, softened
1 cup sugar
2 eggs
2 tablespoons orange juice
1½ teaspoons grated orange zest

1½ cups sifted flour
1½ teaspoons baking powder
7½- ounce package semi-sweet chocolate morsels
½ cup apricot jam
2 tablespoons apricot brandy
Unsweetened baking cocoa

Preheat the oven to 350° F. Lightly grease two large baking sheets with butter or vegetable shortening.

In a large mixing bowl, cream together the butter, cream cheese, and sugar. Beat in the eggs, one at a time. Beat in the orange juice and the orange zest. Sift the flour with the baking powder. Gradually mix the flour into the batter. Stir in the chocolate morsels. Divide the dough in two, wrap each half in waxed paper, and chill in the refrigerator for 30 minutes.

From the chilled dough make 36 2-inch balls. Place the balls on the baking sheets, leaving at least 2 inches between each cookie. Partially flatten each cookie with the bottom of a glass. Use a finger to make an indentation in the middle of each cookie.

In a small saucepan, heat the jam and brandy together until the jam melts. Remove the pan from the heat. Allow the mixture to cool slightly, then spoon a little of it into each indentation. Bake for 15 minutes, or until the cookies have browned around the edges. Remove from the oven.

After the cookies have cooled for 2 to 3 minutes, but are still warm to the touch, use a spatula to transfer them to wire racks to cool completely. When thoroughly cool, dust the cookies with cocoa powder.


NO. **211**

# MILK CHOCOLATE CHIP CREAM CHEESE COOKIES

*Makes about 24 cookies*

Follow the recipe for Chocolate Chip Cream Cheese Cookies (No. 210), substituting milk chocolate morsels for the semi-sweet chocolate morsels.

NO. **212**                    **MINT CHOCOLATE CHIP**
**CREAM CHEESE COOKIES**
*Makes about 24 cookies*

1½ cups unsalted butter,
   softened
8- ounce package cream
   cheese, softened
1 cup sugar
2 eggs
1 teaspoon vanilla extract

1½ cups sifted flour
1½ teaspoons baking powder
7½- ounce package mint
   chocolate morsels
½ cup raspberry jam
2 tablespoons brandy
Unsweetened baking cocoa

Preheat the oven to 350° F. Lightly grease two large baking sheets
with butter or vegetable shortening.

In a large mixing bowl, cream together the butter, cream cheese,
and sugar. Beat in the eggs, one at a time. Beat in the vanilla extract.
Sift the flour with the baking powder. Gradually mix the flour into
the batter. Stir in the chocolate morsels. Divide the dough in two,
wrap each half in waxed paper, and chill in the refrigerator for 30
minutes.

From the chilled dough make 36 2-inch balls. Place the balls on
the baking sheets, leaving at least 2 inches between each cookie.
Partially flatten each cookie with the bottom of a glass. Use a finger
to make an indentation in the middle of each cookie.

In a small saucepan, heat the jam and brandy together until the
jam melts. Remove the pan from the heat. Allow the mixture to cool
slightly, then spoon a little of it into each indentation. Bake for 15
minutes, or until the cookies have browned around the edges. Remove
from the oven.

After the cookies have cooled for 2 to 3 minutes, but are still
warm to the touch, use a spatula to transfer them to wire racks to
cool completely. When thoroughly cool, dust the cookies with cocoa
powder.

NO. **213**                                    **FILBERT BALLS**
*Makes about 36 cookies*

½ cup unsalted butter,
   softened
1 teaspoon vanilla extract
2 tablespoons superfine sugar

1 cup sifted flour
1 cup blanched filberts, finely
   chopped
Confectioners' sugar

Preheat the oven to 350° F. Lightly grease two large baking sheets
with butter or vegetable shortening.

Cream the butter and vanilla extract together in a large mixing bowl. In another bowl, combine the sugar, flour, and chopped filberts. Work the sugar mixture into the butter mixture, ½ cup at a time. Pinch off small pieces of dough and roll between the palms of the hands into 1-inch balls. Place the balls on baking sheets, about 2 inches apart. Flatten each cookie with the bottom of a glass. Bake for about 15 minutes, or until the cookies have browned around the edges. Remove from the oven.

While the cookies are still hot, dust them with confectioners' sugar and transfer to wire racks to cool completely.

## NO. 214      GERMAN ALMOND COOKIES

*Makes about 24 cookies*

| | |
|---|---|
| 2 eggs | 1 cup sifted flour |
| 1 cup sugar | 1 cup blanched almonds, |
| ½ teaspoon vanilla extract | finely chopped |

Preheat the oven to 350° F. Lightly grease two large baking sheets with butter or vegetable shortening.

In a large mixing bowl, beat the eggs until foamy. Gradually beat in the sugar. Continue beating until the batter is thick and light. Mix in the vanilla extract. Stir in the flour and the chopped almonds. Mix well.

Divide the dough into 24 pieces. Roll each piece into a ball. Arrange the balls 2 inches apart on the baking sheets. Flatten each one slightly with the bottom of a glass. Bake for 12 to 15 minutes, or until the cookies are golden brown. Remove from the oven.

After the cookies have cooled for 2 to 3 minutes, but are still warm to the touch, use a spatula to transfer them to wire racks to cool completely.

## NO. 215      GERMAN ALMOND CRESCENTS

*Makes about 36 cookies*

| | |
|---|---|
| 5 egg whites | 2 cups blanched almonds, |
| 3½ cups sugar | finely chopped |
| 1 teaspoon vanilla extract | Confectioners' sugar |

Preheat the oven to 275° F. Lightly grease two large baking sheets with butter or vegetable shortening.

In a large mixing bowl, beat the egg whites until they hold stiff peaks. Beat in the sugar, ½ cup at a time. Continue to beat until the batter is thick and glossy. Mix in the vanilla extract. Stir the chopped almonds into the batter.

Divide the dough into 36 pieces. Roll each piece between the palms and shape into a crescent. Arrange the crescents 1 inch apart on the baking sheets. Bake for about 30 minutes, or until the cookies have browned around the edges. Remove from the oven.

After the cookies have cooled for 2 to 3 minutes, but are still warm to the touch, use a spatula to transfer them to wire racks to cool completely. When cool, dust each cookie with confectioners' sugar and transfer to a serving plate.

NO. **216**          **GERMAN ALMOND PRETZELS**

*Makes about 30 cookies*

1 cup unsalted butter,
   softened
2 eggs
2 egg yolks

2 cups sifted flour
1 cup ground almonds
1 egg white, beaten
Unrefined sugar crystals

Preheat the oven to 350° F. Lightly grease two large baking sheets with butter or vegetable shortening.

In a large mixing bowl, cream the butter until it is soft. Blend the whole eggs and the egg yolks, one at a time, into the creamed butter. In another bowl, combine the flour and ground almonds and mix well. Gradually add the flour-and-almond mixture to the butter mixture, working the batter into a thick, smooth dough.

Divide the dough into 30 equal balls. Roll each ball between the palms of the hands to form a roll 4 inches long and about the thickness of a pencil. On the baking sheet, shape the roll into a pretzel. Repeat with the remaining balls.

Brush the pretzels with beaten egg white and sprinkle liberally with sugar crystals. Bake for 15 to 20 minutes, or until the cookies have begun to brown. Remove from the oven.

When the cookies are completely cool, gently remove them from the baking sheets with a spatula and transfer to a serving plate.

NO. **217**                    **GOLDEN COOKIES**

*Makes about 24 cookies*

½ cup unsalted butter,
   softened
½ cup confectioners' sugar
3 egg yolks
2 teaspoons grated lemon zest
1 teaspoon lemon juice

1 teaspoon vanilla extract
1⅔ cups sifted flour
⅛ teaspoon salt
1 egg yolk, beaten
½ cup ground pecans

Preheat the oven to 350° F. Lightly grease two large baking sheets with butter or vegetable shortening.

In a large mixing bowl, cream together the butter and sugar. Beat in the 3 egg yolks and mix well. Stir in the lemon zest and lemon juice. Add the vanilla extract. Sift the flour with the salt. Gradually add the flour mixture to the batter, ½ cup at a time. Mix well after each addition.

Knead the mixture to a smooth dough. If the dough is sticky, add more flour, a little at a time, until it is easier to work. Pull off small pieces of dough and roll into 1-inch balls. Place the balls on the baking sheets, about 2 inches apart, and flatten them with the bottom of a glass. Brush each cookie with beaten egg yolk and sprinkle with the ground pecans. Bake for 10 to 12 minutes, or until the cookies have browned around the edges. Remove from the oven.

After the cookies have cooled for 2 to 3 minutes, but are still warm to the touch, use a spatula to transfer them to wire racks to cool completely.

NO. **218**
# HAZELNUT BALLS
*Makes about 36 cookies*

1 cup unsalted butter, softened
1 cup sugar
¼ teaspoon almond extract

3 cups sifted flour
¼ cup ground hazelnuts
3 eggs
1 tablespoon water

Preheat the oven to 400° F. Lightly grease a large baking sheet with butter or vegetable shortening.

In a large mixing bowl, cream together the butter, sugar, and almond extract. In another bowl, combine the sifted flour with the ground hazelnuts and mix well. In a small bowl, using a rotary beater, beat the eggs and water together for 3 to 5 minutes, or until the mixture is foamy. Add the flour mixture, 1 cup at a time, to the butter mixture, alternating with the beaten eggs. Mix well after each addition. Knead to a smooth dough. If the dough is too sticky, add more flour, a little at a time, until it is easier to work.

Pull off small pieces of dough and roll into 1-inch balls. Place the balls on the baking sheet, 1 inch apart. Bake for 18 to 20 minutes, or until the cookies are golden brown. Remove from the oven.

After the cookies have cooled for 2 to 3 minutes, but are still warm to the touch, use a spatula to transfer them to wire racks to cool completely.

NO. **219**          # HAZELNUT CRESCENTS
*Makes about 36 cookies*

2 cups sifted flour
½ cup confectioners' sugar
1½ cups ground hazelnuts
1 cup unsalted butter,
    softened

1 teaspoon vanilla extract
Additional confectioners'
    sugar

Preheat the oven to 350° F. Lightly grease two large baking sheets with butter or vegetable shortening.

In a large mixing bowl, sift the flour with the ½ cup of sugar. Mix in the ground hazelnuts. Cut the butter into large chunks. Using a pastry blender, or two forks, work the butter into the flour mixture until the mixture has the texture of coarse oatmeal. Stir in the vanilla extract. Work the mixture into a smooth dough.

Divide the dough into 36 pieces. Roll each piece of dough into a ball, then shape it into a crescent. Arrange the crescents 1 inch apart on the baking sheets. Bake for 12 to 15 minutes, or until the cookies have browned around the edges. Remove from the oven.

After the cookies have cooled for 2 to 3 minutes, but are still warm to the touch, use a spatula to transfer them to wire racks to cool completely. Roll the cookies in confectioners' sugar and transfer to a serving plate.

NO. **220**          # NORWEGIAN ALMOND BALLS
*Makes about 36 cookies*

1 cup unsalted butter
1 cup sugar
¼ teaspoon almond extract
3 cups sifted flour

¼ cup ground almonds
3 eggs
1 tablespoon water

Preheat the oven to 400° F. Lightly grease two large baking sheets with butter or vegetable shortening.

In a large mixing bowl, cream together the butter, sugar, and almond extract. In another bowl, combine the sifted flour with the ground almonds and mix well. In a small bowl, using a rotary beater, beat the eggs and water together for 3 to 5 minutes, or until the mixture is foamy. Add the flour mixture, 1 cup at a time, to the butter mixture, alternating with the beaten eggs. Mix well after each addition. Knead to a smooth dough. If the dough is too sticky, add more flour, a little at a time, until it is easier to work.

Pull off small pieces of dough and roll into 1-inch balls. Place the balls on the baking sheets, 1 inch apart. Bake for 18 to 20 minutes, or until the cookies are brown around the edges. Remove from the oven.

After the cookies have cooled for 2 to 3 minutes, but are still warm to the touch, use a spatula to transfer them to wire racks to cool completely.

NO. **221**

# ORANGE TWISTS

*Makes about 36 cookies*

¾ cup unsalted butter, softened
¾ cup sugar
½ teaspoon orange extract
2 teaspoons grated orange zest

3 cups sifted flour
2 teaspoons baking powder
¼ teaspoon salt
½ cup milk, warmed
1 egg white, beaten
Unrefined sugar crystals

Preheat the oven to 350° F. Lightly grease two large baking sheets with butter or vegetable shortening.

In a large mixing bowl, cream together the butter and sugar. Beat in the orange extract and orange zest. Sift the flour with the baking powder and salt. Add the flour mixture to the batter, ½ cup at a time, alternating with the warm milk. Mix well after each addition. Knead the mixture to a smooth dough. If the dough is sticky, add more flour, a little at a time, until it is easier to work.

Divide the dough into 36 balls. Using the palms of the hands, shape each ball into a 4-inch-long roll. Take the end of the roll in each hand and twist several times. Place the twists on a baking sheet, brush with beaten egg white, and sprinkle with unrefined sugar. Bake for about 20 minutes, or until the cookies are golden brown. Remove from the oven.

After the cookies have cooled for 2 to 3 minutes, but are still warm to the touch, use a spatula to transfer them to wire racks to cool completely.

NO. **222**

# ORANGE WALNUT WAFERS

*Makes about 48 cookies*

½ cup unsalted butter, softened
1 cup sugar
1 egg
1 tablespoon orange juice

1 tablespoon grated orange zest
2 cups sifted flour
1 teaspoon baking powder
1 cup walnuts, finely chopped

Preheat the oven to 350° F. Lightly grease two large baking sheets with butter or vegetable shortening.

In a large mixing bowl, cream together the butter and sugar. Beat in the egg and mix well. Stir in the orange juice and the orange zest. Sift the flour with the baking powder. Add the flour mixture to the batter, ½ cup at a time. Mix well after each addition. Work the chopped walnuts into the dough.

Divide the dough into two equal parts. Wrap each half in waxed paper and chill for 30 minutes in the freezer.

From each chilled ball of dough, make 24 balls. Place the balls 2 inches apart on the baking sheets, and flatten each cookie with the bottom of a glass. Bake for 12 to 15 minutes, or until the cookies have browned around the edges. Remove from the oven.

After the cookies have cooled for 2 to 3 minutes, but are still warm to the touch, use a spatula to transfer them to wire racks to cool completely.

## NO. 223      POWDERED SUGAR COOKIES
*Makes about 72 cookies*

| | |
|---|---|
| 1 cup unsalted butter, softened | 2½ cups sifted flour |
| 1 cup solid vegetable shortening | ¼ teaspoon baking powder |
| ½ cup sugar | 1½ cups walnuts, finely chopped |
| 3 teaspoons vanilla extract | Confectioners' sugar |

Preheat the oven to 400° F. Lightly grease two large baking sheets with butter or vegetable shortening.

In a large mixing bowl, cream together the butter, vegetable shortening, and sugar. Beat in the vanilla extract. Sift the flour with the baking powder. Add the flour mixture to the batter, ½ cup at a time. Stir in the chopped walnuts.

Knead the mixture to a smooth dough. If the dough is sticky, add more flour, a little at a time, until it is easier to work. Pinch off small pieces of dough. Roll into little sausages no thicker than a pencil. Arrange the rolls 1 inch apart on the baking sheets. Bake for about 10 minutes, or until the cookies are golden brown. Remove from the oven.

After the cookies have cooled for 2 to 3 minutes, roll each one in confectioners' sugar. Transfer to wire racks to cool completely.

NO. **224**

# RASPBERRY ORANGE WALNUT ROUNDS

*Makes about 24 cookies*

1½ cups unsalted butter, softened
8- ounce package cream cheese
1 cup sugar
2 eggs
2 tablespoons orange juice
1½ teaspoons grated orange zest

1½ cups sifted flour
1½ teaspoons baking powder
1 cup walnuts, finely chopped
½ cup raspberry jam
2 tablespoons brandy
Confectioners' sugar

Preheat the oven to 350° F. Lightly grease two large baking sheets with butter or vegetable shortening.

In a large mixing bowl, cream together the butter, cream cheese, and sugar. Beat in the eggs, one at a time. Stir in the orange juice and the orange zest. Sift the flour with the baking powder. Gradually mix the flour into the batter. Work the chopped walnuts into the dough.

Divide the dough in two, wrap each half in waxed paper. Chill in the freezer for 30 minutes.

Divide the chilled dough into 24 pieces. Roll each piece into a ball. Arrange the balls on the baking sheets, about 2 inches apart. Partially flatten each cookie with the bottom of a glass. Using the tip of a finger, make an indentation in the center of each cookie.

Combine the jam and brandy in a small saucepan. Cook over very low heat, stirring frequently, until the jam has melted. Cool slightly, then spoon a little of the jam mixture into the indentation in each cookie. Bake for 15 minutes, or until the cookies have browned around the edges. Remove from the oven.

After the cookies have cooled for 2 to 3 minutes, but are still warm to the touch, use a spatula to transfer them to wire racks to cool completely. When the cookies are thoroughly cool, sprinkle them with confectioners' sugar.

NO. **225**

# ROLLED PECAN COOKIES

*Makes about 36 cookies*

1 cup unsalted butter, softened
¾ cup confectioners' sugar
1 teaspoon vanilla extract
2 cups sifted flour

⅛ teaspoon salt
1 tablespoon ice water
2 cups pecans, coarsely chopped
Confectioners' sugar

Preheat the oven to 325° F. Lightly grease two large baking sheets with butter or vegetable shortening.

In a large mixing bowl, cream together the butter and sugar. Beat in the vanilla extract. Sift the flour with the salt. Beat the flour mixture into the batter, ½ cup at a time. Add the ice water after the first cup of flour. Mix in the chopped pecans.

Break off small pieces of dough. Roll between the palms of the hands into finger lengths and place 1 inch apart on the baking sheets. Bake for about 25 minutes, or until the cookies are golden brown. Remove from the oven.

After the cookies have cooled for 2 to 3 minutes, but are still warm to the touch, roll in confectioners' sugar. Transfer to wire racks to cool completely.

NO. **226**                          # VIRGINIA COOKIES
*Makes about 36 cookies*

½ cup unsalted butter,          2 egg yolks
   softened          1½ cups sifted flour
½ cup confectioners' sugar      Blanched almond halves

Preheat the oven to 325° F. Lightly grease two large baking sheets with butter or vegetable shortening.

In a large mixing bowl, cream together the butter and sugar. Beat in the egg yolks and mix well. Stir the flour into the batter, ½ cup at time. Work the mixture into a smooth dough.

Break off small pieces of dough and roll into balls between the palms of the hands. Arrange the balls 2 inches apart on the baking sheets. Flatten each cookie slightly with the bottom of a glass. Press an almond half into the center of each cookie. Bake for about 20 minutes, or until the cookies have browned around the edges. Remove from the oven.

After the cookies have cooled for 2 to 3 minutes, but are still warm to the touch, use a spatula to transfer them to wire racks to cool completely.

NO. **227**                    # WHIPPED CREAM COOKIES
*Makes about 30 cookies*

1 cup heavy cream              ½ cup unsalted butter,
2 cups sifted flour               softened
2 tablespoons sugar            1 egg white, beaten
1 teaspoon baking powder       Unrefined sugar crystals

Preheat the oven to 400° F. Lightly grease two large baking sheets with butter or vegetable shortening.

In a small mixing bowl, beat the cream until stiff. Sift the flour with the sugar and baking powder. In a large mixing bowl, cut the butter into chunks. Using a pastry blender, or two forks, work the flour mixture into the butter until the dough resembles coarse oatmeal. Mix in the whipped cream.

Knead the mixture to a smooth dough. If the dough is sticky, add more flour, a little at a time, until it is easier to work. Divide the dough into 30 balls. Roll each ball between the palms of the hands to form a roll 4 inches long and about the thickness of a pencil. On the baking sheet, shape the roll into a pretzel. Repeat with the remaining dough.

Brush the cookies with beaten egg white and sprinkle liberally with sugar crystals. Bake for 12 to 15 minutes, or until the cookies have begun to brown. Remove from the oven.

Cool completely, then gently remove the cookies from the baking sheets with a spatula and transfer to a serving plate.

# Cookie Cutter and Pressed Cookies

Anyone who collects cookie cutters will attest to the wide variety and quality of the cookie cutters on the market. Additionally, antique or reproductions of antique cutters are available, and these, like the modern variety, may also be used with mixed results. A well-made cookie cutter does not have a closed top. When the top of the cutter is open, it is easier to push the cookie dough gently out of the cutter without damaging the shape. Beware of solid molds requiring seasoning or chilling—they are more difficult and more time-consuming to use. A pastry cloth and rolling pin cover will make rolling out the dough for cookie cutter cookies much more efficient. Always cut out as many cookies as possible from the sheet of dough before rerolling it. If the dough is handled too much it may become tough. If you want to make a cookie cutter cookie in a particular shape, you can always draw a paper pattern and cut out the cookie around it.

If you do not own a cookie press, and want to make some of the cookie press cookies, you may slice the dough as noted in the recipes. Always press out a few preliminary test cookies from the cookie press to make sure it is working properly—the first few cookies may not be as attractive as those that follow.

NO. **228**

## ALMOND TEA CAKES

*Makes about 36 cookies*

¾ cup unsalted butter, softened  
½ cup sugar  
2 egg yolks, beaten  

2 cups sifted flour  
1 egg white, beaten  
¼ cup cinnamon sugar  
¼ cup ground almonds  

Preheat the oven to 350° F. Lightly grease two large baking sheets with butter or vegetable shortening.

In a large mixing bowl, cream together the butter and sugar. Beat in the egg yolks. Work the flour into the batter, ½ cup at a time. Knead the mixture to a smooth dough. If the dough is sticky, add more flour, a little at a time, until it is easier to work.

On a floured work surface, roll out the dough to a thickness of ¼ inch. Cut out the cookies using a 2-inch, curly-edged biscuit or cookie cutter. Place the cookies 1 inch apart on the baking sheets. Brush each one with beaten egg white, then sprinkle with cinnamon sugar and ground almonds. Bake for 12 to 15 minutes, or until the cookies have browned around the edges. Remove from the oven.

After the cookies have cooled for 2 to 3 minutes, but are still warm to the touch, use a spatula to transfer them to wire racks to cool completely.

## NO. 229 BLACK-AND-WHITE COOKIES
*Makes about 20 cookies*

1½ cups sugar
1 cup unsalted butter, softened

4 eggs
3 cups sifted flour
1 teaspoon baking soda

### Chocolate Fudge Icing

3 ounces unsweetened baking chocolate
⅔ cup sugar
⅓ cup strong coffee

¼ cup heavy cream
⅛ teaspoon salt
1 tablespoon unsalted butter
1 teaspoon vanilla extract

### Vanilla Icing

2 tablespoons butter, softened
1 tablespoon heavy cream

2 teaspoons vanilla extract
2 cups confectioners' sugar

Preheat the oven to 400° F. Lightly grease two large baking sheets with butter or vegetable shortening.

In a large mixing bowl, cream together the sugar and butter. Beat in the eggs, one at a time, and continue to beat until the mixture is creamy. Sift the flour with the baking soda. Add the flour mixture to the batter, ½ cup at a time, and work into a soft dough.

On a floured work surface, roll out the dough to a thickness of ¼ inch. Cut out the cookies using a 4-inch, round cookie cutter or a small bowl. Place the cookies 1 inch apart on the baking sheets. Bake for 8 to 10 minutes, or until the cookies have browned around the edges. Remove from the oven.

After the cookies have cooled for 2 to 3 minutes, but are still warm to the touch, use a spatula to transfer them to wire racks to cool completely.

When the cookies have thoroughly cooled, prepare the icing. In a saucepan over low heat, combine the chocolate, sugar, coffee, cream, and salt. Bring to a boil and cook, stirring constantly, until the mixture reaches the soft-ball stage (when a teaspoon of liquid dropped into a glass of water forms a soft ball). Remove the pan from the heat. Stir in the butter and vanilla, then set aside.

In another bowl, combine the butter, cream, and vanilla extract. Beat until the mixture is creamy. Gradually add the sugar until the icing thickens. Spread half of each cookie with the chocolate icing and the other half with the vanilla icing. Let the icing harden and dry before storing the cookies.

## NO. 230     BLACK WALNUT SQUARES

*Makes about 48 cookies*

1 cup unsalted butter, softened
1½ cups sugar
3 eggs
3 cups sifted flour
½ teaspoon baking soda

1 teaspoon cream of tartar
½ teaspoon salt
1 cup milk
1 cup black walnuts, finely chopped

Preheat the oven to 450° F. Lightly grease two large baking sheets with butter or vegetable shortening.

In a large mixing bowl, cream together the butter and sugar. Beat in the eggs, one at a time. Sift the flour together with the baking soda, cream of tartar, and salt. Add the flour mixture to the butter and sugar mixture, alternating with the milk. Beat until smooth, then gently mix in the chopped walnuts.

On a floured work surface, roll out the dough to a thickness of ¼ inch, adding more flour if it is too sticky. Using a sharp knife, cut the dough into 2-inch squares. Transfer the squares to the baking sheets. Bake for 10 minutes, then reduce the oven temperature to 350° F and bake for an additional 5 to 8 minutes or until the squares have browned. Remove from the oven.

After the squares have cooled for 2 to 3 minutes, but are still warm to the touch, gently remove them from the baking sheets with a spatula and transfer to wire racks to cool completely.

## NO. 231     BONNEFEADAS

*Makes about 36 cookies*

¼ cup dark brown sugar, firmly packed
2 tablespoons cinnamon
1 teaspoon lemon juice
2 cups sifted flour

2 tablespoons sugar
¼ teaspoon salt
⅔ cup unsalted butter, softened
4 to 5 tablespoons water

Preheat the oven to 375° F. Lightly grease two large baking sheets with butter or vegetable shortening.

In a small bowl, combine the brown sugar, cinnamon, and lemon juice. Set aside. In a large mixing bowl, combine the flour with the sugar and salt. Cut the butter into chunks. Using a pastry blender, or two forks, work the butter into the flour mixture until the dough has the texture of coarse oatmeal. Sprinkle on 4 tablespoons of water (add more if the dough does not hold together), and lightly knead into a ball. Wrap the dough in waxed paper and chill in the freezer for 30 minutes.

On a floured work surface, roll out the dough to a thickness of ¼ inch. Spread the sugar mixture evenly over the dough. Using a sharp knife, cut into strips ½ inch wide and 4 inches long. Roll the strips up tightly and place, with the wide side down, on the baking sheets. Bake for 20 to 25 minutes, or until golden brown. Remove from the oven.

After the cookies have cooled for 2 to 3 minutes, but are still warm to the touch, use a spatula to transfer them to wire racks to cool completely.

## NO. 232     BUTTER COOKIES I

*Makes about 48 cookies*

1 cup unsalted butter, softened
1½ cups light brown sugar
2 eggs
2 tablespoons grated lemon zest

4 cups sifted flour
1 teaspoon cinnamon
1 tablespoon ground ginger
½ teaspoon salt

Preheat the oven to 400° F. Lightly grease two large baking sheets with butter or vegetable shortening.

In a large mixing bowl, cream together the butter and sugar. Beat in the eggs, one at a time. Add the lemon zest and mix well. Sift together the flour, cinnamon, ginger, and salt. Gradually add the flour mixture to the batter, ½ cup at a time. Work the batter into a smooth, stiff dough, finishing the kneading on a floured work surface.

Roll out the dough to a thickness of ¼ inch. Cut out the cookies using a 2-inch, curly-edged biscuit or cookie cutter. Place the cookies 1 inch apart on the baking sheets. Bake for 10 to 12 minutes, or until the cookies have browned around the edges. Remove from the oven.

After the cookies have cooled for 2 to 3 minutes, but are still warm to the touch, use a spatula to transfer them to wire racks to cool completely.

NO. **233**                        # BUTTER COOKIES II
                                    *Makes about 48 cookies*

2 cups unsalted butter,            2 eggs, beaten
   slightly softened           4 cups sifted flour
1 cup sugar

Cut the butter into large pieces and place in a mixing bowl. Add the sugar and eggs all at once. Work the mixture with a pastry blender until it has a creamy texture. Continuing to use the pastry blender, add enough flour to make the dough firm.

Mold the dough into 6 small rolls and wrap each roll in waxed paper. Chill in the refrigerator for 3 hours. Do not freeze.

Preheat the oven to 400° F. Lightly grease two large baking sheets with butter or vegetable shortening.

Place one roll of dough in a cookie press with a decorative shape, and press out cookies onto a baking sheet. Continue to press out cookies until all the dough has been used. (Alternatively, the dough rolls may be cut into ½-inch-thick rounds.) Bake for 10 to 12 minutes, or until the cookies are brown around the edges. Remove from the oven.

After the cookies have cooled for 2 to 3 minutes, but are still warm to the touch, use a spatula to transfer them to wire racks to cool completely.

NO. **234**                       # HOT BUTTER TEA COOKIES
                                   *Makes about 36 cookies*

½ cup unsalted butter             1 cup sugar
2 cups sifted flour               2 eggs

Preheat the oven to 400° F. Lightly grease two large baking sheets with butter or vegetable shortening.

Melt the butter in the top of a double boiler over simmering water. Do not remove from the heat until the melted butter is very hot.

While the butter is melting, pour the flour into a large mixing bowl. Pour the hot, melted butter over the flour and mix well. Stir in the sugar. Beat in the eggs, one at a time. Knead the mixture to a smooth dough. If the dough is sticky, add more flour, a little at a time, until it is easier to work.

On a floured work surface, roll out the dough to a thickness of ¼ inch. Cut out the cookies using a 3-inch, curly-edged biscuit or cookie cutter. Place the cookies 1 inch apart on the baking sheets. Bake for 10 to 12 minutes, or until the cookies have browned around the edges. Remove from the oven.

After the cookies have cooled for 2 to 3 minutes, but are still warm to the touch, use a spatula to transfer them to wire racks to cool completely.

## NO. 235     BUTTERMILK SUGAR COOKIES

*Makes about 36 cookies*

½ cup unsalted butter, softened  
1¼ cups sugar  
1 egg  
½ teaspoon vanilla extract  

2 cups sifted flour  
½ teaspoon baking soda  
¼ teaspoon salt  
½ cup buttermilk  
Sugar  

Preheat the oven to 400° F. Lightly grease two large baking sheets with butter or vegetable shortening.

In a large mixing bowl, cream together the butter and sugar. Beat in the egg and the vanilla extract. Mix well. Sift the flour with the baking soda and salt. Add the flour to the batter, ½ cup at a time, alternating with the buttermilk. Knead the mixture to a smooth dough. If the dough is sticky, add more flour, a little at a time, until it is easier to work.

On a floured work surface, roll out the dough to a thickness of ½ inch. Cut out the cookies using a 3-inch, curly-edged biscuit or cookie cutter. Place the cookies 1 inch apart on the baking sheets. Sprinkle each cookie with sugar. Bake for 12 to 15 minutes, or until the cookies are golden brown. Remove from the oven.

After the cookies have cooled for 2 to 3 minutes, but are still warm to the touch, use a spatula to transfer them to wire racks to cool completely.

## NO. 236     CARAWAY COOKIES

*Makes about 50 cookies*

½ cup unsalted butter, softened  
2 cups sugar  
1 egg, beaten  
½ teaspoon lemon extract  

1 teaspoon grated lemon zest  
4 cups sifted flour  
1 teaspoon baking soda  
½ cup caraway seeds  
½ cup milk  

Preheat the oven to 400° F. Lightly grease two large baking sheets with butter or vegetable shortening.

In a large mixing bowl, cream together the butter and sugar. Beat in the egg, and mix well. Add the lemon extract and lemon zest. Sift the flour with the baking soda into another bowl. Stir in the caraway seeds. Add the flour mixture and milk alternately to the butter mixture. Knead to a smooth dough. If the dough is sticky, add more flour, a little at a time, until it is easier to work. On a floured work surface, roll out the dough to a thickness of ¼ inch.

Cut out the cookies using a 3-inch, curly-edged biscuit or cookie cutter. Place the cookies 1 inch apart on the baking sheets. Bake for 8 to 10 minutes, or until the cookies have browned around the edges. Remove from the oven.

After the cookies have cooled for 2 to 3 minutes, but are still warm to the touch, use a spatula to transfer them to wire racks to cool completely.

NO. **237**                        # CHOCOLATE COOKIES
*Makes about 30 cookies*

4 ounces (4 squares) unsweetened baking chocolate
½ cup unsalted butter, softened
1 tablespoon solid vegetable shortening
1 cup sugar

1 egg
1 teaspoon vanilla extract
2½ cups sifted flour
¼ teaspoon salt
1 teaspoon cinnamon
½ teaspoon baking soda
2 tablespoons cold strong coffee

Preheat the oven to 400° F. Lightly grease two large baking sheets with butter or vegetable shortening.

Melt the chocolate in the top of a double boiler over simmering water, stirring frequently. Remove from the heat and set aside.

In a large mixing bowl, cream together the butter, vegetable shortening, and sugar. Beat in the egg and vanilla extract. Add the melted chocolate and mix well. Sift the flour with the salt and cinnamon. Dissolve the baking soda in the coffee. Gradually add the flour mixture to the batter, ½ cup at a time, alternating with the coffee mixture.

On a floured work surface, roll out the dough to a thickness of ¼ inch. Cut out the cookies using a 3-inch, curly-edged biscuit or cookie cutter. Place the cookies 1 inch apart on the baking sheets. Bake for 6 to 8 minutes, or until the cookies have browned around the edges. Remove from the oven.

After the cookies have cooled for 2 to 3 minutes, but are still warm to the touch, use a spatula to transfer them to wire racks to cool completely.

## NO. 238    CINNAMON RAISIN COOKIES

*Makes about 36 cookies*

1 cup unsalted butter,
    softened
2 cups sugar
2 eggs
4 cups sifted flour
1 teaspoon baking soda

1 teaspoon cinnamon
½ teaspoon nutmeg
¼ teaspoon ground cloves
¼ teaspoon salt
½ cup milk
1 cup golden raisins, coarsely
    chopped

Preheat the oven to 400° F. Lightly grease two large baking sheets with butter or vegetable shortening.

In a large mixing bowl, cream together the butter and sugar. Beat in the eggs, one at a time, mixing thoroughly after each addition. Sift the flour with the baking soda, cinnamon, nutmeg, cloves, and salt. Add the flour to the batter, ½ cup at a time, alternating with the milk. Mix the chopped raisins into the batter.

Knead the mixture to a smooth dough. If the dough is sticky, add more flour, a little at a time, until it is easier to work. On a floured work surface, roll out the dough to a thickness of ¼ inch. Cut out the cookies using a 3-inch, curly-edged biscuit or cookie cutter. Place the cookies 1 inch apart on the baking sheets. Bake for about 15 minutes, or until the cookies have browned around the edges. Remove from the oven.

After the cookies have cooled for 2 to 3 minutes, but are still warm to the touch, use a spatula to transfer them to wire racks to cool completely.

## NO. 239    CINNAMON PINE NUT COOKIES

*Makes about 36 cookies*

1 cup unsalted butter,
    softened
⅔ cup light brown sugar
3 egg yolks, beaten
2 teaspoons grated orange zest
    1½ cups sifted cake flour
1½ cups cornmeal

1 teaspoon baking powder
2 teaspoons cinnamon
¼ teaspoon salt
½ cup pine nuts
1 egg white, beaten
    Confectioners' sugar

Preheat the oven to 350° F. Lightly grease two large baking sheets with butter or vegetable shortening.

In a large mixing bowl, cream together the butter and sugar. Beat in the egg yolks and the orange zest. Sift together the flour, cornmeal, baking powder, cinnamon, and salt. Gradually add the flour mixture to the batter, ½ cup at a time, mixing thoroughly after each addition. Stir in the pine nuts.

Knead the mixture to a smooth dough. If the dough is sticky, add more flour, a little at a time, until it is easier to work. On a floured work surface, roll out the dough to a thickness of ½ inch. Cut out the cookies using a 2-inch, curly-edged biscuit or cookie cutter. Place the cookies 1 inch apart on the baking sheets. Brush each cookie with beaten egg white and dust with confectioners' sugar. Bake for about 20 minutes, or until the cookies are golden and slightly puffy around the edges. Remove from the oven.

After the cookies have cooled for 2 to 3 minutes, but are still warm to the touch, use a spatula to transfer them to wire racks to cool completely.

## NO. 240                                          CINNAMON STARS
*Makes about 36 cookies*

3 egg whites
2 cups confectioners' sugar
1 teaspoon cinnamon

2 teaspoons grated lemon zest
2 cups ground almonds

Preheat the oven to 350° F. Lightly grease two large baking sheets with butter or vegetable shortening.

In a large mixing bowl, beat the egg whites until they hold stiff peaks. Gradually beat in the confectioners' sugar, ½ cup at a time, until the mixture is glossy and stiff. Beat in the cinnamon and the lemon zest. Stir in the ground almonds.

On a work surface sprinkled with confectioners' sugar, roll out the dough to a thickness of ½ inch. If the dough seems too sticky, add more confectioners' sugar. Cut out the cookies using a 2-inch, star-shaped cookie cutter. Place the cookies 1 inch apart on the baking sheets. Bake for 12 to 15 minutes, or until the cookies have browned around the edges. Remove from the oven.

After the cookies have cooled for 2 to 3 minutes, but are still warm to the touch, use a spatula to transfer them to wire racks to cool completely.

## NO. 241                                            CLOVE COOKIES
*Makes about 50 cookies*

½ cup unsalted butter,
    softened
2 cups dark brown sugar,
    firmly packed
1 egg, beaten
1 teaspoon grated lemon zest
4 cups sifted flour

1 teaspoon baking soda
1 teaspoon ground cloves
1 teaspoon cinnamon
2 teaspoons unsweetened
    baking cocoa
½ cup milk

Preheat the oven to 400° F. Lightly grease two large baking sheets with butter or vegetable shortening.

In a large mixing bowl, cream together the butter and sugar. Beat in the egg, and mix well. Add the lemon zest. Into another bowl, sift the flour with the baking soda, cloves, cinnamon, and cocoa. Add the flour mixture and milk alternately to the butter mixture.

Knead the mixture to a smooth dough. If the dough is sticky, add more flour, a little at a time, until it is easier to work. On a floured work surface, roll out the dough to a thickness of ¼ inch. Cut out the cookies using a 3-inch, curly-edged biscuit or cookie cutter. Place the cookies 1 inch apart on the baking sheets. Bake for 8 to 10 minutes, or until the cookies have browned around the edges. Remove from the oven.

After the cookies have cooled for 2 to 3 minutes, but are still warm to the touch, use a spatula to transfer them to wire racks to cool completely.

## NO. 242 COFFEE COOKIES
*Makes about 30 cookies*

½ cup unsalted butter, softened
1 tablespoon solid vegetable shortening
1 cup sugar
1 egg
1 teaspoon vanilla extract
2½ cups sifted flour

¼ teaspoon salt
1 teaspoon cinnamon
1 teaspoon espresso coffee powder
2 tablespoons boiling water
½ teaspoon baking soda
1 tablespoon cold strong black coffee

Preheat the oven to 400° F. Lightly grease two large baking sheets with butter or vegetable shortening.

In a large mixing bowl, cream together the butter, vegetable shortening, and sugar. Beat in the egg and the vanilla extract. Sift the flour with the salt and cinnamon. Dissolve the instant coffee in the boiling water. Dissolve the baking soda in the cold coffee. Combine both coffee mixtures in one cup. Gradually add the flour mixture to the batter, ½ cup at a time, alternating with the coffee mixture.

Knead the mixture to a smooth dough. If dough is sticky, add more flour, a little at a time, until it is easier to work. On a floured work surface, roll out the dough to a thickness of ¼ inch. Cut out the cookies using a 3-inch, curly-edged biscuit or cookie cutter. Place the cookies 1 inch apart on the baking sheets. Bake for 6 to 8 minutes, or until the cookies have browned around the edges. Remove from the oven.

After the cookies have cooled for 2 to 3 minutes, but are still

warm to the touch, use a spatula to transfer them to wire racks to cool completely.

NO. **243**             # COFFEE GINGER COOKIES
*Makes about 24 cookies*

½ cup unsalted butter,
    softened
1 cup sugar
1½ teaspoons baking soda
½ cup hot strong black coffee
½ cup dark molasses

1 egg, beaten
1 teaspoon vanilla extract
2½ cups sifted flour
½ teaspoon salt
1 teaspoon ground ginger

Preheat the oven to 400° F. Lightly grease two large baking sheets with butter or vegetable shortening.

In a large mixing bowl, cream together the butter and sugar. Dissolve the baking soda in the coffee. Beat the hot coffee mixture into the batter. Beat in the molasses. Allow the batter to cool, then mix in the egg and vanilla extract. Sift the flour with the salt and ginger. Gradually add the flour to the batter, ½ cup at a time, until the mixture forms a soft dough. Knead until smooth. If the dough is sticky, add more flour, a little at a time, until it is easier to work.

On a floured work surface, roll out the dough to a thickness of ¼ inch. Cut out the cookies using a 3-inch, curly-edged biscuit or cookie cutter. Place the cookies 1 inch apart on the baking sheets. Bake for 10 to 15 minutes, or until the cookies have browned around the edges. Remove from the oven.

After the cookies have cooled for 2 to 3 minutes, but are still warm to the touch, use a spatula to transfer them to wire racks to cool completely.

NO. **244**                # CORNMEAL COOKIES
*Makes about 36 cookies*

1 cup unsalted butter,
    softened
⅔ cup light brown sugar
3 egg yolks, lightly beaten
2 teaspoons grated orange
    zest

1½ cups sifted cake flour
1½ cups cornmeal
1 teaspoon baking powder
¼ teaspoon salt
1 egg white, lightly beaten
    Confectioners' sugar

Preheat the oven to 350° F. Lightly grease two large baking sheets with butter or vegetable shortening.

In a large mixing bowl, cream together the butter and sugar. Beat in the egg yolks and the orange zest. Sift together the flour, cornmeal, baking powder, and salt. Gradually add the flour mixture to the batter, ½ cup at a time, mixing thoroughly after each addition. Knead the mixture to a smooth dough. If the dough is sticky, add more flour, a little at a time, until it is easier to work.

On a floured work surface, roll out the dough to a thickness of ½ inch. Cut out the cookies using a 2-inch, curly-edged biscuit or cookie cutter. Place the cookies 1 inch apart on the baking sheets. Brush each cookie with beaten egg white and dust with confectioners' sugar. Bake for about 20 minutes, or until the cookies are golden and slightly puffy around the edges. Remove from the oven.

After the cookies have cooled for 2 to 3 minutes, but are still warm to the touch, use a spatula to transfer them to wire racks to cool completely.

NO. **245**                     **CREAM TEA COOKIES**

*Makes about 24 cookies*

½ cup unsalted butter, softened
1½ cups sugar
2 eggs

2½ cups sifted flour
¼ teaspoon baking soda
⅓ cup heavy cream

Preheat the oven to 400° F. Lightly grease two large baking sheets with butter or vegetable shortening.

In a large mixing bowl, cream together the butter and sugar. Beat in the eggs, one at a time, mixing well after each addition. Sift the flour with the baking soda. Add the flour mixture to the batter, ½ cup at a time, alternating with the cream.

On a floured work surface, knead the mixture to a smooth dough. If the dough is sticky, add more flour, a little at a time, until it is easier to work. Roll out the dough to a thickness of ¼ inch. Cut out the cookies using a 3-inch, curly-edged biscuit or cookie cutter. Place the cookies 1 inch apart on the baking sheets. Bake for 10 to 12 minutes, or until the cookies have browned around the edges. Remove from the oven.

After the cookies have cooled for 2 to 3 minutes, but are still warm to the touch, use a spatula to transfer them to wire racks to cool completely.

NO. **246**                              # CURRANT CAKES

*Makes about 48 cookies*

1 cup unsalted butter,           1½ cups dried currants
   softened                      1 egg, beaten
1½ cups sifted flour             ½ cup milk
1½ cups dark brown sugar,
   firmly packed

Preheat the oven to 400° F. Lightly grease two large baking sheets
with butter or vegetable shortening.

In a large mixing bowl, cut the butter into large chunks. Using a
pastry blender, or two forks, work the flour into the butter until the
mixture has the texture of coarse oatmeal. Mix in the sugar and the
currants. Add the egg and the milk. Mix well. Knead the mixture to
a smooth dough. If the dough is sticky, add more flour, a little at a
time, until it is easier to work.

On a floured work surface, roll out the dough to a thickness of ¼
inch. Cut out the cookies using a 3-inch, curly-edged biscuit or cookie
cutter. Place the cookies 1 inch apart on the baking sheets. Bake for
8 to 10 minutes, or until the cookies have browned around the edges.
Remove from the oven.

After the cookies have cooled for 2 to 3 minutes, but are still
warm to the touch, use a spatula to transfer them to wire racks to
cool completely.

NO. **247**                    # LITTLE CURRANT SPICE
# COOKIES

*Makes about 60 cookies*

½ cup unsalted butter,           1 tablespoon rose water
   softened                      1 cup confectioners' sugar
4 cups sifted flour              ¼ teaspoon nutmeg
1 egg, beaten                    1 cup dried currants

Preheat the oven to 400° F. Lightly grease two large baking sheets
with butter or vegetable shortening.

In a large mixing bowl, cut the butter into large chunks. Using a
pastry blender, or two forks, work the flour into the butter until the
mixture resembles coarse oatmeal. Stir in the beaten egg and the
rose water. Mix well. Work the confectioners' sugar and nutmeg into
the dough. Add the currants and mix well.

Knead the mixture to a smooth dough. If the dough is sticky, add
more flour, a little at a time, until it is easier to work. On a floured
work surface, roll out the dough to a thickness of ¼ inch. Cut out

the cookies using a 1-inch, curly-edged biscuit or cookie cutter. Place the cookies 1 inch apart on the baking sheets. Bake for 8 to 10 minutes, or until the cookies have browned around the edges. Remove from the oven.

After the cookies have cooled for 2 to 3 minutes, but are still warm to the touch, use a spatula to transfer them to wire racks to cool completely.

NO. **248**

# DARK GINGERSNAPS

*Makes about 48 cookies*

½ cup unsalted butter, softened
½ cup sugar
½ cup dark molasses
½ teaspoon baking soda
¼ cup plus 1 tablespoon ice water

3 cups sifted flour
½ teaspoon ground cloves
2 teaspoons ground ginger
½ teaspoon salt

Preheat the oven to 400° F. Lightly grease two large baking sheets with butter or vegetable shortening.

In a large mixing bowl, cream together the butter and sugar. Beat in the molasses. Dissolve the baking soda in the ice water. Sift the flour with the cloves, ginger, and salt. Add the flour mixture to the batter, ½ cup at a time, alternating with the water mixture. Stir well after each addition. Knead the mixture to a smooth dough. If the dough is sticky, add more flour, a little at a time, until it is easier to work.

On a floured work surface, roll out the dough to a thickness of ¼ inch. Cut out the cookies using a 3-inch, curly-edged biscuit or cookie cutter. Place the cookies 1 inch apart on the baking sheets. Bake for 8 to 10 minutes, or until the cookies have browned around the edges. Remove from the oven.

After the cookies have cooled for 2 to 3 minutes, but are still warm to the touch, use a spatula to transfer them to wire racks to cool completely.

NO. **249**

# DOVES

*Makes about 30 cookies*

½ cup unsalted butter, softened
½ cup sugar
2 egg yolks

1 teaspoon vanilla extract
2 tablespoons heavy cream
2 cups sifted flour
Raisins

Preheat the oven to 350° F. Lightly grease two large baking sheets with butter or vegetable shortening.

In a large mixing bowl, cream together the butter and sugar. Beat in the egg yolks and mix well. Stir in the vanilla extract and the cream. Add the flour to the batter, ½ cup at a time, mixing well after each addition. Knead to a smooth dough. If the dough is sticky, add more flour, a little at a time, until it is easier to work.

On a floured work surface, roll out the dough to a thickness of ¼ inch. Cut out the cookies using a bird-shaped cookie cutter. Place the cookies 1 inch apart on the baking sheets. With raisins, make eyes on the doves. Bake for 12 to 15 minutes, or until the cookies have browned around the edges. Remove from the oven.

After the cookies have cooled for 2 to 3 minutes, but are still warm to the touch, use a spatula to transfer them to wire racks to cool completely.

NO. **250**                        **EASY TEA CAKES**

*Makes about 40 cookies*

| | |
|---|---|
| ½ cup unsalted butter, softened | ¼ teaspoon nutmeg |
| 4 cups sifted flour | 2 eggs, beaten |
| ½ teaspoon baking soda | 1½ cups sugar |
| | ½ cup heavy cream |

Preheat the oven to 400° F. Lightly grease two large baking sheets with butter or vegetable shortening.

In a large mixing bowl, cut the butter into large chunks. Sift the flour with the baking soda and nutmeg. Using a pastry blender, or two forks, work the flour mixture into the butter until the mixture has the texture of coarse oatmeal. Mix in the beaten eggs, then add the sugar and the cream.

Knead the mixture to a smooth dough. If the dough is sticky, add more flour, a little at a time, until it is easier to work. On a floured work surface, roll out the dough to a thickness of ¼ inch. Cut out the cookies using a 3-inch, curly-edged biscuit or cookie cutter. Place the cookies 1 inch apart on the baking sheets. Bake for 8 to 10 minutes, or until the cookies have browned around the edges. Remove from the oven.

After the cookies have cooled for 2 to 3 minutes, but are still warm to the touch, use a spatula to transfer them to wire racks to cool completely.

NO. **251** ELIZABETH'S COOKIES

*Makes about 36 cookies*

2 eggs
¾ cup sugar
1 tablespoon unsalted butter, melted
1 teaspoon orange juice

3 cups sifted flour
1 teaspoon baking powder
1 cup citron, cut in thin strips

Preheat the oven to 400° F. Lightly grease two large baking sheets with butter or vegetable shortening.

In a large mixing bowl, beat the eggs until foamy. Gradually add the sugar, and continue to beat until the batter is light and thick. Mix in the melted butter and the orange juice. Sift ½ cup of the flour with the baking powder. Beat the remaining flour into the batter. Finally, knead in the flour and baking powder mixture. Knead to a smooth dough. If the dough is sticky, add more flour, a little at a time, until it is easier to work.

On a floured work surface, roll out the dough to a thickness of ¼ inch. Cut out the cookies using a 3-inch, curly-edged biscuit or cookie cutter. Place the cookies 1 inch apart on the baking sheets. Decorate the top of each cookie with a strip of citron. Bake for 8 to 10 minutes, or until the cookies have browned around the edges. Remove from the oven.

After the cookies have cooled for 2 to 3 minutes, but are still warm to the touch, use a spatula to transfer them to wire racks to cool completely.

NO. **252** FRUIT SNAPS

*Makes about 48 cookies*

½ cup unsalted butter, softened
½ cup sugar
½ cup dark molasses
½ teaspoon baking soda
¼ cup plus 1 tablespoon ice water

3 cups sifted flour
½ teaspoon ground cloves
2 teaspoons ground ginger
½ teaspoon salt
1 cup dried currants
½ cup golden raisins

Preheat the oven to 400° F. Lightly grease two large baking sheets with butter or vegetable shortening.

In a large mixing bowl, cream together the butter and sugar. Beat in the molasses and mix well. Dissolve the baking soda in the ice water. Sift the flour with the cloves, ginger, and salt. Mix the currants and raisins into the flour mixture. Add the flour mixture to the batter,

½ cup at a time, alternating with the baking soda mixture. Stir well after each addition. Knead the mixture to a smooth dough. If the dough is sticky, add more flour, a little at a time, until it is easier to work.

On a floured work surface, roll out the dough to a thickness of ¼ inch. Cut out the cookies using a 3-inch, curly-edged biscuit or cookie cutter. Place the cookies 1 inch apart on the baking sheets. Bake for 8 to 10 minutes, or until the cookies have browned around the edges. Remove from the oven.

After the cookies have cooled for 2 to 3 minutes, but are still warm to the touch, use a spatula to transfer them to wire racks to cool completely.

NO. **253**                                  **GINGERBREAD CREAM COOKIES**

*Makes about 60 cookies*

| | |
|---|---|
| 1 cup unsalted butter, softened | ¼ teaspoon salt |
| 5 cups sifted flour | 1 cup sugar |
| 1 tablespoon ground ginger | ½ cup dark molasses |
| ½ teaspoon nutmeg | ¼ cup heavy cream |

Preheat the oven to 400° F. Lightly grease two large baking sheets with butter or vegetable shortening.

In a large mixing bowl, cut the butter into chunks. Sift the flour with the ginger, nutmeg, and salt. Using a pastry blender, or two forks, work the butter into the flour mixture until the texture resembles that of coarse oatmeal.

In a medium saucepan over low heat, combine the sugar, molasses, and cream. Cook over low heat, stirring constantly with a wooden spoon, until the sugar has dissolved and the mixture thins. Pour into the butter mixture.

Knead to a smooth dough. If the dough is sticky, add more flour, a little at a time, until it is easier to work. On a floured work surface, roll out the dough to a thickness of ¼ inch. Cut out the cookies using a 3-inch, curly-edged biscuit or cookie cutter. Place the cookies 1 inch apart on the baking sheets. Bake for about 8 minutes, or until the cookies have browned around the edges. Remove from the oven.

After the cookies have cooled for 2 to 3 minutes, but are still warm to the touch, use a spatula to transfer them to wire racks to cool completely.

NO. **254**

# HARD GINGERBREAD

*Makes about 48 bars*

½ cup unsalted butter
1 cup dark molasses
½ cup buttermilk
½ teaspoon baking soda
½ teaspoon ground cloves

1 tablespoon ground ginger
2 teaspoons grated lemon zest
3 cups sifted flour
½ cup confectioners' sugar

Preheat the oven to 400° F. Lightly grease two large baking sheets with butter or vegetable shortening.

Cut the butter into large chunks and place in a medium saucepan. Add the molasses. Cook the mixture over low heat, stirring constantly with a wooden spoon, until the butter has melted. Remove from the heat and turn the mixture into a large mixing bowl. Beat in the buttermilk, baking soda, cloves, ginger, and lemon zest. Mix well. Put the flour in a separate bowl. Pour the batter over the flour.

Knead the mixture to a smooth dough. If the dough is sticky, add more flour, a little at a time, until it is easier to work. Divide the dough in half. On a floured work surface, roll out one half of the dough in a rectangle, ¼ inch thick. Transfer to a baking sheet. Roll out the remaining dough and transfer to the other baking sheet. Sprinkle the dough with the confectioners' sugar. Bake for 12 to 15 minutes, or until a toothpick inserted in the center comes out clean. Remove from the oven.

Cut each cake into 3-inch squares while still warm. Gently remove the cookies from the baking sheets with a spatula and transfer to wire racks to cool completely.

NO. **255**

# GINGERBREAD MEN

*Makes about 48 cookies*

This dough should be refrigerated overnight before baking.

¼ cup unsalted butter,
  softened
½ cup dark brown sugar,
  firmly packed
1 teaspoon baking soda
1 teaspoon salt
½ teaspoon cinnamon

½ teaspoon ground ginger
½ teaspoon ground cloves
½ teaspoon allspice
¾ cup dark molasses
⅓ cup water
3¼ cups sifted flour
Raisins

In a large mixing bowl, cream together the butter and sugar. Beat in the baking soda, salt, cinnamon, ginger, cloves, and allspice. Mix well. Stir in the molasses, then add the water. Gradually work the flour into the batter, 1 cup at a time.

Knead the mixture to a smooth dough. If the dough is sticky, add more flour, a little at a time, until it is easier to work. Divide the dough into two equal parts. Wrap each half in waxed paper and refrigerate overnight. Do not freeze.

The next day, preheat the oven to 350° F. Lightly grease two large baking sheets with butter or vegetable shortening.

On a floured work surface, roll out the dough to a thickness of ¼ inch. Cut out the cookies using a 3-inch-tall gingerbread man cookie cutter. Place the cookies 1 inch apart on the baking sheets. Create the eyes and buttons with the raisins. Bake for 10 to 12 minutes, or until the cookies have browned around the edges. Remove from the oven.

After the cookies have cooled for 2 to 3 minutes, but are still warm to the touch, use a spatula to transfer them to wire racks to cool completely.

## NO. 256 GINGERBREAD SQUARES
*Makes about 60 bars*

½ cup sugar
½ cup solid vegetable
   shortening
½ cup dark molasses
4 cups sifted flour
2 teaspoons ground ginger

2 teaspoons cinnamon
¼ teaspoon ground cloves
½ teaspoon salt
½ teaspoon baking soda
¼ cup hot water

Preheat the oven to 400° F. Lightly grease two large baking sheets with butter or vegetable shortening.

In a large mixing bowl, cream together the sugar and shortening. Stir in the molasses and mix well. Sift the flour with the ginger, cinnamon, cloves, and salt. Dissolve the baking soda in the water. Add the flour mixture to the batter, ½ cup at a time, alternating with the water mixture. Stir vigorously after each addition. Knead to a smooth dough. If the dough is sticky, add more flour, a little at a time, until it is easier to work.

On a floured work surface, roll out the dough to a thickness of ¼ inch. Using a sharp knife, cut the dough into 2-inch squares. Transfer the squares to the baking sheets. Bake for 10 to 12 minutes, or until the cookies have browned around the edges. Remove from the oven.

After the cookies have cooled for 2 to 3 minutes, but are still warm to the touch, use a spatula to transfer them to wire racks to cool completely.

NO. **257**

# GLAZED COOKIES

*Makes about 50 cookies*

½ cup unsalted butter,
    softened
2 cups sugar
1 egg, beaten
½ teaspoon lemon extract

1 teaspoon grated lemon zest
4 cups sifted flour
1 teaspoon baking soda
2 tablespoons caraway seeds
½ cup milk

*Glaze*

2 cups sugar
1 cup water

Preheat the oven to 400° F. Lightly grease two large baking sheets with butter or vegetable shortening.

In a large mixing bowl, cream together the butter and sugar. Beat in the egg, and mix well. Add the lemon extract and lemon zest. In another bowl, sift the flour with the baking soda. Stir the caraway seeds into the flour mixture. Add the flour mixture and milk alternately to the butter mixture.

Knead the mixture to a smooth dough. If the dough is sticky, add more flour, a little at a time, until it is easier to work. On a floured work surface, roll out the dough to a thickness of ¼ inch. Cut out the cookies using a 3-inch, curly-edged biscuit or cookie cutter. Place the cookies 1 inch apart on the baking sheets. Bake for 8 to 10 minutes, or until the cookies have browned around the edges. Remove from the oven. Leave the oven on.

After the cookies have cooled for 2 to 3 minutes, but are still warm to the touch, use a spatula to transfer them to wire racks to cool completely.

While the cookies are baking, make the glaze. Combine the sugar and water in a small saucepan and, stirring constantly, bring to a rolling boil. Continue to boil until the mixture reaches the soft ball stage (240° F on a candy thermometer or when a soft ball forms when a teaspoon of syrup is dropped into a glass of cold water). Return the cooled cookies to the baking sheets. Using a pastry brush, spread the top of each cookie with glaze. Place the baking sheet in the oven, turn off the heat, and let the cookies dry out for 5 minutes. Remove from the oven and transfer to wire racks to cool.

NO. **258**     # GREEK BUTTER COOKIES
*Makes about 48 cookies*

1 cup unsalted butter,
    softened
2½ cups confectioners' sugar
1 egg yolk
¼ cup Amaretto liqueur

1 teaspoon grated lemon zest
1 teaspoon rose water
2½ cups sifted flour
½ teaspoon baking powder
Confectioners' sugar

Preheat the oven to 300° F. Lightly grease two large baking sheets with butter or vegetable shortening.

In a large mixing bowl, cream together the butter and sugar. Beat in the egg yolk. Mix in the liqueur, lemon zest, and rose water. Set aside ½ cup of the flour. Sift the remaining 2 cups of flour with the baking powder. Add the flour mixture to the batter, ½ cup at a time, mixing well after each addition. Knead the mixture to a smooth dough. The dough will be sticky, so add more flour from the reserved flour, a little at a time, until it is easier to work.

Using a cookie press, press circles or crescents of dough onto the baking sheets. (Alternatively, the dough may be cut into ½-inch-thick rounds.) Bake for 15 to 20 minutes, or until the cookies are golden brown. Remove from the oven.

After the cookies have cooled for 2 to 3 minutes, but are still warm to the touch, use a spatula to transfer them to wire racks to cool completely. When cool, dust each cookie with confectioners' sugar and arrange on a serving plate.

NO. **259**     # GROUND OATMEAL COOKIES
*Makes about 36 cookies*

½ cup unsalted butter,
    softened
½ cup dark brown sugar,
    firmly packed
1 cup rolled oats

1 cup sifted flour
½ teaspoon baking soda
¼ teaspoon salt
¼ teaspoon nutmeg
¼ cup buttermilk

Preheat the oven to 400° F. Lightly grease two large baking sheets with butter or vegetable shortening.

In a large mixing bowl, cream together the butter and sugar. In a blender, grind the oatmeal to a fine consistency. Sift the flour with the baking soda, salt, and nutmeg. Stir the ground oats into the flour mixture. Add the flour mixture to the batter, ½ cup at a time, alternating with the buttermilk. Knead the mixture to a smooth dough. If the dough is sticky, add more flour, a little at a time, until it is easier to work.

On a floured work surface, roll out the dough to a thickness of ¼ inch. Cut out the cookies using a 3-inch, curly-edged biscuit or cookie cutter. Place the cookies 1 inch apart on the baking sheets. Bake for 10 to 15 minutes, or until the cookies have browned around the edges. Remove from the oven.

After the cookies have cooled for 2 to 3 minutes, but are still warm to the touch, use a spatula to transfer them to wire racks to cool completely.

NO. **260**                                        **HAZELNUT STARS**

*Makes about 36 cookies*

2 egg whites                          2 cups confectioners' sugar
¼ teaspoon cream of tartar            2 cups ground hazelnuts

Preheat the oven to 325° F. Lightly grease two large baking sheets with butter or vegetable shortening.

In a large mixing bowl, beat the egg whites with the cream of tartar until they hold stiff peaks. Beat in the sugar, ½ cup at a time. Continue to beat until the meringue is thick and glossy. Mix in the ground hazelnuts. Knead the mixture to a smooth dough. If the dough is sticky, add more ground hazelnuts, a little at a time, until it is easier to work.

On a floured work surface, roll out the dough to a thickness of ½ inch. Cut out the cookies using a 2-inch, star-shaped cookie cutter. Place the cookies 1 inch apart on the baking sheets. Bake for about 30 minutes, or until the cookies have browned around the edges. Remove from the oven.

After the cookies have cooled for 2 to 3 minutes, but are still warm to the touch, use a spatula to transfer them to wire racks to cool completely.

NO. **261**                                          **HONEY CAKES**

*Makes about 36 cookies*

To make these cookies, the honey mixture must stand overnight before the dough can be prepared.

1 cup honey                           ½ cup unsalted butter,
⅔ cup thinly sliced citron                 softened
⅔ cup thinly sliced candied           1 cup sugar
    orange peel                       2 eggs, beaten
                                      3 cups sifted flour

One day before you want to bake these cookies, prepare the honey mixture. In a small saucepan over low heat, cook the honey until it becomes liquid, stirring constantly with a wooden spoon. Place the citron and orange peel in a mixing bowl, and pour the heated honey on top. Mix well. Cover the bowl with plastic wrap and let the mixture stand overnight. Do not refrigerate.

The following day, preheat the oven to 400° F. Lightly grease two large baking sheets with butter or vegetable shortening.

In a large mixing bowl, cream together the butter and sugar. Beat in the eggs and mix well. Stir in the honey mixture. Add the flour to the batter, ½ cup at a time, mixing well after each addition. Knead the mixture to a smooth dough. If the dough is sticky, add more flour, a little at a time, until it is easier to work.

On a floured work surface, roll out the dough to a thickness of ¼ inch. Cut out the cookies using a 3-inch, curly-edged biscuit or cookie cutter. Place the cookies 1 inch apart on the baking sheets. Bake for about 10 minutes, or until the cookies have browned around the edges. Remove from the oven.

After the cookies have cooled for 2 to 3 minutes, but are still warm to the touch, use a spatula to transfer them to wire racks to cool completely.

NO. **262**       # ITALIAN NUT COOKIES
*Makes about 30 cookies*

½ cup hot water
1 cup dark brown sugar, firmly packed
1 cup walnuts, coarsely chopped
⅓ cup coarsely chopped candied orange peel

⅛ teaspoon nutmeg
⅛ teaspoon ground cloves
½ teaspoon cinnamon
½ teaspoon aniseed
2 cups sifted flour

Preheat the oven to 350° F. Lightly grease two large baking sheets with butter or vegetable shortening.

In a small saucepan, bring the water and sugar to a boil over medium heat, stirring frequently. Boil until the sugar syrup makes a thread when a teaspoonful is dripped into a glass of cold water.

In a large mixing bowl, combine the hot sugar syrup with the chopped walnuts, orange peel, nutmeg, cloves, cinnamon, and aniseed. Mix well. Add the flour to the batter, ½ cup at a time, mixing well after each addition.

Knead the mixture to a smooth dough. If the dough is sticky, add more flour, a little at a time, until it is easier to work. On a floured work surface, roll out the dough to a thickness of ¼ inch. Cut out the cookies using a 2-inch, curly-edged biscuit or cookie cutter. Place the cookies 1 inch apart on the baking sheets. Bake for 12 to 15 minutes, or until the cookies have browned around the edges. Remove from the oven.

After the cookies have cooled for 2 to 3 minutes, but are still warm to the touch, use a spatula to transfer them to wire racks to cool completely.

## NO. 263      LEMON PECAN WAFERS

*Makes about 48 cookies*

½ cup unsalted butter,
    softened
1 cup sugar
1 egg
1 tablespoon lemon juice

1 tablespoon grated lemon
    zest
2 cups sifted flour
1 teaspoon baking powder
1 cup pecans, finely chopped

In a large mixing bowl, cream together the butter and sugar. Beat in the egg and mix well. Stir in the lemon juice and lemon zest. Sift the flour with the baking powder. Add the flour mixture to the batter, ½ cup at a time. Mix well after each addition. Work the chopped pecans into the batter.

Divide the dough into two equal parts, then shape into long rolls about 2 inches in diameter. Wrap each roll in waxed paper. Chill for 30 minutes in the freezer.

Preheat the oven to 350° F. Lightly grease two large baking sheets with butter or vegetable shortening.

Cut ¼-inch slices with a sharp knife and transfer the slices to the baking sheets. Bake for 12 to 15 minutes, or until the cookies have browned around the edges. Remove from the oven.

After the cookies have cooled for 2 to 3 minutes, but are still warm to the touch, use a spatula to transfer them to wire racks to cool completely.

## NO. 264      LEMON WALNUT ROUNDS

*Makes about 24 cookies*

½ cup unsalted butter,
    softened
1 cup sugar
2 eggs
1 tablespoon vanilla extract
¼ cup lemon juice
1 tablespoon grated lemon
    zest

2 teaspoons grated orange
    zest
2 cups sifted flour
¼ teaspoon baking soda
½ cup walnuts, finely chopped
    Confectioners' sugar

Preheat the oven to 375° F. Lightly grease two large baking sheets with butter or vegetable shortening.

In a large mixing bowl, cream together the butter and sugar. Beat in the eggs, one at a time. Stir in the vanilla extract, lemon juice, lemon zest, and orange zest. Sift the flour with the baking soda. Add the flour to the batter, ½ cup at a time, mixing well after each addition. Mix in the chopped walnuts.

Knead the mixture to a smooth dough. If the dough is sticky, add more flour, a little at a time, until it is easier to work. On a floured work surface, roll out the dough to a thickness of ¼ inch. Cut out the cookies using a 2-inch, curly-edged biscuit or cookie cutter. Place the cookies 1 inch apart on the baking sheets. Sprinkle with confectioners' sugar. Bake for about 15 minutes, or until the cookies have browned around the edges. Remove from the oven.

After the cookies have cooled for 2 to 3 minutes, but are still warm to the touch, use a spatula to transfer them to wire racks to cool completely.

## NO. 265            MOLASSES COOKIES

*Makes about 48 cookies*

⅓ cup unsalted butter, softened
1 cup sugar
1 egg
2 tablespoons grated orange zest
1 tablespoon orange juice
1 tablespoon cider vinegar
1 teaspoon baking soda
1 cup light molasses
4 cups sifted flour
1 teaspoon ground ginger
½ teaspoon ground cloves
1 teaspoon cinnamon

Preheat the oven to 375° F. Lightly grease two large baking sheets with butter or vegetable shortening.

In a large mixing bowl, cream together the butter and sugar. Beat in the egg and mix well. Stir in the orange zest, orange juice, and vinegar. In another bowl, mix the baking soda with the molasses. Sift the flour with the ginger, cloves, and cinnamon. Add the flour mixture to the batter, 1 cup at a time, alternating with the molasses mixture. Knead to a smooth dough. If the dough is sticky, add more flour, a little at a time, until it is easier to work.

On a floured work surface, roll out the dough to a thickness of ¼ inch. Cut out the cookies using an assortment of fancy-shaped cookie cutters. Place the cookies 1 inch apart on the baking sheets. Bake for 10 to 12 minutes, or until the cookies have browned around the edges. Remove from the oven.

After the cookies have cooled for 2 to 3 minutes, but are still warm to the touch, use a spatula to transfer them to wire racks to cool completely.

NO. **266**

# ORANGE BISCUITS
*Makes about 48 cookies*

½ cup unsalted butter,
   softened
½ cup sugar
6 egg yolks
1 tablespoon grated orange
   zest

1 tablespoon sweet sherry
3 cups sifted flour
1 egg white, beaten
   Confectioners' sugar

Preheat the oven to 375° F. Lightly grease two large baking sheets with butter or vegetable shortening.

In a large mixing bowl, cream together the butter and sugar. Beat in the egg yolks and mix well. Mix in the orange zest and the sherry. Add the flour to the batter, ½ cup at a time, mixing well after each addition.

Knead the mixture to a smooth dough. If the dough is sticky, add more flour, a little at a time, until it is easier to work. On a floured work surface, roll out the dough to a thickness of ¼ inch. Cut out the cookies using a 3-inch, curly-edged biscuit or cookie cutter. Place the cookies 1 inch apart on the baking sheets. Brush each cookie with beaten egg white and sprinkle with confectioners' sugar. Bake for 10 to 12 minutes, or until the cookies have browned around the edges. Remove from the oven.

After the cookies have cooled for 2 to 3 minutes, but are still warm to the touch, use a spatula to transfer them to wire racks to cool completely.

NO. **267**

# PINK ELEPHANTS
*Makes about 40 cookies*

½ cup unsalted butter,
   softened
1 cup sugar
1 egg
3 cups sifted flour

1 teaspoon baking powder
½ teaspoon baking soda
½ teaspoon salt
1 cup cold strong coffee

*Icing*

2 tablespoons unsalted butter,
   softened
1 tablespoon heavy cream
2 teaspoons vanilla extract

2 cups confectioners' sugar
   Red food coloring
   Silver dragees

Preheat the oven to 400° F. Lightly grease two large baking sheets with butter or vegetable shortening.

In a large mixing bowl, cream together the butter and sugar. Beat in the egg. Mix well. Sift the flour with the baking powder, baking soda, and salt. Add the flour mixture to the batter, ½ cup at a time, alternating with the coffee.

Knead the mixture to a smooth dough. If the dough is sticky, add more flour, a little at a time, until it is easier to work. On a floured work surface, roll out the dough to a thickness of ¼ inch. Cut out the cookies using a large, elephant-shaped cookie cutter, or make a paper pattern to use in place of a cookie cutter. Place the cookies 1 inch apart on the baking sheets. Bake for 8 to 10 minutes, or until the cookies have browned around the edges. Remove from the oven.

After the cookies have cooled for 2 to 3 minutes, but are still warm to the touch, use a spatula to transfer them to wire racks to cool completely.

When the cookies have thoroughly cooled, prepare the icing. In a large mixing bowl, combine the butter, cream, and vanilla extract. Beat until smooth. Gradually beat in the sugar. Still beating, carefully add red food coloring, 1 drop at a time, until the icing turns the desired shade of pink. Spread each cookie with icing. Decorate with silver dragees. Let the icing harden and dry before storing the cookies.

NO. **268**                                 # PINWHEELS
*Makes about 48 cookies*

2 ounces (2 squares) unsweetened baking chocolate
¾ cup unsalted butter, softened
1 cup dark brown sugar, firmly packed
2 eggs

½ teaspoon almond extract
1 teaspoon grated lemon zest
2½ cups sifted flour
1 teaspoon baking powder
½ teaspoon salt
Red food coloring
1 egg white, beaten

Melt the chocolate in the top of a double boiler over simmering water, stirring frequently. Remove the pan from the heat and set aside.

In a large mixing bowl, cream together the butter and sugar. Beat in the eggs, one at a time. Add the almond extract and lemon zest. Sift the flour with the baking powder and salt. Beat the flour into the batter, ½ cup at time. Mix well until the dough is smooth. Divide the dough in half.

Put the dough into two bowls. Work the melted chocolate into half of the dough. Add the red food coloring, one drop at a time, to the other half of the dough, working it in until the mixture turns bright pink. Wrap each dough ball in waxed paper and chill in the freezer for 10 minutes.

On a floured work surface, roll out the red dough in a rectangle, ¼ inch thick. Brush the top of the dough with beaten egg white. Roll out the chocolate dough to a rectangle the same size. Place the chocolate dough on top of the red dough. Roll the two layers of dough together until they are ¼ inch thick. Roll the dough up tightly and wrap in waxed paper. Chill in the freezer for an additional 10 minutes.

Preheat the oven to 375° F. Lightly grease two large baking sheets with butter or vegetable shortening.

Using a sharp knife, cut the dough roll into ¼-inch slices. Arrange the dough slices 1 inch apart on the baking sheets. (Chill the remaining dough while the first batch of cookies are baking.) Bake for 8 to 10 minutes, or until the cookies have browned around the edges. Remove from the oven.

After the cookies have cooled for 2 to 3 minutes, but are still warm to the touch, use a spatula to transfer them to wire racks to cool completely.

## NO. 269               ROUT CAKES

*Makes about 48 cookies*

| | |
|---|---|
| 4  cups ground almonds | 2  cups sugar |
| 2  tablespoons grated lemon zest | 4  egg yolks |
| | Confectioners' sugar |

Preheat the oven to 400° F. Lightly grease two large baking sheets with butter or vegetable shortening.

In a large mixing bowl, combine the ground almonds, lemon zest, and sugar. Mix well. Stir in the egg yolks, one at a time.

Knead the mixture to a smooth dough. If the dough is sticky, add more ground almonds, a little at a time, until it is easier to work. On a work surface dusted with confectioners' sugar, roll out the dough to a thickness of ¼ inch. Cut out the cookies using a 3-inch, curly-edged biscuit or cookie cutter. Place the cookies 1 inch apart on the baking sheets. Bake for 8 to 10 minutes, or until the cookies are lightly browned. Remove from the oven.

After the cookies have cooled for 2 to 3 minutes, but are still warm to the touch, use a spatula to transfer them to wire racks to cool completely.

No. **270**                                        # RYE ROUNDS
*Makes about 30 cookies*

½ cup unsalted butter,              ½ teaspoon vanilla extract
   softened                   1 cup unsifted rye flour
⅓ cup sugar                            ½ cup sifted all-purpose flour

Preheat the oven to 400° F. Lightly grease two large baking sheets
with butter or vegetable shortening.

In a large mixing bowl, cream together the butter and sugar. Mix
in the vanilla extract. In a separate bowl, mix the two flours together.
Add the flour mixture to the butter and sugar mixture. Using a pastry
blender, or two forks, work the flour mixture until it resembles coarse
oatmeal.

Knead to a smooth dough. If the dough is sticky, add more flour,
a little at a time, until it is easier to work. On a floured work surface,
roll out the dough to a thickness of ⅛ inch. Cut out the cookies
using a 3-inch, curly-edged biscuit or cookie cutter. Place the cookies
1 inch apart on the baking sheets. Prick the top of each cookie in
an attractive pattern, using the tines of a fork. Bake for 5 to 7 minutes,
or until the cookies have browned around the edges. Remove from
the oven.

After the cookies have cooled for 2 to 3 minutes, but are still
warm to the touch, use a spatula to transfer them to wire racks to
cool completely.

No. **271**                                        # SAND CAKES
*Makes about 36 cookies*

1 cup unsalted butter,             2½ cups sifted flour
   softened                   1 teaspoon cinnamon
1 cup sugar                            ½ teaspoon ground cardamon
1 egg, beaten                          Confectioners' sugar

Preheat the oven to 400° F. Lightly grease two large baking sheets
with butter or vegetable shortening.

In a large mixing bowl, cream together the butter and sugar. Beat
in the egg. Mix well. Sift the flour with the cinnamon and cardamon.
Add the flour mixture to the batter, 1 cup at a time, mixing well
after each addition.

Knead to a smooth dough. If the dough is sticky, add more flour,
a little at a time, until it is easier to work. Cut out the cookies using
a 3-inch, curly-edged biscuit or cookie cutter. Place the cookies 1
inch apart on the baking sheets. Dust each cookie with confectioners'
sugar. Bake for about 10 minutes, or until the cookies are golden
brown. Remove from the oven.

After the cookies have cooled for 2 to 3 minutes, but are still warm to the touch, use a spatula to transfer them to wire racks to cool completely.

NO. **272**  SCOTCH OAT CAKES

*Makes about 36 cookies*

1 cup unsalted butter
4 cups rolled oats
1½ cups confectioners' sugar

1½ teaspoons cinnamon
½ teaspoon mace

Preheat the oven to 400° F. Lightly grease two large baking sheets with butter or vegetable shortening.

Melt the butter in a small saucepan over very low heat. Remove the pan from the heat and set aside to cool.

Crush the oats to a fine consistency in a food processor, blender, or with a rolling pin. Sift the sugar with the cinnamon and mace. In a large mixing bowl, combine the crushed oats and sugar mixture. Add the melted butter. Work the mixture into a thick dough. Add a little water if necessary.

On a floured work surface, roll out the dough to a thickness of ¼ inch. Cut out the cookies using a 3-inch, curly-edged biscuit or cookie cutter. Place the cookies 1 inch apart on the baking sheets. Bake for 10 to 12 minutes, or until the cookies have browned around the edges. Remove from the oven.

After the cookies have cooled for 2 to 3 minutes, but are still warm to the touch, use a spatula to transfer them to wire racks to cool completely.

NO. **273**  SCOTCH OAT CURRANT CAKES

*Makes about 36 cookies*

Follow the recipe for Scotch Oat Cakes (No. 272), adding 1½ cups of dried currants to the mixture before stirring in the butter.

NO. **274**  SEED CAKES

*Makes about 60 cookies*

¾ cup unsalted butter,
   softened
1 cup sugar
3 eggs
2 teaspoons coriander seeds

4 cups sifted flour
½ teaspoon baking soda
½ cup milk
Sugar

Preheat the oven to 400° F. Lightly grease two large baking sheets with butter or vegetable shortening.

In a large mixing bowl, cream together the butter and sugar. Beat in the eggs, one at a time. Stir in the coriander seeds and mix well. Sift the flour with the baking soda. Add the flour mixture to the batter, 1 cup at a time, alternating with the milk.

Knead the mixture to a smooth dough. If the dough is sticky, add more flour, a little at a time, until it is easier to work. On a floured work surface, roll out the dough to a thickness of ¼ inch. Cut out the cookies using a 3-inch, curly-edged biscuit or cookie cutter. Place the cookies 1 inch apart on the baking sheets. Sprinkle each cookie with sugar. Bake for 8 to 10 minutes, or until the cookies have browned around the edges. Remove from the oven.

After the cookies have cooled for 2 to 3 minutes, but are still warm to the touch, use a spatula to transfer them to wire racks to cool completely.

## NO. 275          SOUR CREAM GINGER COOKIES

*Makes about 36 cookies*

| | |
|---|---|
| ½ cup unsalted butter, softened | ½ cup sour cream |
| ½ cup sugar | 2½ cups sifted flour |
| 1 egg | 1 teaspoon baking soda |
| 1 cup dark molasses | ½ teaspoon cinnamon |
| | 2 teaspoons ground ginger |

Preheat the oven to 350° F. Lightly grease two large baking sheets with butter or vegetable shortening.

In a large mixing bowl, cream together the butter and sugar. Add the egg and beat well. Stir in the molasses and the sour cream. Sift the flour with the baking soda, cinnamon, and ginger. Add the flour to the batter, ½ cup at a time. Mix well after each addition.

Knead the mixture to a smooth dough. If the dough is sticky, add more flour, a little at a time, until it is easier to work. On a floured work surface, roll out the dough to a thickness of ¼ inch. Cut out the cookies using a 3-inch, curly-edged biscuit or cookie cutter. Place the cookies 1 inch apart on the baking sheets. Bake for about 15 minutes, or until the cookies have browned around the edges. Remove from the oven.

After the cookies have cooled for 2 to 3 minutes, but are still warm to the touch, use a spatula to transfer them to wire racks to cool completely.

NO. **276**          **SOUR CREAM RAISIN COOKIES**

*Makes about 36 cookies*

¾ cup unsalted butter,
  softened
1 cup dark brown sugar,
  firmly packed
2 eggs, separated
½ cup sour cream

½ teaspoon baking soda
2 teaspoons hot water
2½ cups sifted flour
⅛ teaspoon nutmeg
½ teaspoon cinnamon
½ teaspoon mace

Preheat the oven to 350° F. Lightly grease two large baking sheets with butter or vegetable shortening.

In a large mixing bowl, cream together the butter and sugar. Beat in the egg yolks, and mix well. In a separate bowl, beat the egg whites until stiff peaks form. Gently fold the egg whites into the batter. Stir in the sour cream. Dissolve the baking soda in the hot water, then beat into the batter. Sift the flour with the nutmeg, cinnamon, and mace. Add the flour mixture to the batter, ½ cup at a time.

Knead the mixture to a smooth dough. If the dough is sticky, add more flour, a little at a time, until it is easier to work. On a floured work surface, roll out the dough to a thickness of ¼ inch. Cut out the cookies using a 3-inch, curly-edged biscuit or cookie cutter. Place the cookies 1 inch apart on the baking sheets. Bake for about 20 minutes, or until the cookies have browned around the edges. Remove from the oven.

After the cookies have cooled for 2 to 3 minutes, but are still warm to the touch, use a spatula to transfer them to wire racks to cool completely.

NO. **277**          **SPICE COOKIES**

*Makes about 48 cookies*

1 cup sugar
1 cup dark molasses
2 teaspoons grated orange
  zest
1½ teaspoons baking soda

3 cups sifted flour
½ teaspoon allspice
1 teaspoon cinnamon
¼ teaspoon nutmeg
¼ teaspoon ground cloves

Preheat the oven to 350° F. Lightly grease two large baking sheets with butter or vegetable shortening.

Combine the sugar, molasses, and orange zest in a saucepan. Bring the mixture to a boil over low heat, stirring constantly with a wooden spoon. When it is boiling, add the baking soda and stir well. The mixture will foam. Remove the pan from the heat and set aside.

Into a large mixing bowl, sift the flour with the allspice, cinnamon, nutmeg, and cloves. Pour in the hot syrup. Mix well, then knead to a smooth dough. If the dough is sticky, add more flour, a little at a time, until it is easier to work.

On a floured work surface, roll out the dough to a thickness of ½ inch. Cut out the cookies using a 2-inch, curly-edged biscuit or cookie cutter. Place the cookies 1 inch apart on the baking sheets. Bake for about 20 minutes, or until the cookies have browned around the edges. Remove from the oven.

After the cookies have cooled for 2 to 3 minutes, but are still warm to the touch, use a spatula to transfer them to wire racks to cool completely.

NO. 278                                              # SUGAR COOKIES I
*Makes about 36 cookies*

¾ cup unsalted butter,              1 tablespoon rose water
   softened                          3 cups sifted flour
¾ cup sugar                              ¼ teaspoon salt
2 eggs, beaten                           Sugar

Preheat the oven to 400° F. Lightly grease two large baking sheets with butter or vegetable shortening.

In a large mixing bowl, cream together the butter and sugar. Beat in the eggs and the rose water. Continue to beat until the batter is thick and creamy. Sift the flour with the salt. Add the flour mixture to the batter, 1 cup at a time, mixing well after each addition. Knead to a smooth dough. If the dough is sticky, add more flour, a little at a time, until it is easier to work.

On a floured work surface, roll out the dough to a thickness of ¼ inch. Cut out the cookies using a 3-inch, curly-edged biscuit or cookie cutter. Place the cookies 1 inch apart on the baking sheets. Sprinkle each cookie with sugar. Bake for 8 to 10 minutes, or until the cookies have browned around the edges. Remove from the oven.

After the cookies have cooled for 2 to 3 minutes, but are still warm to the touch, use a spatula to transfer them to wire racks to cool completely.

NO. 279                                              # SUGAR COOKIES II
*Makes about 40 cookies*

1 cup unsalted butter,              3 cups sifted flour
   softened                          1 teaspoon baking soda
1½ cups sugar                            Sugar
4 eggs

Preheat the oven to 400° F. Lightly grease two large baking sheets with butter or vegetable shortening.

In a large mixing bowl, cream together the butter and sugar. Beat in the eggs, one at a time. Continue to beat until the mixture is thick and creamy. Sift the flour with the baking soda. Add the flour mixture to the batter, ½ cup at a time. Knead into a soft dough.

On a floured work surface, roll out the dough to a thickness of ¼ inch. Cut out the cookies using a 2-inch, round cookie cutter. Place the cookies 1 inch apart on the baking sheets. Sprinkle each cookie with sugar. Bake for 8 to 10 minutes, or until the cookies are light brown. Remove from the oven.

After the cookies have cooled for 2 to 3 minutes, but are still warm to the touch, use a spatula to transfer them to wire racks to cool completely.

NO. **280**   # HARD SUGAR BISCUITS

*Makes about 50 cookies*

½ cup sugar
⅓ cup plus 1 tablespoon milk
½ cup unsalted butter,
   softened

2 teaspoons caraway seeds
2 cups sifted flour
½ teaspoon baking soda
1 teaspoon cinnamon

Preheat the oven to 450° F. Lightly grease two large baking sheets with butter or vegetable shortening.

In a small mixing bowl, combine the sugar with the milk. Stir until the sugar dissolves. In another bowl, cut the butter into large chunks. Add the caraway seeds. Sift the flour with the baking soda and cinnamon. Using a pastry blender, or two forks, work the flour mixture into the butter until the texture resembles that of coarse oatmeal. Gradually add the milk mixture. Knead to a smooth dough. If the dough is sticky, add more flour, a little at a time, until it is easier to work.

On a floured work surface, roll out the dough to a thickness of ½ inch. Cut out the cookies using a 2-inch, curly-edged biscuit or cookie cutter. Place the cookies 1 inch apart on the baking sheets. Bake for 12 to 15 minutes, or until the cookies have browned around the edges. Remove from the oven.

After the cookies have cooled for 2 to 3 minutes, but are still warm to the touch, use a spatula to transfer them to wire racks to cool completely.

NO. **281**            **SWEDISH BUTTER RINGS**
*Makes about 60 cookies*

A cookie press is required to make classic Swedish butter rings. If
you do not have a cookie press, the dough rolls may be cut into
rounds, ½ inch thick.

| | |
|---|---|
| 1 cup unsalted butter, softened | 3 egg yolks, beaten |
| 1 cup sugar | 2 teaspoons grated lemon zest |
| | 3½ cups sifted flour |

Cut the butter into large pieces and place in a mixing bowl. Add
the sugar and beaten egg yolks. Work the mixture with a pastry
blender until it is creamy. Mix in the lemon zest. Continuing to use
the pastry blender, gradually add the flour, ½ cup at a time, until
the dough becomes firm. It may not be necessary to use all the flour.
Mold the dough into 6 small rolls. Wrap each roll in waxed paper.
Chill in the refrigerator for 3 hours.

Preheat the oven to 350° F. Lightly grease two large baking sheets
with butter or vegetable shortening.

Place one chilled dough roll in a cookie press with a ring shape,
then press out cookies onto the baking sheets. Continue to press out
cookies until you have used all the dough. Bake for 12 to 15 minutes,
or until the cookies are golden brown. Remove from the oven.

After the cookies have cooled for 2 to 3 minutes, but are still
warm to the touch, use a spatula to transfer them to wire racks to
cool completely.

NO. **282**                  **VANILLA WAFERS**
*Makes about 40 cookies*

| | |
|---|---|
| ½ cup unsalted butter, softened | 3 cups sifted flour |
| 1½ cups sugar | 2 teaspoons baking powder |
| 2 eggs | ¼ teaspoon salt |
| 2 teaspoons vanilla extract | 2 tablespoons milk |

Preheat the oven to 400° F. Lightly grease two large baking sheets
with butter or vegetable shortening.

In a large mixing bowl, cream together the butter and sugar. Beat
in the eggs, one at a time. Mix in the vanilla extract. Sift the flour
with the baking powder and salt. Add the flour mixture to the batter,
1 cup at a time, alternating with the milk. Knead the mixture to a
smooth dough. If the dough is sticky, add more flour, a little at a
time, until it is easier to work.

On a floured work surface, roll out the dough to a thickness of ¼ inch. Cut out the cookies using a 2-inch, round cookie cutter. Place the cookies 1 inch apart on the baking sheets. Bake for 8 to 10 minutes, or until the cookies have browned around the edges. Remove from the oven.

After the cookies have cooled for 2 to 3 minutes, but are still warm to the touch, use a spatula to transfer them to wire racks to cool completely.

NO. 283      # WILD HONEY COOKIES

*Makes about 60 cookies*

1 cup unsalted butter
2 cups wild or strong dark
    honey
3 teaspoons baking soda

5 cups sifted flour
1 teaspoon salt
2 tablespoons ground ginger

Preheat the oven to 400° F. Lightly grease two large baking sheets with butter or vegetable shortening.

In a large saucepan, combine the butter and the honey. Cook over low heat, stirring constantly with a wooden spoon, until the mixture comes to a boil. Remove the pan from the heat and set aside to cool.

Pour the cooled honey mixture into a large mixing bowl. Beat in the baking soda until it foams. Sift the flour with the salt and ginger. Add the flour mixture to the honey mixture, 1 cup at a time, mixing well after each addition. Knead the mixture to a smooth dough. If the dough is sticky, add more flour, a little at a time, until it is easier to work.

On a floured work surface, roll out the dough to a thickness of ¼ inch. Cut out the cookies using a 3-inch, curly-edged biscuit or cookie cutter. Place the cookies 1 inch apart on the baking sheets. Bake for 8 to 10 minutes, or until the cookies have browned around the edges. Remove from the oven.

After the cookies have cooled for 2 to 3 minutes, but are still warm to the touch, use a spatula to transfer them to wire racks to cool completely.

# Sandwich Cookies

Sandwich cookies are exactly that—two cookies sandwiched together around a sweet filling. They are also dream cookies—split them in two and you have double the pleasure. Some of these "sandwiches" are simple and some are more complicated. All are scrumptious.

NO. 284

## CHOCOLATE APRICOT MERINGUES

*Makes about 12 cookies*

To make these elegant cookies, a pastry bag is required.

| | |
|---|---|
| 2 egg whites | ¼ teaspoon almond extract |
| ¼ teaspoon cream of tartar | 4 ounces semi-sweet chocolate |
| ¼ cup sugar | ¼ cup apricot jam |
| ½ teaspoon vanilla extract | 1 tablespoon brandy |

Preheat the oven to 200° F. Line two baking sheets with baking parchment. Using a 1½-inch round cookie cutter as a guide, draw 24 circles on the parchment (12 on each baking sheet).

In a large mixing bowl, beat the egg whites with the cream of tartar until the mixture is foamy. Gradually add the sugar, a little at a time, and continue to beat until the mixture forms stiff peaks. Beat in the vanilla extract and the almond extract.

Fit a pastry bag with a smooth tip and fill, reserving a quarter of the meringue. Pipe out meringue bases onto 12 circles, filling in the outlines of the circles on one baking sheet. Smooth the tops with a rubber spatula. Spoon the remaining meringue into a pastry bag with a fluted, decorated tip, and pipe out a ring of rosettes around each of the remaining circles on the other baking sheet.

Place both baking sheets in the oven. Remove the sheet with the rings after 25 minutes. Carefully loosen the rings from the parchment with the tip of a sharp knife, and transfer to a wire rack to cool. Continue to bake the bases for an additional 15 minutes, or until they are dry to the touch. Remove from the parchment as with the rings.

Melt the chocolate in the top of a double boiler over hot water. Set aside to cool. Combine the jam and brandy in a small saucepan, and heat until the jam has melted. Set aside to cool.

Spread each meringue base first with a layer of chocolate and then with a layer of jam. Top with a meringue ring and arrange on a serving plate.

NO. 285  CHOCOLATE RASPBERRY
HAZELNUT MERINGUES

*Makes about 12 cookies*

To make these elegant cookies, a pastry bag and some care in handling
are required.

2 egg whites·                    ¼ cup ground hazelnuts
¼ teaspoon cream of tartar       4 ounces semi-sweet chocolate
¼ cup sugar                      ¼ cup raspberry jam
¼ teaspoon almond extract        1 tablespoon cherry brandy

Preheat the oven to 200° F. Line two standard baking sheets with
baking parchment. Using a 1½-inch round cookie cutter as a guide,
draw 24 circles on the parchment (12 on each baking sheet).

In a large mixing bowl, beat the egg whites with the cream of
tartar until foamy. Gradually add the sugar, a little at a time, and
continue to beat until stiff peaks form. Beat in the almond extract.
Gently fold in the ground hazelnuts.

Fit a pastry bag with a smooth tip and fill, reserving one quarter
of the meringue. Pipe out meringue bases on 12 circles. Smooth the
tops with a rubber spatula. Change to a pastry bag with a fluted,
decorated tip, and using the remaining meringue, pipe out a ring of
rosettes around each remaining circle.

Place both baking sheets in the oven. Remove the rings after 25
minutes. Carefully loosen them from the parchment with the tip of
a sharp knife and transfer to a wire cooling rack. Continue to bake
the bases for an additional 15 minutes, or until they are dry to the
touch. Remove from the parchment as with the rings.

Melt the chocolate in the top of a double boiler over simmering
water, stirring frequently. Remove the pan from the heat and set
aside. Combine the jam and brandy in a small saucepan. Cook over
low heat, stirring frequently, until the jam has melted. Remove the
pan from the heat and cool.

Spread each meringue base first with a layer of chocolate and then
with a layer of jam. Top with a meringue ring and arrange on a
serving plate.

No. **286**           **CHOCOLATE SANDWICHES**
                                *Makes about 24 cookies*

4 ounces (4 squares)            2 eggs
    unsweetened baking          1 teaspoon vanilla extract
    chocolate                   1 tablespoon heavy cream
1 cup unsalted butter,          3 cups sifted flour
    softened                    1½ teaspoons baking soda
1¼ cups sugar

*Filling*

1½ cups confectioners' sugar    2 tablespoons finely chopped
1 teaspoon vanilla extract          candied orange peel
2 tablespoons sweet white
    wine

Preheat the oven to 400° F. Lightly grease two large baking sheets
with butter or vegetable shortening.

Melt the chocolate in the top of a double boiler over simmering
water, stirring frequently. Remove the pan from the heat and set
aside.

In a large mixing bowl, cream together the butter and sugar. Beat
in the eggs, one at a time, and mix well. Add the melted chocolate.
Stir in the vanilla extract and the cream. Sift the flour with the baking
soda. Add the flour mixture to the batter, ½ cup at a time.

Knead the mixture to a smooth dough. If the dough is sticky, add
more flour, a little at a time, until it is easier to work. On a floured
work surface, roll out the dough to a thickness of ¼ inch. Cut out
48 cookies using a 2-inch, curly-edged biscuit or cookie cutter. Place
the cookies 1 inch apart on the baking sheets. Bake for 8 to 10
minutes, or until the cookies have browned around the edges. Remove
from the oven.

After the cookies have cooled for 2 to 3 minutes, but are still
warm to the touch, use a spatula to transfer them to wire racks to
cool completely.

While the cookies are cooling, make the filling. In a large mixing
bowl, combine the confectioners' sugar, vanilla extract, and wine.
Beat until smooth. Mix in the chopped candied orange peel. Spread
half of the cookies with the filling. Top each one with another cookie.
Transfer to a serving plate.

NO. 287

# DOUBLE CHOCOLATE SANDWICHES
*Makes about 24 cookies*

4 ounces (4 squares)
    unsweetened baking
    chocolate
1 cup unsalted butter,
    softened
1¼ cups sugar

2 eggs
1 teaspoon vanilla extract
1 tablespoon heavy cream
3 cups sifted flour
1½ teaspoons baking soda

## Filling
10 ounces semi-sweet chocolate
2 tablespoons finely chopped candied orange peel

Preheat the oven to 400° F. Lightly grease two large baking sheets with butter or vegetable shortening.

Melt the baking chocolate in the top of a double boiler over simmering water, stirring frequently. Remove the pan from the heat and set aside.

In a large mixing bowl, cream together the butter and sugar. Beat in the eggs, one at a time, and mix well. Add the melted chocolate. Stir in the vanilla extract and the cream. Sift the flour with the baking soda. Add the flour mixture to the batter, ½ cup at a time.

Knead the mixture to a smooth dough. If the dough is sticky, add more flour, a little at a time, until it is easier to work. On a floured work surface, roll out the dough to a thickness of ¼ inch. Cut out 48 cookies using a 2-inch, curly-edged biscuit or cookie cutter. Place the cookies 1 inch apart on the baking sheets. Bake for 8 to 10 minutes, or until the cookies have browned around the edges. Remove from the oven.

After the cookies have cooled for 2 to 3 minutes, but are still warm to the touch, use a spatula to transfer them to wire racks to cool completely.

While the cookies are cooling, make the filling. Melt the semi-sweet chocolate in the top of a double boiler over simmering water, stirring frequently. Remove the pan from the heat. Mix in the chopped candied orange peel. Spread half of the cookies with the filling. Top each one with another cookie. Transfer to a serving plate.

NO. **288**                          # FILLED COOKIES
                              *Makes about 36 cookies*

½ cup unsalted butter,          3½ cups sifted flour
   softened          3 teaspoons baking powder
1 cup sugar                     ¼ teaspoon salt
2 eggs                          ½ cup milk
1 teaspoon vanilla extract

## Filling

1 tablespoon flour              ½ cup raisins, coarsely
½ cup sugar                        chopped
½ cup water                     ½ cup finely chopped candied
¼ cup unsalted butter              orange peel

Preheat the oven to 400° F. Lightly grease two large baking sheets
with butter or vegetable shortening.

In a large mixing bowl, cream together the butter and sugar. Beat
in the eggs, one at a time, mixing well after each addition. Stir in
the vanilla extract. Sift the flour with the baking powder and salt.
Add the flour mixture to the batter, ½ cup at a time, alternating
with the milk. Knead the mixture to a smooth dough. If the dough
is sticky, add more flour, a little at a time, until it is easier to work.
Set the dough aside while you prepare the filling.

In a medium saucepan, mix together the flour, sugar, and water.
Add the butter and raisins, and cook over low heat, stirring constantly,
until the mixture thickens. Remove the pan from the heat and stir
in the chopped candied orange peel.

On a floured work surface, roll out the dough to a thickness of ¼
inch. Cut out 72 cookies using a 2-inch, curly-edged biscuit or cookie
cutter. Place 36 cookies 1 inch apart on the baking sheets. Place 1
small teaspoonful of filling on each cookie, then top with another
cookie. Press the edges of the filled dough together with your fingers
or a pie crimper. Bake for about 15 minutes, or until the cookies
have browned around the edges. Remove from the oven.

After the cookies have cooled for 2 to 3 minutes, but are still
warm to the touch, use a spatula to transfer them to wire racks to
cool completely.

NO. **289**        **FLORENTINES**

*Makes about 12 cookies*

Bake these cookies in batches of six cookies each. Be sure to regrease the baking sheet before each use.

| | |
|---|---|
| 3 tablespoons unsalted butter | ⅓ cup sifted flour |
| ½ cup heavy cream | 1¼ cups blanched almonds, |
| ½ cup sugar |     finely chopped |
| ⅛ teaspoon salt | ¾ cup finely chopped candied |
| 1 teaspoon grated orange zest |     orange peel |
| 1 teaspoon vanilla extract | |

*Icing*

| | |
|---|---|
| 8 ounces semi-sweet chocolate | 2 tablespoons unsalted butter |

Preheat the oven to 350° F. Lightly grease a large baking sheet with butter or vegetable shortening.

In a large saucepan over low heat, combine the butter, cream, sugar, salt, orange zest, and vanilla extract. Bring to a boil over medium heat, stirring constantly with a wooden spoon. Remove the pan from the heat. Turn the mixture into a large bowl. Stir in the flour, chopped almonds, and orange peel. Mix well.

Drop rounded teaspoonfuls of batter onto the baking sheets, at least 2 inches apart. Bake for 8 to 10 minutes, or until the cookies have browned around the edges. Remove from the oven.

While the cookies are still very hot, use a buttered knife or spatula to remove them from the baking sheet and transfer them to a wire rack to cool completely.

When all the cookies have been baked and are cool, make the icing. Melt the chocolate with the butter in the top of a double boiler over simmering water, stirring frequently. Cool slightly, then spread the icing on half of the cookies and top with a plain cookie. Let the icing set, then transfer the florentines to a serving plate.

NO. **290**        **FRUIT-FILLED COOKIES**

*Makes about 36 cookies*

| | |
|---|---|
| ½ cup unsalted butter, | 3½ cups sifted flour |
|     softened | 3 teaspoons baking powder |
| 1 cup sugar | 1 teaspoon allspice |
| 2 eggs | ¼ teaspoon salt |
| 1 teaspoon vanilla extract | ½ cup milk |

## Filling

| | |
|---|---|
| 1 tablespoon flour | ½ cup finely chopped dried |
| ½ cup sugar | apricots |
| ½ cup water | ½ cup finely chopped pitted |
| ¼ cup unsalted butter | dates |
| | ½ cup walnuts, finely chopped |

Preheat the oven to 400° F. Lightly grease two large baking sheets with butter or vegetable shortening.

In a large mixing bowl, cream together the butter and sugar. Beat in the eggs, one at a time, mixing well after each addition. Stir in the vanilla extract. Sift the flour with the baking powder, allspice, and salt. Add the flour mixture to the batter, ½ cup at a time, alternating with the milk. Knead the mixture to a smooth dough. If the dough is sticky, add more flour, a little at a time, until it is easier to work. Set the dough aside while you prepare the filling.

In a medium saucepan, mix together the flour, sugar, and water. Add the butter, apricots, and dates and cook over low heat, stirring constantly, until the mixture thickens. Remove the pan from the heat. Stir in the chopped walnuts and set aside.

On a floured work surface, roll out the dough to a thickness of ¼ inch. Cut out 72 cookies using a 2-inch, curly-edged biscuit or cookie cutter. Place 36 cookies 1 inch apart on the baking sheets. Place 1 small teaspoonful of filling on each cookie, then top with another cookie. Press the edges of the filled cookie together with your fingers or a pie crimper. Bake for about 15 minutes, or until the cookies have browned around the edges. Remove from the oven.

After the cookies have cooled for 2 to 3 minutes, but are still warm to the touch, use a spatula to transfer them to wire racks to cool completely.

---

NO. 291

# LEMON SANDWICHES
*Makes about 24 cookies*

| | |
|---|---|
| 1 cup unsalted butter, softened | ½ teaspoon lemon extract |
| 1¼ cups sugar | 1 tablespoon heavy cream |
| 2 eggs | 3 cups sifted flour |
| | 1½ teaspoons baking soda |

## Filling

| | |
|---|---|
| 1½ cups confectioners' sugar | 2 tablespoons finely chopped |
| 2 tablespoons lemon juice | candied lemon peel |
| 1 tablespoon sweet white wine | |

Preheat the oven to 400° F. Lightly grease two large baking sheets with butter or vegetable shortening.

In a large mixing bowl, cream together the butter and sugar. Beat in the eggs, one at a time, and mix well. Stir in the lemon extract and the cream. Sift the flour with the baking soda. Add the flour mixture to the batter, ½ cup at a time.

Knead the mixture to a smooth dough. If the dough is sticky, add more flour, a little at a time, until it is easier to work. On a floured work surface, roll out the dough to a thickness of ¼ inch. Cut out 48 cookies using a 2-inch, curly-edged biscuit or cookie cutter. Place the cookies 1 inch apart on the baking sheets. Bake for 8 to 10 minutes, or until the cookies have browned around the edges. Remove from the oven.

After the cookies have cooled for 2 to 3 minutes, but are still warm to the touch, use a spatula to transfer them to wire racks to cool completely.

While the cookies are cooling, make the filling. In a large mixing bowl, combine the confectioners' sugar, lemon juice, and wine. Beat until smooth. Mix in the chopped candied lemon peel. Spread half of the cookies with the filling. Top each one with another cookie. Transfer to a serving plate.

NO. **292**

# ORANGE SANDWICHES

*Makes about 24 cookies*

| | |
|---|---|
| 1 cup unsalted butter, softened | ½ teaspoon orange extract |
| 1¼ cups sugar | 1 tablespoon heavy cream |
| 2 eggs | 3 cups sifted flour |
| | 1½ teaspoons baking soda |

## Filling

| | |
|---|---|
| 1½ cups confectioners' sugar | 2 tablespoons finely chopped candied orange peel |
| 2 tablespoons orange juice | |
| 1 tablespoon rum | |

Preheat the oven to 400° F. Lightly grease two large baking sheets with butter or vegetable shortening.

In a large mixing bowl, cream together the butter and sugar. Beat in the eggs, one at a time, and mix well. Stir in the orange extract and the cream. Sift the flour with the baking soda. Add the flour mixture to the batter, ½ cup at a time.

Knead the mixture to a smooth dough. If the dough is sticky, add more flour, a little at a time, until it is easier to work. On a floured work surface, roll out the dough to a thickness of ¼ inch. Cut out 48 cookies using a 2-inch, curly-edged biscuit or cookie cutter. Place the cookies 1 inch apart on the baking sheets. Bake for 8 to 10 minutes, or until the cookies have browned around the edges. Remove from the oven.

After the cookies have cooled for 2 to 3 minutes, but are still warm to the touch, use a spatula to transfer them to wire racks to cool completely.

While the cookies are cooling, make the filling. Combine the confectioners' sugar, orange juice, and rum in a mixing bowl. Beat until smooth. Add the chopped candied orange peel and mix well. Spread half of the cookies with the filling, and top each one with another cookie. Transfer to a serving plate.

NO. **293**                              ## SUGAR SANDWICHES

*Makes about 20 cookies*

Following the recipe for Sugar Cookies II (No. 279), make the dough and roll it out. Then follow the recipe below.

### Filling

1 cup raspberry jam
1 tablespoon brandy

Preheat the oven to 400° F.

Cut out 40 2-inch rounds of dough. Place 20 of the rounds 1 inch apart on the prepared baking sheets.

Combine the raspberry jam and brandy in a small saucepan. Cook over low heat, stirring constantly, until the jam has melted. Remove the pan from the heat and set aside to cool.

Spread the 20 dough rounds with the cooled jam filling. Place a plain round on top. Press the edges of each cookie together with the tines of a fork that has been dipped in flour. Sprinkle each cookie with sugar. Bake for 8 to 10 minutes, or until the cookies have lightly browned. Remove from the oven.

After the cookies have cooled for 2 to 3 minutes, but are still warm to the touch, use a spatula to transfer them to wire racks to cool completely.

NO. **294**                    **VANILLA SANDWICHES**

*Makes about 24 cookies*

| | |
|---|---|
| 1 cup unsalted butter, softened | 2 teaspoons vanilla extract |
| 1¼ cups sugar | 1 tablespoon heavy cream |
| 2 eggs | 3 cups sifted flour |
| | 1½ teaspoons baking soda |

*Filling*

| | |
|---|---|
| 1½ cups confectioners' sugar | 2 tablespoons finely chopped citron |
| 2 tablespoons ice water | |
| 2 teaspoons vanilla extract | |

Preheat the oven to 400° F. Lightly grease two large baking sheets with butter or vegetable shortening.

In a large mixing bowl, cream together the butter and sugar. Add the eggs, one at a time, and beat well. Stir in the vanilla extract. Add the cream. Sift the flour with the baking soda. Add the flour mixture to the batter, ½ cup at a time.

Knead the mixture to a smooth dough. If the dough is sticky, add more flour, a little at a time, until it is easier to work. On a floured work surface, roll out the dough to a thickness of ¼ inch. Cut out 48 cookies using a 2-inch, curly-edged biscuit or cookie cutter. Place the cookies 1 inch apart on the baking sheets. Bake for 8 to 10 minutes, or until the cookies have browned around the edges. Remove from the oven.

After the cookies have cooled for 2 to 3 minutes, but are still warm to the touch, use a spatula to transfer them to wire racks to cool completely.

While the cookies are cooling, make the filling. In a large mixing bowl, combine the confectioners' sugar, ice water, and vanilla extract. Beat until smooth. Mix in the chopped citron. Spread 24 cookies with the filling. Top each one with another cookie. Transfer to a serving plate.

# Icebox Cookies

A thin, crispy chocolate icebox cookie goes very well with a tall glass of cold milk. Icebox cookies got their name back in the days when a refrigerator was known as an icebox. They are made from dough that is refrigerated overnight before baking. All the recipes in this section require the dough to be refrigerated overnight. When making icebox cookies in batches, be sure to return the unused dough to the refrigerator while the cookies are baking.

NO. **295**

## BROWN BUTTER ICEBOX COOKIES

*Makes about 64 cookies*

½ cup unsalted butter, softened
½ cup sugar
1 egg
½ cup maple syrup
1 tablespoon dark molasses
½ teaspoon grated lemon zest

2 cups sifted flour
½ teaspoon baking soda
1 teaspoon cinnamon
¼ teaspoon ground cloves
¼ teaspoon nutmeg
¼ teaspoon ground ginger

In a large mixing bowl, cream together the butter and sugar. Beat in the egg, then add the maple syrup, molasses, and lemon zest. Sift together the flour, baking soda, cinnamon, cloves, nutmeg, and ginger. Gradually add the flour mixture to the butter and sugar mixture, working the dough until it becomes stiff. Add more flour if the dough is sticky.

Divide the dough into two equal parts. Shape into long rolls about 2 inches in diameter and wrap each roll in waxed paper. Chill overnight in the refrigerator. Do not freeze.

The next day, preheat the oven to 375° F. Lightly grease two large baking sheets with butter or vegetable shortening. Cut the dough rolls into ¼-inch slices. Arrange the slices 2 inches apart on the baking sheets. Bake for 12 to 15 minutes, or until the cookies are light brown. Remove from the oven.

After the cookies have cooled for 2 to 3 minutes, but are still warm to the touch, use a spatula to transfer them to wire racks to cool completely.

NO. **296**

# BUTTERSCOTCH ICEBOX COOKIES

*Makes about 100 cookies*

3½ cups sifted flour
½ teaspoon baking soda
½ teaspoon salt
½ teaspoon cream of tartar

2 cups dark brown sugar, firmly packed
½ cup unsalted butter, softened
2 eggs, beaten

Sift together the flour, baking soda, salt, and cream of tartar. In a large mixing bowl, combine the flour mixture with the brown sugar. Cut the butter into pieces and add to the mixture. Using a pastry blender, or two forks, work the butter into the flour mixture. Add the eggs, and knead to a smooth dough. If the dough is too sticky, add more flour, a little at a time, until it is easier to work.

Divide the dough into two equal parts. Shape into long rolls about 2 inches in diameter, and wrap each roll in waxed paper. Chill overnight in the refrigerator. Do not freeze.

The next day, preheat the oven to 400° F. Lightly grease two large baking sheets with butter or vegetable shortening. Using a sharp knife, cut the rolls into ¼-inch slices. Arrange the cookies 1 inch apart on the baking sheets. Bake for 10 to 12 minutes, or until the cookies have browned around the edges. Remove from the oven.

After the cookies have cooled for 2 to 3 minutes, but are still warm to the touch, use a spatula to transfer them to wire racks to cool completely.

NO. **297**

# BUTTERSCOTCH WALNUT ICEBOX COOKIES

*Makes about 100 cookies*

3½ cups sifted flour
½ teaspoon baking soda
½ teaspoon salt
½ teaspoon cream of tartar
1½ cups dark brown sugar, firmly packed

½ cup unsalted butter, softened
2 eggs, beaten
1 teaspoon grated lemon zest
1½ cups walnuts, finely chopped
1 cup butterscotch morsels

Sift together the flour, baking soda, salt, and cream of tartar. Combine the flour mixture with the brown sugar in a large mixing bowl. Cut the butter into pieces and add to the mixture. Using a pastry blender, or two forks, work the butter into the flour mixture until the texture resembles that of coarse oatmeal. Add the eggs and the lemon zest. Mix well. Stir the chopped walnuts and butterscotch morsels into the mixture.

Knead the dough. If the dough is too sticky, add more flour, a little at a time, until it is easier to work. Divide the dough into two equal parts, shape into long rolls about 2 inches in diameter, and wrap each roll in waxed paper. Chill overnight in the refrigerator. Do not freeze.

The next day, preheat the oven to 400° F. Lightly grease two large baking sheets with butter or vegetable shortening. Using a sharp knife, cut the rolls into ¼-inch slices. Arrange the dough slices 1 inch apart on the baking sheets. Bake for 10 to 12 minutes, or until the cookies have browned around the edges. Remove from the oven.

After the cookies have cooled for 2 to 3 minutes, but are still warm to the touch, use a spatula to transfer them to wire racks to cool completely.

## NO. 298     CHERRY WALNUT ICEBOX COOKIES

*Makes about 64 cookies*

2 cups sifted flour
½ teaspoon baking soda
⅓ teaspoon salt
¼ teaspoon cream of tartar
¾ cup dark brown sugar, firmly packed
¼ cup unsalted butter, softened

1 egg, beaten
1 tablespoon cherry liqueur
½ teaspoon vanilla extract
¾ cup coarsely chopped maraschino cherries, drained
1 cup walnuts, finely chopped

Sift together the flour, baking soda, salt, and cream of tartar. In a large mixing bowl, combine the flour mixture with the sugar. Cut the butter into chunks and add to the flour mixture. Using a pastry blender, or two forks, work the butter into the flour mixture until the texture resembles that of coarse oatmeal. Add the beaten egg. Mix in the liqueur and the vanilla extract. Stir in the chopped cherries and walnuts.

Knead until smooth. If the dough is too sticky, add more flour, a little at a time, until it is easier to work. Divide the dough into two equal parts. Shape into rolls about 2 inches in diameter. Wrap each roll in waxed paper. Chill overnight in the refrigerator. Do not freeze.

The next day, preheat the oven to 400° F. Lightly grease two large baking sheets with butter or vegetable shortening. Using a sharp knife, cut the dough rolls into ¼-inch slices. Arrange the dough slices

1 inch apart on the baking sheets. Bake for 10 to 12 minutes, or until the cookies have browned around the edges. Remove from the oven.

After the cookies have cooled for 2 to 3 minutes, but are still warm to the touch, use a spatula to transfer them to wire racks to cool completely.

## NO. 299 CHOCOLATE ICEBOX COOKIES

*Makes about 100 cookies*

4 ounces (4 squares) unsweetened baking chocolate
3½ cups sifted flour
½ teaspoon baking soda
½ teaspoon salt

½ teaspoon cream of tartar
1 teaspoon cinnamon
2 cups sugar
½ cup unsalted butter, softened
2 eggs, beaten

Melt the chocolate in the top of a double boiler over simmering water, stirring frequently. Remove the pan from the heat and set aside.

Sift together the flour, baking soda, salt, cream of tartar, and cinnamon. Combine the flour mixture with the sugar in a large mixing bowl. Cut the butter into pieces and add to the flour mixture. Using a pastry blender, or two forks, work the butter into the flour mixture until the texture resembles that of coarse oatmeal. Stir in the beaten eggs, then add the melted chocolate. Mix well.

On a floured work surface, knead the dough until smooth. If the dough is too sticky, add more flour, a little at a time, until it is easier to work. Divide the dough into two equal parts and shape into long rolls 2 inches in diameter. Wrap each roll in waxed paper and chill overnight in the refrigerator. Do not freeze.

The next day, preheat the oven to 400° F. Lightly grease two large baking sheets with butter or vegetable shortening. Using a sharp knife, cut the dough into ¼-inch slices. Arrange the slices 1 inch apart on the baking sheets. Bake for 10 to 12 minutes, or until the cookies have browned around the edges. Remove from the oven.

After the cookies have cooled for 2 to 3 minutes, but are still warm to the touch, use a spatula to transfer them to wire racks to cool completely.

NO. 300                       COFFEE ICEBOX COOKIES
                                                *Makes about 64 cookies*

2 cups sifted flour                  ½ teaspoon espresso coffee
½ teaspoon baking soda                  powder
¼ teaspoon salt                      1 tablespoon hot water
¼ teaspoon cream of tartar           1 egg, beaten
¾ cup dark brown sugar,              ½ teaspoon vanilla extract
   firmly packed                     1 cup walnuts, finely chopped
¼ cup unsalted butter,
   softened

Sift together the flour, baking soda, salt, and cream of tartar. In a
large mixing bowl, combine the flour mixture with the brown sugar.
Cut the butter into pieces and add to the mixture. Using a pastry
blender, or two forks, work the butter into the flour until the mixture
resembles coarse oatmeal. Dissolve the coffee powder in the hot water
and add to the beaten egg. Stir the egg mixture into the batter and
mix well. Add the vanilla extract and the chopped walnuts.

Knead the dough until it is smooth. If the dough is too sticky, add
more flour, a little at a time, until it is easier to work. Divide the
dough into two equal parts and shape into long rolls 2 inches in
diameter. Wrap each roll in waxed paper and chill overnight in the
refrigerator. Do not freeze.

The next day, preheat the oven to 400° F. Lightly grease two large
baking sheets with butter or vegetable shortening. Using a sharp
knife, cut the chilled dough into ¼-inch slices. Arrange the dough
slices 1 inch apart on the baking sheets. Bake for 10 to 12 minutes,
or until the cookies have browned around the edges. Remove from
the oven.

After the cookies have cooled for 2 to 3 minutes, but are still
warm to the touch, use a spatula to transfer them to wire racks to
cool completely.

NO. 301                        CREAM ICEBOX COOKIES
                                                *Makes about 64 cookies*

2 cups sifted flour                  ½ cup heavy cream
1 cup sugar                          1 teaspoon vanilla extract
1 cup unsalted butter,
   softened

In a large mixing bowl, combine the flour with the sugar. Cut the
butter into chunks, then add to the flour mixture. Using a pastry
blender, or two forks, work in the butter until it has the texture of
coarse oatmeal. Stir in the cream and vanilla extract.

Knead until smooth. If the dough is too sticky, add more flour, a little at a time, until it is easier to work. Divide the dough into two equal parts and shape into long rolls about 2 inches in diameter. Wrap each roll in waxed paper. Chill overnight in the refrigerator. Do not freeze.

The next day, preheat the oven to 400° F. Lightly grease two large baking sheets with butter or vegetable shortening. Using a sharp knife, cut the dough rolls into ¼-inch slices. Arrange the dough slices 1 inch apart on the baking sheets. Bake for 10 to 12 minutes, or until the cookies have browned around the edges. Remove from the oven.

After the cookies have cooled for 2 to 3 minutes, but are still warm to the touch, use a spatula to transfer them to wire racks to cool completely.

## NO. 302     LEMON ICEBOX COOKIES
*Makes about 100 cookies*

3½ cups sifted flour
½ teaspoon baking soda
½ teaspoon salt
½ teaspoon cream of tartar
1½ cups confectioners' sugar

½ cup unsalted butter, softened
2 eggs, beaten
2 teaspoons grated lemon zest
1 teaspoon lemon juice
1½ cups walnuts, finely chopped

Sift together the flour, baking soda, salt, and cream of tartar. In a large mixing bowl, combine the flour mixture with the sugar. Cut the butter into pieces and add to the mixture. Using a pastry blender, or two forks, work the butter into the flour until the mixture resembles coarse oatmeal. Add the beaten eggs, lemon zest, and lemon juice. Mix well. Stir in the chopped walnuts.

Knead the batter until smooth. If the dough is too sticky, add more flour, a little at a time, until it is easier to work. Divide the dough into two equal parts and shape into long rolls 2 inches in diameter. Wrap each roll in waxed paper. Chill overnight in the refrigerator. Do not freeze.

The next day, preheat the oven to 400° F. Lightly grease two large baking sheets with butter or vegetable shortening. Using a sharp knife, cut each roll of dough into ¼-inch slices. Arrange the dough slices 1 inch apart on the baking sheets. Bake for 10 to 12 minutes, or until the cookies have browned around the edges. Remove from the oven.

After the cookies have cooled for 2 to 3 minutes, but are still warm to the touch, use a spatula to transfer them to wire racks to cool completely.

NO. **303** MOCHA ALMOND ICEBOX
COOKIES

*Makes about 100 cookies*

4 ounces (4 squares)
  unsweetened baking
  chocolate
1 tablespoon espresso coffee
  powder
3½ cups sifted flour
½ teaspoon baking soda
½ teaspoon salt

½ teaspoon cream of tartar
1 teaspoon cinnamon
2 cups sugar
½ cup unsalted butter,
  softened
2 eggs, beaten
1 cup blanched almonds,
  finely chopped

Melt the chocolate in the top of a double boiler over simmering water, stirring frequently. When the chocolate is melted, add the coffee powder and stir until it dissolves. Remove the pan from the heat and set aside.

Sift together the flour, baking soda, salt, cream of tartar, and cinnamon. In a large mixing bowl, combine the flour mixture with the sugar. Cut the butter into pieces and add to the flour mixture. Using a pastry blender, or two forks, work the butter into the flour mixture until the texture resembles that of coarse oatmeal. Mix in the eggs, one at a time. Add the melted chocolate and mix well. Stir in the chopped almonds.

Knead the batter until smooth. If the dough is too sticky, add more flour, a little at a time, until it is easier to work. Divide the dough into two equal parts and shape into long rolls about 2 inches in diameter. Wrap each roll in waxed paper. Chill overnight in the refrigerator. Do not freeze.

The next day, preheat the oven to 400° F. Lightly grease two large baking sheets with butter or vegetable shortening. Using a sharp knife, cut the rolls into ¼-inch slices. Arrange the dough slices 1 inch apart on the baking sheets. Bake for 10 to 12 minutes, or until the cookies have browned around the edges. Remove from the oven.

After the cookies have cooled for 2 to 3 minutes, but are still warm to the touch, use a spatula to transfer them to wire racks to cool completely.

NO. **304**  # VANILLA WALNUT ICEBOX COOKIES

*Makes about 64 cookies*

2 cups sifted flour
½ teaspoon baking soda
¼ teaspoon salt
¼ teaspoon cream of tartar
¾ cup sugar

¼ cup unsalted butter, softened
1 egg, beaten
½ tablespoon vanilla extract
¼ teaspoon almond extract
1 cup walnuts, finely chopped

Sift together the flour, baking soda, salt, and cream of tartar. Combine the flour mixture with the sugar in a large mixing bowl. Cut the butter into pieces and add to the flour mixture. Using a pastry blender, or two forks, work the butter into the flour mixture until the texture resembles that of coarse oatmeal. Mix in the beaten egg and the vanilla and almond extracts. Stir in the chopped walnuts. Knead until smooth. If the dough is too sticky, add more flour, a little at a time, until it is easier to work. Divide the dough into two equal parts, and shape into long rolls about 2 inches in diameter. Wrap each roll in waxed paper. Chill overnight in the refrigerator. Do not freeze.

The next day, preheat the oven to 400° F. Lightly grease two large baking sheets with butter or vegetable shortening. Using a sharp knife, cut the dough rolls into ¼-inch slices. Arrange the dough slices 1 inch apart on the baking sheets. Bake for 10 to 12 minutes, or until the cookies have browned around the edges. Remove from the oven.

After the cookies have cooled for 2 to 3 minutes, but are still warm to the touch, use a spatula to transfer them to wire racks to cool completely.

# Shortbread Cookies

The basic dough for shortbread cookies is made from butter, sugar, and flour, and they have a special texture all their own. Before baking, you can press a cookie stamp into the surface of shortbread cookies to give them an attractive look, or you can prick the cookies with the tines of a fork in attractive patterns.

## NO. 305 ALMOND SHORTBREAD

*Makes about 24 cookies*

½ cup unsalted butter,
    softened
2 cups sifted flour

½ cup sugar
1 tablespoon water
½ cup ground almonds

Preheat the oven to 350° F. Lightly grease two large baking sheets with butter or vegetable shortening.

In a large mixing bowl, cut the butter into large pieces. Gradually add the flour and sugar to the butter. Blend thoroughly, using a pastry blender or two forks. Add the water and mix well. Stir in the ground almonds and work the mixture into a thick dough. Divide the dough in half.

On a floured work surface, roll out the dough to a thickness of ½ inch. Cut out the cookies using a 2-inch, curly-edged biscuit or cookie cutter. Place the cookies 1 inch apart on the baking sheets. Prick the top of each cookie with a fork, making a pattern if desired. Bake for 25 to 30 minutes.

After the cookies have cooled for 2 to 3 minutes, but are still warm to the touch, use a spatula to transfer them to wire racks to cool completely.

## NO. 306 BROWN SUGAR SHORTBREAD

*Makes about 24 cookies*

½ cup unsalted butter,
    softened
½ cup light brown sugar

1 egg
2 cups sifted flour

Preheat the oven to 400° F. Lightly grease two large baking sheets with butter or vegetable shortening.

In a large mixing bowl, cream together the butter and sugar. Beat in the egg thoroughly. Blend in the flour, ½ cup at a time. Work the mixture into a smooth dough. This dough will probably be too stiff to use an electric mixer or food processor, and is best kneaded by hand.

On a floured work surface, roll out the dough to a thickness of ½ inch. Cut the dough into 2-inch squares. Transfer the squares to the baking sheet. Bake for about 15 minutes, or until the cookies feel firm to a light touch. Remove from the oven.

After the cookies have cooled completely, use a spatula to remove them from the baking sheets and transfer to a serving plate.

## NO. 307     CASHEW SHORTBREAD

*Makes about 24 cookies*

1 cup unsalted butter,
   softened
½ cup light brown sugar
1 teaspoon almond extract
1 teaspoon vanilla extract

2 cups sifted cake flour
½ teaspoon baking powder
1 cup salted cashew nuts,
   finely chopped

Preheat the oven to 350° F. Lightly grease two large baking sheets with butter or vegetable shortening.

In a large mixing bowl, cream together the butter and sugar. Mix in the almond extract and the vanilla extract. Sift the flour with the baking powder. Using a pastry blender, or two forks, work the flour mixture into the butter mixture until thoroughly blended. Mix the chopped cashew nuts into the dough by hand.

On a floured work surface, roll out the dough to a thickness of ½ inch. Cut out the cookies using a 2-inch, curly-edged biscuit or cookie cutter. Place the cookies 1 inch apart on the baking sheets. Bake for about 15 minutes, or until the cookies are light brown. Remove from the oven.

After the cookies have cooled for 2 to 3 minutes, but are still warm to the touch, use a spatula to transfer them to wire racks to cool completely.

## NO. 308     CHOCOLATE SHORTBREAD

*Makes about 24 cookies*

4 ounces (4 squares)
   unsweetened baking
   chocolate
1 cup unsalted butter,
   softened
1 cup light brown sugar

2 teaspoons vanilla extract
2 cups sifted cake flour
½ teaspoon baking powder
1 cup walnuts, coarsely
   chopped

Preheat the oven to 350° F. Lightly grease two large baking sheets with butter or vegetable shortening.

Melt the chocolate in the top of a double boiler over simmering water, stirring frequently. Remove the pan from the heat and set aside.

In a large mixing bowl, cream together the butter and sugar. Mix in the vanilla extract. Beat in the melted chocolate and mix thoroughly. Sift the flour with the baking powder. Using a pastry blender, or two forks, work the flour mixture into the butter mixture until it is thoroughly blended. Mix the chopped walnuts into the dough by hand.

On a floured work surface, roll out the dough to a thickness of ½ inch. Cut out the cookies using a 2-inch, curly-edged biscuit or cookie cutter. Place the cookies 1 inch apart on the baking sheets. Bake for about 15 minutes, or until the cookies are light brown. Remove from the oven.

After the cookies have cooled for 2 to 3 minutes, but are still warm to the touch, use a spatula to transfer them to wire racks to cool completely.

## NO. 309     DOUBLE DELIGHT CHOCOLATE SHORTBREAD

*Makes about 30 cookies*

Follow the recipe for Chocolate Shortbread (No. 308), adding ¾ cup of semi-sweet chocolate morsels to the batter.

## NO. 310     DOUBLE DELIGHT CHOCOLATE MINT SHORTBREAD

*Makes about 30 cookies*

Follow the recipe for Chocolate Shortbread (No. 308), adding ¾ cup of mint chocolate morsels to the batter.

## NO. 311     CINNAMON SHORTBREAD

*Makes about 24 cookies*

| | |
|---|---|
| 1 cup unsalted butter, softened | 2 cups sifted cake flour |
| 1 cup superfine sugar | ½ teaspoon baking powder |
| 1 teaspoon vanilla extract | 2 tablespoons cinnamon |
| | ½ cup walnuts, finely chopped |

Preheat the oven to 350° F. Lightly grease two large baking sheets with butter or vegetable shortening.

In a large mixing bowl, cream together the butter and sugar. Mix in the vanilla extract. Sift the flour with the baking powder and cinnamon. Using a pastry blender or two forks, work the flour mixture into the butter mixture until the texture resembles that of coarse oatmeal. Stir in the chopped walnuts and mix well.

On a floured work surface, roll out the dough to a thickness of ½ inch. Cut out the cookies using a 2-inch, curly-edged biscuit or cookie cutter. Place the cookies 1 inch apart on the baking sheets. Bake for about 15 minutes, or until the cookies are light brown. Remove from the oven.

After the cookies have cooled for 2 to 3 minutes, but are still warm to the touch, use a spatula to transfer them to wire racks to cool completely.

## NO. 312       GINGER SHORTBREAD

*Makes about 24 cookies*

½ cup unsalted butter, softened
½ cup dark brown sugar, firmly packed
1 teaspoon vanilla extract

1 tablespoon heavy cream
1½ cups sifted cake flour
1 teaspoon ground ginger
¼ teaspoon salt

Preheat the oven to 350° F. Lightly grease two large baking sheets with butter or vegetable shortening.

In a large mixing bowl, cream together the butter and sugar. Mix in the vanilla extract and the heavy cream. Sift the flour with the ginger and salt. Using a pastry blender or two forks, work the flour mixture into the butter mixture until the texture resembles that of coarse oatmeal.

On a floured work surface, roll out the dough to a thickness of ½ inch. Cut out the cookies using a 2-inch, curly-edged biscuit or cookie cutter. Place the cookies 1 inch apart on the baking sheets. Prick each cookie in the center with the tines of a fork. Bake for 25 to 30 minutes, or until the cookies are light brown. Remove from the oven.

After the cookies have cooled for 2 to 3 minutes, but are still warm to the touch, use a spatula to transfer them to wire racks to cool completely.

## NO. 313      OLD-FASHIONED AMERICAN SHORTBREAD

*Makes about 48 cookies*

| | |
|---|---|
| 1 cup unsalted butter, softened | 3 eggs |
| 1 cup sugar | ½ teaspoon caraway seeds |
| | 4 cups sifted flour |

Preheat the oven to 400° F. Lightly grease two large baking sheets with butter or vegetable shortening.

In a large mixing bowl, cream together the butter and sugar. Beat in the eggs, one at a time. Mix in the caraway seeds. Blend in the flour, ½ cup at a time, and work the mixture into a smooth dough. The dough will probably be too stiff to use an electric mixer or food processor, and is best kneaded by hand.

On a floured work surface, roll out the dough to a thickness of ½ inch. Cut the dough into 2-inch squares and transfer the squares to the baking sheets. Slash each cookie with a knife or stamp with a decorative cookie press.

Bake for about 15 minutes, or until the cookies feel firm to a light touch. Remove from the oven. After the cookies have cooled, remove them from the baking sheets with a spatula and transfer to a serving plate.

## NO. 314      WHOLE WHEAT SHORTBREAD

*Makes about 24 cookies*

| | |
|---|---|
| 1 cup unsalted butter, softened | 2 cups sifted whole wheat flour |
| ½ cup light brown sugar | ½ teaspoon baking powder |
| 1 teaspoon vanilla extract | 1 cup walnuts, finely chopped |

Preheat the oven to 300° F. Lightly grease two large baking sheets with butter or vegetable shortening.

In a large mixing bowl, cream together the butter and sugar. Mix in the vanilla extract. Sift the flour with the baking powder. Using a pastry blender, or two forks, work the flour mixture into the butter mixture until it has the texture of coarse oatmeal. Work the chopped walnuts into the dough by hand.

On a floured work surface, roll out the dough to a thickness of ½ inch. Cut out the cookies using a 2-inch, curly-edged biscuit or cookie cutter. Place the cookies 1 inch apart on the baking sheets. Bake for 25 to 30 minutes, or until the cookies are light brown. Remove from the oven.

After the cookies have cooled for 2 to 3 minutes, but are still warm to the touch, use a spatula to transfer them to wire racks to cool completely.

# Rusks

Rusks are cookies that are baked twice, once as free-form loaves, and a second time in slices. The rusk, like many delicious and unusual cookies, originates in Italian cuisine. Not too sweet, and with a hard, yet subtly satisfying texture achieved by the double baking, a rusk makes an elegant accompaniment to a sorbet or a fresh fruit salad. An additional recipe for Christmas rusks may be found in the section on Holiday Cookies.

NO. 315

## ALMOND RUSKS

*Makes about 32 rusks*

6 tablespoons unsalted butter, softened
½ cup sugar
2 eggs
½ teaspoon almond extract
1 teaspoon Amaretto liqueur
1⅔ cups sifted flour

2 teaspoons baking powder
¼ teaspoon salt
¼ teaspoon allspice
¼ teaspoon ground ginger
⅔ cup blanched almonds, coarsely chopped

Preheat the oven to 325° F. Lightly grease two large baking sheets with butter or vegetable shortening.

In a large mixing bowl, cream together the butter and sugar. Beat in the eggs, one at a time. Add the almond extract and liqueur. Sift together the flour, baking powder, salt, allspice, and ginger. Combine the flour mixture with the batter, mixing thoroughly. Stir in the chopped almonds.

Divide the dough in half, and then into quarters. Shape the dough into four equal loaves no more than 1 inch high. Place two loaves on each baking sheet. Bake for 20 minutes, or until the loaves are golden. Remove from the oven, but leave the oven turned on.

While the loaves are still hot, cut them into ¾-inch slices using a sharp, serrated knife (a tomato knife is ideal). Turn off the oven, arrange the rusk slices on the baking sheets, and return them to the oven for an additional 15 minutes. Turn the rusks once after 5 minutes. Remove from the oven and transfer the rusks to wire racks to cool completely.

NO. **316**                 # BISCOTTI (ITALIAN RUSKS)
*Makes about 64 rusks*

½ cup unsalted butter,            3 cups sifted flour
   softened         ½ teaspoon salt
¾ cup sugar                       3 teaspoons baking powder
3 eggs                            1 tablespoon ground aniseed
1 tablespoon orange juice         1 cup blanched almonds,
2 tablespoons grated orange          finely chopped
   zest
1 tablespoon grated lemon
   zest

Preheat the oven to 400° F. Lightly grease two large baking sheets with butter or vegetable shortening.

In a large mixing bowl, cream together the butter and the sugar. Beat in the eggs, one at a time. Add the orange juice, orange zest, and lemon zest. Mix well. Sift together the flour, salt, baking powder, and aniseed. Gradually beat the flour mixture into the batter. Stir in the chopped almonds.

Divide the dough in half, and then into quarters. Shape the dough into four equal loaves no more than 1 inch high. Place two loaves on each baking sheet. Flatten the top of each loaf slightly with a rolling pin. Bake for 15 minutes.

Remove from the oven, leaving the oven on. Cut each loaf into ¾-inch slices. Return the slices to the cookie sheets. Bake for an additional 15 minutes. Turn the rusks once after 5 minutes. Remove from the oven and transfer to wire racks to cool.

NO. **317**                      # CHOCOLATE RUSKS
*Makes about 32 rusks*

4 ounces (4 squares)              1 teaspoon chocolate liqueur
   unsweetened baking    1⅔ cups sifted flour
   chocolate         2 teaspoons baking powder
6 tablespoons unsalted butter,    ¼ teaspoon salt
   softened         1 teaspoon mace
¾ cup sugar                       ⅔ cup walnuts, coarsely
2 eggs                               chopped
1 teaspoon vanilla extract

Preheat the oven to 325° F. Lightly grease two large baking sheets with butter or vegetable shortening.

Melt the chocolate in the top of a double boiler over simmering water, stirring frequently. Remove the pan from the heat and set aside.

In a large mixing bowl, cream together the butter and sugar. Beat in the eggs, one at a time. Add the vanilla extract and liqueur. Mix in the melted chocolate. Sift together the flour, baking powder, salt, and mace. Combine the flour mixture with the batter, mixing thoroughly. Stir in the chopped walnuts.

Divide the dough in half, and then into quarters. Form the dough into four equal loaves no more than 1 inch high. Place two loaves on each baking sheet. Bake for 20 minutes, or until the loaves are firm to a light touch. Remove from the oven, but leave the oven turned on.

While the loaves are still hot, cut them into ¾-inch slices using a sharp, serrated knife (a tomato knife is ideal). Turn off the oven, arrange the rusk slices on the baking sheets, and return them to the oven for an additional 15 minutes. Turn the rusks once after 5 minutes. Remove from the oven and transfer to wire racks to cool completely.

NO. **318**        **CINNAMON RUSKS**

*Makes about 32 rusks*

| | |
|---|---|
| 6 tablespoons unsalted butter, softened | 1⅔ cups sifted flour |
| ½ cup sugar | 2 teaspoons baking powder |
| 2 eggs | ¼ teaspoon salt |
| 1 teaspoon vanilla extract | 1 tablespoon cinnamon |
| 1 teaspoon brandy | ⅔ cup blanched almonds, finely chopped |

Preheat the oven to 325° F. Lightly grease two large baking sheets with butter or vegetable shortening.

In a large mixing bowl, cream together the butter and sugar. Beat in the eggs, one at a time. Add the vanilla extract and brandy. Sift together the flour, baking powder, salt, and cinnamon. Combine the flour mixture with the batter, mixing thoroughly. Stir in the chopped almonds.

Divide the dough in half, and then into quarters. Form the dough into four equal loaves no more than 1 inch high. Place two loaves on each baking sheet. Bake for 20 minutes, or until the loaves are firm to a light touch. Remove from the oven, but leave the oven turned on.

While the loaves are still hot, cut them into ¾-inch slices using a sharp, serrated knife (a tomato knife is ideal). Turn off the oven, arrange the rusk slices on the baking sheets, and return them to the oven for an additional 15 minutes. Turn the rusks once after 5 minutes. Remove from the oven and transfer to wire racks to cool completely.

NO. **319**                                                   **ORANGE RUSKS**

*Makes about 32 rusks*

6 tablespoons unsalted butter,
  softened
½ cup sugar
2 eggs
2 teaspoons brandy
½ teaspoon orange extract
2 teaspoons grated orange
  zest

1⅔ cups sifted flour
2 teaspoons baking powder
¼ teaspoon salt
⅔ cup blanched almonds,
  coarsely chopped
⅔ cup finely chopped candied
  orange peel

Preheat the oven to 325° F. Lightly grease two large baking sheets with butter or vegetable shortening.

In a large mixing bowl, cream the butter and sugar together. Beat in the eggs, one at a time, and add the brandy, orange extract, and orange zest. Sift together the flour, baking powder, and salt. Combine the flour mixture with the batter, mixing thoroughly. Stir in the chopped almonds and orange peel.

Divide the dough in half, and then into quarters. Form into four equal loaf shapes no more than 1 inch high. Place two loaves on each baking sheet. Bake for 20 minutes, or until the loaves are golden. Remove from the oven, but leave the oven turned on.

While the loaves are still hot, cut them into ¾-inch slices using a sharp, serrated knife (a tomato knife is ideal). Turn off the oven, arrange the rusk slices on the baking sheets, and return them to the oven for an additional 15 minutes. Turn the rusks once after 5 minutes. Remove from the oven. Transfer the rusks to wire racks to cool completely.

# Holiday Cookies

The busiest times of the year for any cookie baker are the fall and winter holidays. Perhaps the cold air outside brings an increased desire for something sweet, or maybe it's the extra visitors or parties, not to mention festive holiday dinners. This selection of holiday recipes will supplement any treasured family recipes. To make edible Christmas tree ornaments, using a skewer, make a small hole in the top of each cookie before it is baked, then add a loop of gold or silver thread or a colorful ribbon after the cookie has cooled. Halloween and Valentine's Day cookies are also included here.

## NO. 320     CHRISTMAS FRUIT COOKIES

*Makes about 48 cookies*

1 cup unsalted butter, softened
1 cup light brown sugar
3 eggs
3 cups sifted flour
1 teaspoon baking soda
1 teaspoon cinnamon
¼ teaspoon nutmeg
½ cup heavy cream

1 cup raisins
½ cup dried currants
1 cup pitted dates, coarsely chopped
1 cup unsweetened shredded coconut
1 egg white, beaten
Unrefined sugar crystals
Cinnamon

Preheat the oven to 400° F. Lightly grease two large baking sheets with butter or vegetable shortening.

In a large mixing bowl, cream together the butter and sugar. Beat in the eggs, one at a time, mixing thoroughly after each addition. Sift the flour with the baking soda, cinnamon, and nutmeg. Work the flour mixture into the batter, ½ cup at a time, alternating with the cream. In another bowl, mix together the raisins, currants, dates, and coconut. Stir the fruit mixture into the batter.

On a floured work surface, knead the mixture to a smooth dough. If the dough is sticky, add more flour, a little at a time, until it is easier to work. Divide the dough into 48 balls. Shape each ball between the palms of the hands to form a roll 3 inches long and about the thickness of a pencil. On the baking sheet, shape each roll into a ring.

Brush the rings with beaten egg white and sprinkle liberally with sugar crystals and cinnamon. Bake for 12 to 15 minutes, or until the cookies have browned around the edges. Remove from the oven.

After the cookies have cooled for 2 to 3 minutes, but are still warm to the touch, use a spatula to transfer them to wire racks to cool completely.

NO. 321                 **CHRISTMAS RUSKS**

*Makes about 32 rusks*

| | |
|---|---|
| 6 tablespoons unsalted butter, softened | 2 teaspoons baking powder |
| ½ cup sugar | ¼ teaspoon salt |
| 2 eggs | ⅔ cup blanched almonds, coarsely chopped |
| 2 teaspoons rum | |
| ½ teaspoon almond extract | ⅓ cup red candied cherries, coarsely chopped |
| 1 teaspoon grated lemon zest | |
| 1⅔ cups sifted flour | ⅓ cup green candied cherries, coarsely chopped |

Preheat the oven to 325° F. Lightly grease two large baking sheets with butter or vegetable shortening.

In a large mixing bowl, cream together the butter and sugar. Beat in the eggs, one at a time. Add the rum, almond extract, and lemon zest. Mix well. Sift together the flour, baking powder, and salt. Combine the flour mixture with the batter, mixing thoroughly. Stir in the chopped almonds and cherries.

Divide the dough in half, and then into quarters. Form the dough into four equal loaves no more than 1 inch high. Place two loaves on each baking sheet. Bake for 20 minutes, or until the loaves are golden. Remove from the oven, but leave the oven turned on.

While the loaves are still hot, cut them into ¾-inch slices using a sharp, serrated knife (a tomato knife is ideal). Turn off the oven, arrange the rusk slices on the baking sheets, and return them to the oven for an additional 15 minutes. Turn the rusks once after 5 minutes. Remove from the oven and transfer to wire racks to cool completely.

NO. 322             **CHRISTMAS TREE COOKIES**

*Makes about 48 cookies*

| | |
|---|---|
| ½ cup unsalted butter, softened | 1 teaspoon baking powder |
| 1 cup sugar | ½ teaspoon baking soda |
| 1 egg | ½ teaspoon salt |
| 1 teaspoon grated lemon zest | 1 cup heavy cream |
| 3 cups sifted flour | 1 egg white, beaten |
| | Green colored sugar |

Preheat the oven to 400° F. Lightly grease two large baking sheets with butter or vegetable shortening.

In a large mixing bowl, cream together the butter and sugar. Beat in the egg and the lemon zest. Mix well. Sift the flour with the baking powder, baking soda, and salt. Add the flour mixture to the batter, ½ cup at a time, alternating with the cream.

Knead the mixture to a smooth dough. If the dough is sticky, add more flour, a little at a time, until it is easier to work. On a floured work surface, roll out the dough to a thickness of ¼ inch. Cut out the cookies using a Christmas-tree-shaped cookie cutter. Place the cookies 1 inch apart on the baking sheets. Brush each cookie with beaten egg white and sprinkle generously with green colored sugar. Bake for 8 to 10 minutes, or until the cookies have browned around the edges. Remove from the oven.

After the cookies have cooled for 2 to 3 minutes, but are still warm to the touch, use a spatula to transfer them to wire racks to cool completely.

## NO. 323 GERMAN CHRISTMAS COOKIES

*Makes about 60 cookies*

| | |
|---|---|
| 1 cup unsalted butter | ½ teaspoon ground cardamon |
| ¾ cup sugar | ½ cup blanched almonds, |
| ¾ cup dark corn syrup | coarsely chopped |
| 3 teaspoons grated lemon zest | ½ cup thinly sliced citron |
| 5 cups sifted flour | ½ cup thinly sliced candied |
| 1½ teaspoons baking soda | orange peel |

Preheat the oven to 350° F. Lightly grease two large baking sheets with butter or vegetable shortening.

Melt the butter in a small saucepan over very low heat. In a large mixing bowl, combine the melted butter, sugar, corn syrup, and lemon zest. Mix well. Sift the flour with the baking soda and cardamon. Combine the flour mixture with the chopped almonds, citron, and orange peel. Add the flour mixture to the batter, 1 cup at a time, mixing well after each addition.

Knead the mixture to a smooth dough. If the dough is sticky, add more flour, a little at a time, until it is easier to work. On a floured work surface, roll out the dough to a thickness of ¼ inch. Cut out the cookies using a 2-inch, curly-edged biscuit or cookie cutter. Place the cookies 1 inch apart on the baking sheets. Bake for 12 to 15 minutes, or until the cookies have browned around the edges. Remove from the oven.

After the cookies have cooled for 2 to 3 minutes, but are still

warm to the touch, use a spatula to transfer them to wire racks to cool completely.

NO. 324

# HOLIDAY BELLS

*Makes about 48 cookies*

½ cup unsalted butter,
  softened
1 cup sugar
1 egg
3 cups sifted flour
1 teaspoon baking powder

½ teaspoon baking soda
½ teaspoon salt
1 cup cold strong black coffee
1 egg white, beaten
Red and green colored
  sugar

Preheat the oven to 400° F. Lightly grease two large baking sheets with butter or vegetable shortening.

In a large mixing bowl, cream together the butter and sugar. Beat in the egg. Mix well. Sift the flour with the baking powder, baking soda, and salt. Add the flour mixture to the batter, ½ cup at a time, alternating with the coffee.

Knead the mixture to a smooth dough. If the dough is sticky, add more flour, a little at a time, until it is easier to work. On a floured work surface, roll out the dough to a thickness of ¼ inch. Cut out the cookies using a bell-shaped cookie cutter or a paper pattern. Place the cookies 1 inch apart on the baking sheets. Brush each cookie with beaten egg white and sprinkle generously with red or green colored sugar. Bake for 8 to 10 minutes, or until the cookies have browned around the edges. Remove from the oven.

After the cookies have cooled for 2 to 3 minutes, but are still warm to the touch, use a spatula to transfer them to wire racks to cool completely.

NO. 325

# LEBKUCHEN

*Makes about 48 cookies*

¾ cup honey
1 cup sugar
2½ cups sifted flour
1 teaspoon cinnamon
½ teaspoon ground cloves
½ teaspoon ground ginger

½ cup finely chopped citron
1 teaspoon baking soda
2 teaspoons water
1 egg, beaten
Confectioners' sugar

Preheat the oven to 325° F. Lightly grease two large baking sheets with butter or vegetable shortening.

Combine the honey and sugar in a small saucepan. Cook over low heat, stirring constantly with a wooden spoon, until the mixture begins to boil. Remove the pan from the heat and set aside to cool.

Sift the flour with the cinnamon, cloves, and ginger. Mix in the citron. Dissolve the baking soda in the water. Gradually add the honey mixture to the flour, alternating with the beaten egg and the baking soda mixture.

Knead the mixture to a smooth dough. If the dough is sticky, add more flour, a little at a time, until it is easier to work. On a floured work surface, roll out the dough to a thickness of ¼ inch. Cut out the cookies using a 1-inch, round cookie cutter. Place the cookies 1 inch apart on the baking sheets. Bake for about 20 minutes, or until the cookies have browned around the edges. Remove from the oven.

After the cookies have cooled for 2 to 3 minutes, but are still warm to the touch, use a spatula to transfer them to wire racks to cool completely. When cool, dust each cookie with confectioners' sugar and arrange on a serving plate.

NO. **326**       **MINCEMEAT COOKIES**

*Makes about 48 cookies*

¾ cup unsalted butter, softened
1½ cups sugar
3 eggs, beaten
1 teaspoon grated lemon zest
1 cup mincemeat

3 cups sifted flour
1 teaspoon baking soda
½ teaspoon salt
3 tablespoons water
1 cup walnuts, coarsely chopped

Preheat the oven to 350° F. Lightly grease two large baking sheets with butter or vegetable shortening.

In a large mixing bowl, cream together the butter and sugar. Beat in the eggs and the lemon zest. Mix well. Stir in the mincemeat. Sift the flour with the baking soda and salt. Add half the flour mixture to the batter and mix well. Add the water, then beat in the remaining flour mixture. Stir in the chopped walnuts.

Drop rounded teaspoonfuls of batter onto the baking sheets, about 2 inches apart. Bake for 10 to 15 minutes, or until the cookies have browned around the edges. Remove from the oven.

After the cookies have cooled for 2 to 3 minutes, but are still warm to the touch, use a spatula to transfer them to wire racks to cool completely.

NO. **327**                         # PEPPER COOKIES
                                    *Makes about 48 cookies*

1½ cups raisins
1 tablespoon grated orange
    zest
1 cup unsalted peanuts,
    coarsely chopped
1 cup coarsely chopped,
    unsweetened canned
    pineapple, drained
⅛ cup unsalted butter,
    softened
1 cup solid vegetable
    shortening
1 cup sugar

½ cup dark brown sugar,
    firmly packed
3 eggs
⅛ teaspoon salt
1 tablespoon freshly ground
    black pepper
2 teaspoons cinnamon
1 teaspoon nutmeg
1 teaspoon ground cloves
3 cups sifted flour
¼ cup unsweetened baking
    cocoa
4 teaspoons baking powder

Preheat the oven to 400° F. Lightly grease two large baking sheets
with butter or vegetable shortening.

In a large saucepan, combine the raisins, orange zest, peanuts, and
pineapple. Add just enough water to barely cover the mixture. Simmer
over low heat, stirring occasionally, for about 20 minutes. Remove
the pan from the heat and set aside.

In a large mixing bowl, cream together the butter, vegetable shortening, and sugars. Add the eggs, one at a time, beating well after
each addition. Beat in the salt, pepper, cinnamon, nutmeg, and cloves.
Stir in the cooled fruit mixture. Sift the flour with the cocoa and
baking powder. Work the flour mixture into the batter, 1 cup at a
time.

Knead to a smooth dough. If the dough is sticky, add more flour,
a little at a time, until it is easier to work. On a floured work surface,
roll out the dough to a thickness of ¼ inch. Cut out the cookies
using a 3-inch, curly-edged biscuit or cookie cutter. Place the cookies
1 inch apart on the baking sheets. Bake for about 8 minutes, or until
the cookies have browned around the edges. Remove from the oven.

After the cookies have cooled for 2 to 3 minutes, but are still
warm to the touch, use a spatula to transfer them to wire racks to
cool completely.

NO. **328** # PFEFFERNUSSE
*Makes about 72 cookies*

The dough for these cookies must be chilled for 1 hour in the freezer and must also stand for 2 hours before baking.

| | |
|---|---|
| ½ cup unsalted butter | 1 teaspoon coarsely ground |
| ¾ cup dark molasses | black pepper |
| ½ cup water | 1 teaspoon allspice |
| 2 teaspoons grated lemon zest | 1 teaspoon cinnamon |
| 2 teaspoons grated orange | ½ teaspoon ground cloves |
| zest | 4 cups sifted flour |

In a medium saucepan, combine the butter, molasses, water, lemon zest, orange zest, pepper, allspice, cinnamon, and cloves. Bring the mixture to a boil over low heat, stirring constantly with a wooden spoon. Remove the pan from the heat. Pour the mixture into a large mixing bowl. Cool slightly, cover, and chill in the freezer for about 1 hour.

When the mixture is very cold and stiff, work in the flour, 1 cup at a time. Knead to a smooth dough. If the dough is sticky, add more flour, a little at a time, until it is easier to work. Cover the bowl with a dish towel and let it stand for 2 hours.

Preheat the oven to 350° F. Lightly grease two large baking sheets with butter or vegetable shortening. Place rounded teaspoonfuls of batter onto the baking sheets, about 2 inches apart. Bake for 10 to 12 minutes, or until the cookies are dry to the touch. Remove from the oven.

After the cookies have cooled for 2 to 3 minutes, but are still warm to the touch, use a spatula to transfer them to wire racks to cool completely.

NO. **329** # CHOCOLATE PFEFFERNUSSE
*Makes about 72 cookies*

Follow the recipe for Pfeffernusse (No. 328), adding 1 ounce (1 square) of grated unsweetened baking chocolate to the butter and molasses mixture while it is boiling.

NO. 330                **WHITE PFEFFERNUSSE**
                        *Makes about 36 cookies*

4 eggs
2 cups sugar
1 tablespoon grated lemon
    zest
3 cups sifted flour
2 teaspoons baking powder

1 teaspoon coarsely ground
    black pepper
1 teaspoon ground cloves
1 tablespoon cinnamon
½ teaspoon nutmeg
1 cup finely chopped citron
    Confectioners' sugar

Preheat the oven to 325° F. Lightly grease two large baking sheets with butter or vegetable shortening.

In a large mixing bowl, beat the eggs until foamy. Gradually add the sugar. Continue to beat until the mixture is thick and light. Mix in the lemon zest. Sift the flour with the baking powder, pepper, cloves, cinnamon, and nutmeg. Work the flour into the batter, 1 cup at a time. Mix in the chopped citron.

Knead the mixture to a smooth dough. If the dough is sticky, add more flour, a little at a time, until it is easier to work. On a floured work surface, roll out the dough to a thickness of ¼ inch. Cut out the cookies using a 2-inch, round cookie cutter. Place the cookies 1 inch apart on the baking sheets. Bake for 12 to 15 minutes, or until the cookies have browned around the edges. Remove from the oven.

After the cookies have cooled for 2 to 3 minutes, but are still warm to the touch, roll them in confectioners' sugar. Transfer to wire racks to cool completely.

NO. 331                **HALLOWEEN COOKIES**
                        *Makes about 40 cookies*

½ cup unsalted butter,
    softened
1 cup sugar
1 egg
3 cups sifted flour

1 teaspoon baking powder
½ teaspoon baking soda
½ teaspoon salt
1 cup cold strong black coffee

*Icing*

2 tablespoons unsalted butter,
    softened
1 tablespoon heavy cream
2 teaspoons vanilla extract

2 cups confectioners' sugar
    Red food coloring
    Yellow food coloring
    Raisins

Preheat the oven to 400° F. Lightly grease two large baking sheets with butter or vegetable shortening.

In a large mixing bowl, cream together the butter and sugar. Beat in the egg. Mix well. Sift the flour with the baking powder, baking soda, and salt. Add the flour mixture to the batter, ½ cup at a time, alternating with the coffee.

Knead the mixture to a smooth dough. If the dough is sticky, add more flour, a little at a time, until it is easier to work. On a floured work surface, roll out the dough to a thickness of ¼ inch. Draw a 3-inch pumpkin on a piece of paper and cut out a pattern. Using the pattern and a sharp kitchen knife, cut each cookie into the shape of a pumpkin. Place the cookies 1 inch apart on the baking sheets. Bake for 8 to 10 minutes, or until the cookies have browned around the edges. Remove from the oven.

After the cookies have cooled for 2 to 3 minutes, but are still warm to the touch, use a spatula to transfer them to wire racks to cool completely.

When the cookies have thoroughly cooled, prepare the icing. In a large mixing bowl, combine the butter, cream, and vanilla extract and beat until creamy. Gradually beat in the sugar until the frosting is thick (it may not be necessary to add all of the sugar). Still beating, carefully add a few drops of red and yellow food coloring, one at a time, until the icing is the desired shade of bright orange. Spread each cookie with icing and decorate with raisin faces. Let the icing harden and dry before storing the cookies.

NO. **332**        # VALENTINE'S DAY HEARTS

*Makes about 36 cookies*

| | |
|---|---|
| 1 cup unsalted butter, softened | 4 eggs |
| 1½ cups sugar | 3 cups sifted flour |
| | 1 teaspoon baking soda |

## Icing

| | |
|---|---|
| 2 tablespoons unsalted butter, softened | 2 cups confectioners' sugar |
| 1 tablespoon heavy cream | Red food coloring |
| 2 teaspoons vanilla extract | Silver dragees |

Preheat the oven to 400° F. Lightly grease two large baking sheets with butter or vegetable shortening.

In a large mixing bowl, cream together the butter and sugar. Beat in the eggs, one at a time, continuing to beat until the mixture is creamy. Sift the flour with the baking soda. Add the flour mixture to the batter, ½ cup at a time.

Knead into a soft dough. On a floured work surface, roll out the dough to a thickness of ¼ inch. Cut out the cookies using a 3-inch, heart-shaped cookie cutter or a heart-shaped paper pattern. Place the cookies 1 inch apart on the baking sheets. Bake for 8 to 10 minutes, or until the cookies have browned around the edges. Remove from the oven.

After the cookies have cooled for 2 to 3 minutes, but are still warm to the touch, use a spatula to transfer them to wire racks to cool completely.

When the cookies have thoroughly cooled, prepare the icing. In a large mixing bowl, combine the butter, cream, and vanilla extract. Beat until smooth. Gradually add the sugar. Continue to beat until the icing is thick. Still beating, add the red food coloring, one drop at a time, until the icing is the desired shade of bright pink. Spread each cookie with icing and decorate with silver dragees. Let the icing harden and dry before storing the cookies.

# Special Cookies

Special Cookies is our catchall category for anything so unique (and delicious) that it doesn't really fit in other categories. According to *Webster's Dictionary*, the word cookie comes from the Dutch *Koekje*—the diminutive of the Dutch *Koek*, or cake. A cookie, under this definition, must be small—but it can also be a small cake. You'll find an elegant assortment of chess cakes, ladyfingers, cream puffs, rugelach, and the incomparable, memorable madeleine, among others. As noted in the introduction, purists may find some of these recipes a bit off the beaten cookie track, but they extend across a wide range of cultures and tastes to bring you the broadest assortment of cookies possible.

NO. 333

## APRICOT RUGELACH
*Makes about 48 cookies*

### Pastry

2 cups sifted flour
1 tablespoon sugar
½ teaspoon salt
1 teaspoon baking powder

1 cup margarine or vegetable shortening, softened
½ cup orange juice

### Filling

½ cup dried apricots, coarsely chopped
¼ cup golden raisins

¼ cup light brown sugar
1 teaspoon allspice

In a large mixing bowl, sift the flour with the sugar, salt, and baking powder. Using a pastry blender, work in the shortening until the mixture resembles coarse oatmeal. Mix in the orange juice. Add more flour if the dough seems too sticky. Divide the dough into four equal balls, wrap each ball in waxed paper, and chill overnight in the refrigerator.

The next day, preheat the oven to 375° F. Lightly grease two large baking sheets with vegetable shortening.

In a large mixing bowl, combine the chopped apricots, raisins, brown sugar, and allspice. Mix well. Roll out each ball of dough onto a floured work surface, forming a circle about ¼ inch thick. Sprinkle a quarter of the filling onto each dough circle. Using a sharp knife, cut each circle into 12 wedges. Starting at the wide end, roll each wedge into a crescent shape. Place the crescents on the baking sheets. Bake for 15 to 20 minutes, or until the cookies are golden brown. Using a spatula, transfer the crescents to wire cooling racks.

NO. **334**                      # CINNAMON RUGELACH
*Makes about 48 cookies*

Follow the recipe for Apricot Rugelach (No. 333), but make the filling with ½ cup dried currants, ¼ cup golden raisins, ¼ cup firmly packed dark brown sugar, and 1 tablespoon of cinnamon.

NO. **335**                      # RASPBERRY RUGELACH
*Makes about 48 cookies*

Follow the recipe for Apricot Rugelach (No. 333), but make the filling with 1 cup raspberry jam, 1 tablespoon brandy, 1 cup coarsely chopped walnuts, ¼ cup light brown sugar, and 1 teaspoon of cinnamon.

NO. **336**                      # ALMOND TARTLETS
*Makes 12 tartlets*

*Pastry Shells*

½ cup unsalted butter, softened
½ cup confectioners' sugar
1 egg
½ teaspoon baking powder
¼ teaspoon salt
1 cup sifted flour

*Custard*

⅓ cup unsalted butter, softened
½ cup sugar
2 eggs
1 teaspoon vanilla extract
¼ teaspoon ground ginger
½ cup blanched almonds, toasted and finely chopped

Preheat the oven to 375° F. Generously grease 12 individual 3-inch tartlet pans with butter.

First prepare the pastry shells. In a large mixing bowl, cream the butter until it is smooth. Beat in the sugar, a little at a time. Add the egg and mix well. The mixture should thicken slightly. Sift together the baking powder, salt, and flour. Work the flour mixture into the batter. Divide the dough into 12 equal parts.

On a floured work surface, roll out each dough ball into the shape of a circle to the fit the tartlet pan. Line each tartlet pan with dough. Set aside.

To prepare the custard filling, in a large bowl cream the butter with the sugar. In a separate bowl, beat the eggs until foamy. Beat in the vanilla extract, then add the ginger. Combine the beaten eggs with the butter mixture and mix well. Add the chopped toasted almonds to the custard. Mix well.

Fill each tartlet shell with custard and place on a baking sheet. Bake for about 20 minutes or until the pastry is golden brown and a knife inserted in the custard comes out clean.

Remove from the oven and cool thoroughly. Gently remove the tartlets from the baking pans just before serving.

NO. **337**      # AUSTRIAN BUTTER HORNS

*Makes about 75 cookies*

### Pastry

| | |
|---|---|
| 4 cups sifted flour | ¼ teaspoon salt |
| 1½ cups unsalted butter, softened | 3 egg yolks, beaten |
| 1 package dry yeast | ½ cup sour cream |
| ¼ cup warm water | 1 teaspoon vanilla extract |
| | ¼ cup confectioners' sugar |

### Filling

| | |
|---|---|
| 3 egg whites | 2 cups walnuts, coarsely chopped |
| 1 cup sugar | |
| 1 teaspoon vanilla extract | |

### Icing

| | |
|---|---|
| 2 tablespoons unsalted butter, softened | ½ teaspoon vanilla extract |
| 2 cups confectioners' sugar | 2 to 3 tablespoons milk |

Preheat the oven to 350° F. Lightly grease two large baking sheets with butter or vegetable shortening.

First make the pastry. In a large mixing bowl, combine the flour and butter and blend until the mixture resembles coarse oatmeal. Dissolve the yeast in the warm water. Add to the flour mixture. Stir in the salt, egg yolks, sour cream, and vanilla extract. Mix well. The dough should be soft, but not sticky. Add additional flour if necessary.

Turn the dough out onto a work surface sprinkled with the confectioners' sugar and knead until smooth. Divide the dough into 12 equal parts. Roll out each piece of dough into a circle with an 8-inch diameter. Using a sharp knife, cut each circle into 8 wedges.

To make the filling, beat the egg whites until foamy. Gradually add the sugar, continuing to beat until stiff peaks form. Mix in the vanilla extract and the chopped walnuts.

Place 1 to 2 teaspoons of filling on each wedge of dough. Roll up each wedge, starting at the wide end. Transfer to the baking sheet and curve the filled pastry into the shape of a horn. Bake for 15 minutes. Remove from the oven. When the horns have cooled slightly, transfer them to wire racks to cool completely.

To make the icing, mix together the butter, confectioners' sugar, vanilla extract, and enough milk to give the mixture a consistency that would coat the back of a wooden spoon. Use a pastry brush to ice the cooled cookies.

NO. **338**                                   **BANBURY CAKES**

*Makes about 36 cookies*

| | |
|---|---|
| 3 sheets frozen puff pastry, thawed | ¼ cup coarsely chopped candied lemon peel |
| 1 cup sifted flour | 1½ teaspoons allspice |
| 2½ cups dried currants | ½ cup unsalted butter, softened |
| ¼ cup coarsely chopped candied orange peel | 1 cup sugar |
| | Confectioners' sugar |

Preheat the oven to 400° F. Lightly grease two large baking sheets with butter or vegetable shortening.

Place the sheets of thawed puff pastry on a lightly floured work surface. Using a small oval cookie or biscuit cutter, press out rounds of pastry.

In a large mixing bowl, combine the flour, currants, orange peel, lemon peel, and allspice. Mix well. In another bowl, cream the butter with the sugar and add to the fruit mixture.

Place one teaspoonful of the fruit mixture in the center of each pastry oval, fold up the edges, and flatten, lightly, with a rolling pin. Sprinkle with confectioners' sugar before baking. Bake for 10 to 12 minutes. Remove from the oven.

After the cookies have cooled for 2 to 3 minutes, but are still warm to the touch, use a spatula to transfer them to wire racks to cool completely.

No. **339**                                                  **CHESS CAKES**
*Makes 12 tartlets*

*Pastry Shells*

½ cup unsalted butter,                    ½ teaspoon baking powder
   softened                          ¼ teaspoon salt
½ cup confectioners' sugar                1 cup sifted flour
1 egg

*Custard*

4 tablespoons unsalted butter,            1 egg, beaten
   softened                          4 egg yolks, beaten
1 cup sugar                               1 teaspoon vanilla extract

Preheat the oven to 375° F. Generously grease 12 individual 3-inch tartlet pans with butter.

First prepare the pastry shells. In a large mixing bowl, cream the butter until it is smooth. Beat in the sugar, a little at a time. Add the egg and mix well. The mixture should thicken slightly. Sift together the baking powder, salt, and flour. Add the flour mixture to the batter and mix well. Divide the dough into 12 equal balls.

On a floured work surface, roll out each dough ball into a circle to fit the tartlet pan. Line each tartlet pan with dough and set aside.

Prepare the custard filling. In a large mixing bowl, cream the butter with the sugar. In a separate bowl, beat the egg and egg yolks until the mixture is foamy. Beat in the vanilla extract. Combine the beaten eggs with the butter mixture and mix well.

Fill each tartlet shell with the custard and place on a baking sheet. Bake for about 20 minutes, or until the pastry is golden brown and a knife inserted in the custard comes out clean.

Remove from the oven and cool thoroughly. Gently remove the tartlets from the baking pans just before serving.

No. **340**                              **CHOCOLATE CHESS CAKES**
*Makes 12 tartlets*

Prepare the pastry shells, following the recipe for Chess Cakes (No. 339). Make the custard filling following the recipe below.

*Custard*

| | |
|---|---|
| 2 ounces (2 squares) unsweetened baking chocolate | 1 cup sugar |
| | 1 egg, beaten |
| | 4 egg yolks, beaten |
| 4 tablespoons unsalted butter, softened | 1 teaspoon vanilla extract |

Preheat the oven to 375° F. Melt the chocolate in the top of a double boiler over simmering water, stirring frequently. Remove the pan from the heat and set aside.

In a large mixing bowl, cream the butter with the sugar. In a separate bowl, beat the egg and egg yolks until foamy. Beat in the vanilla extract. Combine the beaten eggs with the butter mixture and mix well. Stir in the melted chocolate.

Fill each tartlet shell with the custard and place on a baking sheet. Bake for about 20 minutes, or until the pastry is golden brown and a knife inserted in the custard comes out clean.

Remove from the oven and cool thoroughly. Gently remove the tartlets from the baking pans just before serving.

NO. **341**          **CITRON CHESS CAKES**

*Makes 12 tartlets*

Prepare the pastry shells, following the recipe for Chess Cakes (No. 339). Make the custard filling following the recipe below.

*Custard*

| | |
|---|---|
| ½ cup unsalted butter | 2 cups candied citron, cut in thin strips |
| 3 cups sugar | |
| 3 eggs, beaten | |

Preheat the oven to 375° F. Cut the butter into small pieces. In a medium saucepan, combine the butter with the sugar and beaten eggs. Cook over low heat, stirring constantly, until the mixture begins to thicken. Remove the pan from the heat. Place a layer of citron in the bottom of each tartlet shell. Spoon the custard on top of the citron. Place the tartlets on a baking sheet. Bake for about 20 minutes, or until the pastry is golden brown and a knife inserted in the custard comes out clean.

Remove from the oven and cool thoroughly. Gently remove the tartlets from the baking pans just before serving.

NO. **342**    COCONUT CHESS CAKES

*Makes 12 tartlets*

Prepare the pastry shells, following the recipe for Chess Cakes (No. 339). Make the custard filling following the recipe below.

## *Custard*

1 cup sugar
⅔ cup water
¾ cup shredded unsweetened
   coconut

¼ cup unsalted butter
4 egg yolks, beaten

Preheat the oven to 375° F. In a medium saucepan, combine the sugar and water. Bring the mixture to a rolling boil, stirring constantly. Continue to boil until the mixture reaches the soft-ball stage (240° F on a candy thermometer, or when a soft ball forms when a little of the mixture is dropped into a glass of cold water). Mix in the coconut and continue to boil for an additional 5 minutes, stirring constantly. Remove the pan from the heat. Add the butter and stir until melted. Beat in the egg yolks, one at a time.

Fill each tartlet shell with custard and place on a baking sheet. Bake for about 20 minutes, or until the pastry is golden brown and a knife inserted in the custard comes out clean.

Remove from the oven and cool thoroughly. Gently remove the tartlets from the baking pans just before serving.

NO. **343**    COLONIAL CHESS CAKES

*Makes 12 tartlets*

Prepare the pastry shells, following the recipe for Chess Cakes (No. 339). Make the custard filling following the recipe below.

## *Custard*

½ cup unsalted butter
½ cup sugar
½ teaspoon nutmeg

⅛ teaspoon salt
4 eggs, beaten

Preheat the oven to 375° F. Melt the butter in the top of a double boiler over boiling water. Add the sugar, nutmeg, salt, and beaten eggs to the melted butter and mix well. Reduce the heat so the water simmers. Cook the custard, stirring constantly, until the mixture begins to thicken.

Fill each tartlet shell with custard and place on a baking sheet.

Bake for about 20 minutes, or until the pastry is golden brown and a knife inserted in the custard comes out clean.

Remove from the oven and cool thoroughly. Gently remove the tartlets from the baking pans just before serving.

NO. **344**                          # CREAM PUFFS
*Makes about 20 cream puffs*

## Pastry Shells

⅓ cup unsalted butter          ¼ teaspoon salt
1 cup water                    1 cup sifted flour
2 tablespoons sugar            4 eggs

## Filling

1 cup heavy cream              ¼ cup blanched almonds,
2 tablespoons superfine sugar      finely chopped
½ teaspoon almond extract

Preheat the oven to 450° F. Lightly grease two large baking sheets with butter or vegetable shortening.

In a large saucepan, combine the butter, water, sugar, and salt. Bring the mixture to a boil over high heat, stirring constantly. Add the flour to the boiling mixture all at once and continue to stir. Reduce the heat to medium, and continue to cook, stirring constantly with a wooden spoon, until the mixture pulls away from the sides of the pan.

Remove the pan from the heat and turn the dough into a large mixing bowl. While the dough is still hot, beat in the eggs, one at a time, mixing well after each addition.

Drop large rounded teaspoonfuls of batter onto the baking sheets, about 2 inches apart. Bake for 20 minutes. Reduce the oven temperature to 325° F and bake for an additional 20 minutes or until the shells are golden brown. Remove from the oven.

After the pastry shells have cooled for 2 to 3 minutes, but are still warm to the touch, use a spatula to transfer them to wire racks to cool completely.

In a large mixing bowl, beat the cream until stiff peaks form. Beat in the sugar and the almond extract. Gently fold in the chopped almonds.

When the pastry shells are completely cool, use a sharp knife to make a slit in the middle of each one. Spoon the whipped cream into a pastry bag with a smooth tip and fill each shell. Transfer to a plate and refrigerate until ready to serve.

NO. 345 ## CHOCOLATE CREAM PUFFS
*Makes about 20 cream puffs*

Prepare the pastry shells, following the recipe for Cream Puffs (No. 344). Make the filling following the recipe below.

### Filling

1 cup heavy cream            1 teaspoon vanilla extract
2 tablespoons superfine sugar

### Icing

8 ounces semi-sweet chocolate

In a large mixing bowl, beat the cream until stiff peaks form. Beat in the sugar and the vanilla extract and set aside.

To make the icing, melt the chocolate in the top of a double boiler over simmering water, stirring frequently. Remove the pan from the heat and set aside.

Using a sharp knife, make a slit in the middle of each cooled pastry shell. Spoon the whipped cream into a pastry bag with a smooth tip and fill each shell. Ice the top of each cream puff with the melted chocolate. Transfer the cream puffs to a plate and refrigerate until ready to serve.

NO. 346 ## MOCHA CREAM PUFFS
*Makes about 20 cream puffs*

Prepare the pastry shells, following the recipe for Cream Puffs (No. 344). Make the filling following the recipe below.

### Filling

1 cup heavy cream            1 teaspoon coffee liqueur
2 tablespoons superfine sugar

### Icing

8 ounces coffee-flavored chocolate

Make the filling. In a large mixing bowl beat the cream until stiff peaks form. Beat in the sugar and the liqueur.

To make the icing, melt the chocolate in the top of a double boiler over simmering water, stirring frequently. Remove the pan from the heat and set aside.

Using a sharp knife, make a slit in the middle of each cooled pastry shell. Spoon the whipped cream into a pastry bag with a smooth tip and fill each shell. Ice the top of each cream puff with melted chocolate. Transfer to a plate and refrigerate until ready to serve.

NO. 347                                        # CRULLERS
*Makes about 24 cookies*

Vegetable oil for deep-fat
   fryer
4 tablespoons unsalted butter
6 tablespoons sugar
4 eggs
½ teaspoon grated orange zest

1 teaspoon baking soda
4 tablespoons milk
2 cups sifted flour
½ teaspoon salt
½ teaspoon nutmeg
Confectioners' sugar

Preheat vegetable oil in a deep-fat fryer to 370° F.

In a small saucepan, melt the butter over very low heat. In a large mixing bowl, combine the melted butter and sugar. Beat in the eggs, one at a time, and mix well. Add the orange zest. Dissolve the baking soda in the milk. Sift the flour with the salt and nutmeg. Beat the flour mixture into the batter, ½ cup at a time, alternating with the milk. Knead to a smooth dough.

On a floured work surface, roll out the dough to a thickness of ¼ inch. Using a sharp knife or pie cutter, cut the dough into 2 × 1-inch strips. Fry until the strips are golden brown. Drain the crullers on absorbent paper towels, then roll them in confectioners' sugar.

NO. 348                                        # FRIED JUMBLES
*Makes about 24 cookies*

Vegetable oil for deep-fat
   fryer
¼ cup unsalted butter
½ cup sugar
1 egg
3 cups sifted flour

1½ teaspoons baking powder
¼ teaspoon salt
½ teaspoon nutmeg
1 teaspoon cinnamon
½ cup milk
Cinnamon sugar

Preheat vegetable oil in a deep-fat fryer to 370° F.

In a large mixing bowl, cream together the butter and sugar. Beat in the egg and mix well. Sift the flour with the baking powder, salt, nutmeg, and cinnamon. Beat the flour mixture into the batter, ½ cup at a time, alternating with the milk as the mixture thickens. Knead into a smooth dough.

Pinch off 2-inch balls of dough. Shape each one into a little ring. Fry the rings until they are golden brown. Drain on absorbent paper towels. Roll each cookie in cinnamon sugar and transfer to a serving plate.

## NO. 349     HOT SYRUP SPONGE COOKIES

*Makes about 24 cookies*

½ cup hot water
1 cup superfine sugar
4 eggs, separated

2 cups sifted cake flour
¼ teaspoon almond extract
Confectioners' sugar

Preheat the oven to 325° F. Lightly grease two sets of madeleine molds with butter.

In a small saucepan, combine the water and sugar. Bring to a boil over medium heat, stirring frequently. Continue boiling until the sugar syrup makes a thread when a spoon is dipped into it. Remove the pan from the heat and set aside.

In a large mixing bowl, beat the egg whites until they form stiff peaks. In a separate bowl, beat the egg yolks until foamy. Gently fold the beaten egg yolks into the egg whites. Gradually fold in the hot syrup. Continue to mix gently until the batter has cooled. Fold in the flour, ½ cup at a time. Stir in the almond extract.

Fill the molds about three-quarters full with the batter. Bake for 18 to 20 minutes, or until the cookies are golden brown. Remove from the oven.

Let the cookies cool completely, then loosen from the molds with a sharp knife. Transfer the finished cookies to a serving plate and dust with confectioners' sugar.

## NO. 350     LADYFINGERS

*Makes about 24 cookies*

2 eggs, separated
2 egg whites
¼ teaspoon cream of tartar
⅔ cup sugar

1 teaspoon vanilla extract
1¼ cups sifted cake flour
½ teaspoon baking powder
⅛ teaspoon salt

Preheat the oven to 325° F. Lightly grease two large baking sheets with butter or vegetable shortening.

In a large mixing bowl, beat the 4 egg whites with the cream of tartar until the mixture begins to hold soft peaks. Gradually beat in ⅓ cup of the sugar. Continue to beat until the mixture is stiff and glossy. Beat in the vanilla extract.

In a separate bowl, beat the 2 egg yolks until foamy. Beat in the remaining sugar. Sift the flour with the baking powder and salt. Using a rubber spatula, gently fold the egg yolks into the egg white mixture. Lightly fold in the flour.

Spoon the batter into a pastry bag with a fluted tip, and pipe out "fingers," 3 inches long and 1 inch wide, onto the baking sheets. Bake for 18 to 20 minutes, or until the cookies are golden brown. Remove from the oven.

After the cookies have cooled for 2 to 3 minutes, but are still warm to the touch, use a spatula to transfer them to wire racks to cool completely.

## NO. 351     CHOCOLATE LADYFINGERS

*Makes about 24 cookies*

2 ounces (2 squares)
    unsweetened baking
    chocolate
2 eggs, separated
2 egg whites
¼ teaspoon cream of tartar

¾ cup sugar
1 teaspoon vanilla extract
1¼ cups sifted cake flour
½ teaspoon baking powder
⅛ teaspoon salt

Preheat the oven to 325° F. Lightly grease two large baking sheets with butter or vegetable shortening.

Melt the chocolate in the top of a double boiler over simmering water, stirring frequently. Remove the pan from the heat and set aside.

In a large mixing bowl, beat the 4 egg whites with the cream of tartar until the mixture begins to hold soft peaks. Gradually beat in ¼ cup of the sugar. Continue to beat until the mixture is stiff and glossy. Beat in the vanilla extract.

In a separate bowl, beat the 2 egg yolks until foamy. Beat in the remaining sugar, then mix in the melted chocolate. Sift the flour with the baking powder and salt. Using a rubber spatula, gently fold the eggs yolks into the egg white mixture. Lightly fold in the flour.

Spoon the batter into a pastry bag with a fluted tip, and pipe out "fingers," 3 inches long and 1 inch wide, onto the baking sheets. Bake for 18 to 20 minutes, or until the cookies are golden brown. Remove from the oven.

After the cookies have cooled for 2 to 3 minutes, but are still warm to the touch, use a spatula to transfer them to wire racks to cool completely.

NO. **352**

# MADELEINES

*Makes about 24 cookies*

| | |
|---|---|
| ¾ cup unsalted butter | ⅔ cup sugar |
| 2 eggs, at room temperature | ½ teaspoon vanilla extract |
| ⅛ teaspoon salt | 1 cup sifted cake flour |

Preheat the oven to 400° F. Butter and flour two sets of madeleine molds.

Melt the butter in a small saucepan over very low heat. Remove the pan from the heat and set aside to cool.

In a large mixing bowl, beat the eggs with the salt. Gradually beat in the sugar. Continue to beat until the batter is very stiff. Beat in the vanilla extract. Sift ¼ cup of the flour over the batter and gently fold in. Repeat with the remaining flour, ¼ cup at a time. Add the melted butter to the batter, 1 tablespoon at a time, folding it in as quickly as possible.

Fill the molds about three-quarters full. Place in the oven immediately. Bake for about 10 minutes, or until the cookies are golden brown. Remove from the oven.

Cool thoroughly, then loosen the cookies from the molds with a sharp kitchen knife. Transfer to a serving plate.

# Gaufrettes

A gaufrette, also known as a krumkake, is a type of rolled cookie prepared with a Swedish cookie iron or a krumkake iron, available in food specialty stores. A krumkake iron fits over a standard 7-inch stove burner. It works very much like a waffle iron, producing a thin pancake that is shaped into the finished cookie while it is still piping hot. Like a waffle iron, a seasoned krumkake iron should never be washed. Wipe any remaining batter off with a damp cloth. Note that gaufrette batter, unlike the batter of most uncooked cookies, is not particularly tasty.

Besides the usual rolled gaufrettes, these cookies can be made in the shape of a fortune cookie. This is an entertaining idea for a party, particularly if you create your own fortunes. To make a gaufrette fortune cookie, take a cookie fresh from the iron and place the fortune in the middle of the pancake. Fold it in half, and holding one end in each hand, press the middle down on a thin, blunt edge such as that of a coffee can. Transfer the fortune cookie to a muffin tin to hold the shape until it cools.

## NO. 353     BROWN SUGAR WALNUT GAUFRETTES

*Makes about 30 gaufrettes*

| | |
|---|---|
| 1 egg plus 1 egg yolk | 2 teaspoons vanilla extract |
| ⅓ cup sugar | 1⅓ cups sifted cake flour |
| ⅓ cup dark brown sugar, firmly packed | ½ teaspoon baking soda |
| | ½ teaspoon salt |
| 3 tablespoons powdered milk | ½ cup ground walnuts |
| ½ cup water | ¼ cup vegetable oil |

Heat the krumkake iron over moderate heat while preparing the batter; it should be ready to use when the batter is made.

In a large mixing bowl, beat the egg and the egg yolk with the sugars until the mixture is creamy. Combine the powdered milk, water, and vanilla extract, and add to the batter mixture. Sift the flour with the baking soda and salt and add to the batter. Mix well. Stir in the ground walnuts and vegetable oil. The batter should be smooth and glossy.

Test the temperature of the krumkake iron by cooking one gaufrette over moderate heat. Pour 1 tablespoon of batter into the center of the iron, close, and cook for 2 minutes on each side. The batter should form a firm pancake that is lightly browned on both sides. If the iron is too hot, the pancake will burn. If it is not hot enough, the pancake will take longer to cook than the time specified above. Adjust the heat as necessary. Open the iron and, very quickly, remove the pancake by running a sharp knife underneath it. While it is still very hot, roll the pancake into a curl around the handle of a wooden spoon. Place the gaufrette in a muffin tin to hold its shape until it cools. Continue to make gaufrettes, one at a time, until all the batter is used.

## NO. 354     CHOCOLATE GAUFRETTES

*Makes about 30 gaufrettes*

2 ounces (2 squares) unsweetened baking chocolate
1 egg plus 1 egg yolk
⅔ cup sugar
3 tablespoons powdered milk

½ cup strong black coffee
2 teaspoons vanilla extract
1⅓ cups sifted cake flour
½ teaspoon salt
3 tablespoons vegetable oil

Heat the krumkake iron over moderate heat while preparing the batter; it should be ready to use when the batter is made.

Melt the chocolate in the top of a double boiler over simmering water, stirring frequently. Remove the pan from the heat and set aside.

In a large mixing bowl, beat the egg and the egg yolk with the sugar until the mixture is creamy. In another bowl, combine the powdered milk, coffee, and vanilla extract. Add to the sugar mixture. Beat in the melted chocolate. Sift the flour with the salt and mix into the batter. Stir in the vegetable oil. The batter should be smooth and glossy.

Test the temperature of the krumkake iron by cooking one gaufrette over moderate heat. Pour 1 tablespoon of batter into the center of the iron, close, and cook for 2 minutes on each side. The batter should form a firm pancake that is lightly browned on both sides. If the iron is too hot, the pancake will burn. If it is not hot enough, the pancake will take longer to cook than the time specified above. Adjust the heat as necessary. Open the iron and, very quickly, remove the pancake by running a sharp knife underneath it. While it is still very hot, roll the pancake into a curl around the handle of a wooden spoon. Place the gaufrette in a muffin tin to hold its shape until it cools. Continue to make gaufrettes, one at a time, until all the batter is used.

NO. **355**                      # CHOCOLATE MINT
                                   # GAUFRETTES
                                 *Makes about 30 gaufrettes*

2 ounces (2 squares)              ½ teaspoon vanilla extract
   unsweetened baking             1 teaspoon peppermint
   chocolate                         flavoring
1 egg plus 1 egg yolk             1¼ cups sifted cake flour
⅔ cup sugar                       ½ teaspoon salt
3 tablespoons powdered milk       ¼ cup vegetable oil
½ cup water

Heat the krumkake iron over moderate heat while preparing the batter; it should be ready to use when the batter is made.

Melt the chocolate in the top of a double boiler over simmering water, stirring frequently. Remove the pan from the heat and set aside.

In a large mixing bowl, beat the egg and the egg yolk with the sugar until the mixture is creamy. In another bowl, combine the powdered milk, water, vanilla extract, and peppermint flavoring. Add to the sugar mixture. Beat in the melted chocolate. Sift the flour with the salt and mix into the batter. Stir in the vegetable oil. The batter should be smooth and glossy.

Test the temperature of the krumkake iron by cooking one gaufrette over moderate heat. Pour 1 tablespoon of batter into the center of the iron, close, and cook for 2 minutes on each side. The batter should form a firm pancake that is lightly browned on both sides. If the iron is too hot, the pancake will burn. If it is not hot enough, the pancake will take longer to cook than the time specified above. Adjust the heat as necessary. Open the iron and, very quickly, remove the pancake by running a sharp knife underneath it. While it is still very hot, roll the pancake into a curl around the handle of a wooden spoon. Place the gaufrette in a muffin tin to hold its shape until it cools. Continue to make gaufrettes, one at a time, until all the batter is used.

NO. **356**

# CHOCOLATE RIPPLE GAUFRETTES

*Makes about 30 gaufrettes*

1 egg plus 1 egg yolk
⅔ cup sugar
3 tablespoons powdered milk
½ cup water
2 teaspoons vanilla extract

1 ounce (1 square) semi-sweet baking chocolate, grated
1½ cups sifted cake flour
½ teaspoon salt
3 tablespoons vegetable oil

Heat the krumkake iron over moderate heat while preparing the batter; it should be ready to use when the batter is made.

In a large mixing bowl, beat the egg and the egg yolk with the sugar until the mixture is creamy. Combine the powdered milk, water, and vanilla extract. Add to the sugar mixture. Beat in the grated chocolate. Sift the flour with the salt and mix into the batter. Stir in the vegetable oil. The batter should be smooth and glossy.

Test the temperature of the krumkake iron by cooking one gaufrette over moderate heat. Pour 1 tablespoon of batter into the center of the iron, close, and cook for 2 minutes on each side. The batter should form a firm pancake that is lightly browned on both sides. If the iron is too hot, the pancake will burn. If it is not hot enough, the pancake will take longer to cook than the time specified above. Adjust the heat as necessary. Open the iron and, very quickly, remove the pancake by running a sharp knife underneath it. While it is still very hot, roll the pancake into a curl around the handle of a wooden spoon. Place the gaufrette in a muffin tin to hold its shape until it cools. Continue to make gaufrettes, one at a time, until all the batter is used.

NO. **357**

# HAZELNUT GAUFRETTES

*Makes about 30 gaufrettes*

1 egg plus 1 egg yolk
⅔ cup sugar
3 tablespoons powdered milk
½ cup water
1 teaspoon vanilla extract

1½ cups sifted cake flour
½ teaspoon baking soda
½ teaspoon salt
½ cup ground hazelnuts
3 tablespoons vegetable oil

Heat the krumkake iron over moderate heat while preparing the batter; it should be ready to use when the batter is made.

In a large mixing bowl, beat the egg and the egg yolk with the sugar until the mixture is creamy. Combine the powdered milk, water, and vanilla extract. Add to the sugar mixture. Sift the flour with the baking soda and salt. Mix into the batter. Stir in the ground hazelnuts and vegetable oil. The batter should be smooth and glossy.

Test the temperature of the krumkake iron by cooking one gaufrette over moderate heat. Pour 1 tablespoon of batter into the center of the iron, close, and cook for 2 minutes on each side. The batter should form a firm pancake that is lightly browned on both sides. If the iron is too hot, the pancake will burn. If it is not hot enough, the pancake will take longer to cook than the time specified above. Adjust the heat as necessary. Open the iron and, very quickly, remove the pancake by running a sharp knife underneath it. While it is still very hot, roll the pancake into a curl around the handle of a wooden spoon. Place the gaufrette in a muffin tin to hold its shape until it cools. Continue to make gaufrettes, one at a time, until all the batter is used.

NO. **358**

# ORANGE CHOCOLATE GAUFRETTES

*Makes about 30 gaufrettes*

1 egg plus 1 egg yolk
¾ cup sugar
3 tablespoons powdered milk
½ cup water
½ teaspoon vanilla extract
½ teaspoon orange extract

1½ cups sifted cake flour
½ teaspoon salt
¼ cup finely chopped candied
   orange peel, dusted with
   flour
¼ cup vegetable oil

## Icing

8 ounces orange-flavored
   chocolate

1 tablespoon unsalted butter

Heat the krumkake iron over moderate heat while preparing the batter; it should be ready to use when the batter is made.

In a large mixing bowl, beat the egg and the egg yolk with the sugar until the mixture is creamy. Combine the powdered milk, water, vanilla extract, and orange extract. Add to the sugar mixture. Sift the flour with the salt, then mix into the batter. Stir in the chopped candied orange peel and the vegetable oil. The batter should be smooth and glossy.

Test the temperature of the krumkake iron by cooking one gaufrette over moderate heat. Pour 1 tablespoon of batter into the center of the iron, close, and cook for 2 minutes on each side. The batter should form a firm pancake that is lightly browned on both sides. If the iron is too hot, the pancake will burn. If it is not hot enough, the pancake will take longer to cook than the time specified above. Adjust the heat as necessary. Open the iron and, very quickly, remove the pancake by running a sharp knife underneath it. While it is still very hot, roll the pancake into a curl around the handle of a wooden spoon. Place the gaufrette in a muffin tin to hold its shape until it cools. Continue to make gaufrettes, one at a time, until all the batter is used.

Make the icing. Melt the chocolate with the butter in the top of a double boiler over simmering water, stirring frequently. Remove the pan from the heat and set aside. Dip half of each cookie curl (or the tips of each fortune cookie) into the melted chocolate. Place the iced gaufrettes on waxed paper until the chocolate sets. Transfer to a serving plate.

## NO. 359 SPICE GAUFRETTES

*Makes about 30 gaufrettes*

1 egg plus 1 egg yolk
⅔ cup sugar
3 tablespoons powdered milk
½ cup water
1 teaspoon vanilla extract
1 teaspoon lemon extract
1½ cups sifted cake flour

1 teaspoon cinnamon
½ teaspoon ground cloves
½ teaspoon nutmeg
½ teaspoon ground ginger
½ teaspoon salt
3 tablespoons vegetable oil

Heat the krumkake iron over moderate heat while preparing the batter; it should be ready to use when the batter is made.

In a large mixing bowl, beat the egg and the egg yolk with the sugar until the mixture is creamy. Combine the powdered milk, water, vanilla extract, and lemon extract. Add to the sugar mixture. Sift the flour with the cinnamon, cloves, nutmeg, ginger, and salt. Mix into the batter. Stir in the vegetable oil. The batter should be smooth and glossy.

Test the temperature of the krumkake iron by cooking one gaufrette over moderate heat. Pour 1 tablespoon of batter into the center of the iron, close, and cook for 2 minutes on each side. The batter should form a firm pancake that is lightly browned on both sides. If the iron is too hot, the pancake will burn. If it is not hot enough, the pancake will take longer to cook than the time specified above. Adjust the heat as necessary. Open the iron and, very quickly, remove the pancake by running a sharp knife underneath it. While it is still very hot, roll the pancake into a curl around the handle of a wooden spoon. Place the gaufrette in a muffin tin to hold its shape until it cools. Continue to make gaufrettes, one at a time, until all the batter is used.

NO. **360**                    # VANILLA GAUFRETTES
*Makes about 30 gaufrettes*

1 egg plus 1 egg yolk
⅔ cup sugar
3 tablespoons powdered milk
½ cup water

1 teaspoon vanilla extract
1½ cups sifted cake flour
½ teaspoon salt
¼ cup vegetable oil

Heat the krumkake iron over moderate heat while preparing the batter; it should be ready to use when the batter is made.

In a large mixing bowl, beat the egg and the egg yolk with the sugar until the mixture is creamy. Combine the powdered milk, water, and vanilla extract. Add to the sugar mixture. Sift the flour with the salt, then mix into the batter. Stir in the vegetable oil. The batter should be smooth and glossy.

Test the temperature of the krumkake iron by cooking one gaufrette over moderate heat. Pour 1 tablespoon of batter into the center of the iron, close, and cook for 2 minutes on each side. The batter should form a firm pancake that is lightly browned on both sides. If the iron is too hot, the pancake will burn. If it is not hot enough, the pancake will take longer to cook than the time specified above. Adjust the heat as necessary. Open the iron and, very quickly, remove the pancake by running a sharp knife underneath it. While it is still very hot, roll the pancake into a curl around the handle of a wooden spoon. Place the gaufrette in a muffin tin to hold its shape until it cools. Continue to make gaufrettes, one at a time, until all the batter is used.

# Sugar-Free Cookies

These spicy applesauce pecan bars, apricot oatmeal cookies, and banana walnut bars, among others, are all naturally sweetened with fruit and fruit juice. Not everyone can eat sugar, and for diabetics, honey and sugar substitutes have the same dangerous chemistry as sugar. Since these tempting recipes use only fruit and fruit juices as sweeteners, they can be eaten, in small amounts, by almost everyone.

NO. 361

## SUGAR-FREE APPLESAUCE PECAN SQUARES

*Makes about 24 bars*

½ cup unsalted butter, softened
2 eggs
1 teaspoon vanilla extract
4 cups sifted flour
2 teaspoons baking soda
2 teaspoons cinnamon

1 teaspoon allspice
¼ teaspoon ground cloves
½ teaspoon mace
1 cup unsweetened applesauce
1½ cups pecans, coarsely chopped

Preheat the oven to 375° F. Thoroughly butter the bottom and sides of a 13 × 9 × 2 inch baking pan.

Cream the butter in a large mixing bowl. Beat in the eggs, one at a time. Add the vanilla extract. Sift the flour with the baking soda, cinnamon, allspice, cloves, and mace. Add the flour mixture to the batter, ½ cup at a time, alternating with the applesauce. Mix the chopped pecans into the batter.

Pour the batter into the baking pan and smooth the surface with a rubber spatula. Bake for 35 to 40 minutes, or until a toothpick inserted in the center comes out clean. Remove from the oven.

Allow the cake to cool completely, then cut it into 2-inch bars. Remove the bars from the pan with a spatula and transfer to a serving plate.

NO. **362**                    **SUGAR-FREE APRICOT**
                              **OATMEAL COOKIES**

*Makes about 36 cookies*

⅓ cup unsalted butter,          1 teaspoon cinnamon
   softened                     ½ teaspoon salt
1 egg                           1 cup quick-cooking oatmeal
2 teaspoons grated lemon zest   ½ cup pecans, coarsely
2 tablespoons apple juice          chopped
1 cup sifted flour              1 cup coarsely chopped dried
½ teaspoon baking soda             apricots

Preheat the oven to 400° F. Lightly grease two large baking sheets
with butter or vegetable shortening.

Cream the butter in a large mixing bowl. Add the egg and mix
well. Stir in the lemon zest and apple juice. Sift the flour with the
baking soda, cinnamon, and salt. Add half the flour to the butter
mixture and stir until thoroughly blended. Mix in the oatmeal. Lightly
stir in the remaining flour. Add the chopped pecans and apricots.
Mix well.

Drop rounded teaspoonfuls of batter onto the baking sheets, about
2 inches apart. Bake for 10 to 12 minutes, or until the cookies have
browned around the edges. Remove from the oven.

After the cookies have cooled for 2 to 3 minutes, but are still
warm to the touch, use a spatula to transfer them to wire racks to
cool completely.

NO. **363**        **SUGAR-FREE BANANA WALNUT**
                                          **BARS**

*Makes about 24 bars*

½ cup unsalted butter,          3 orange sections, seeded and
   softened                        finely chopped
1 teaspoon orange juice         1¾ cups sifted flour
2 teaspoons grated orange       1 teaspoon baking soda
   zest                         ¼ teaspoon salt
2 eggs                          2 teaspoons cinnamon
1 tablespoon plain yogurt       ½ cup walnuts, coarsely
1½ cups mashed ripe bananas        chopped
   (about 3 large bananas)

Preheat the oven to 350° F. Thoroughly butter the bottom and sides
of a 13 × 9 × 2 inch baking pan.

In a large mixing bowl, cream the butter together with the orange juice and orange zest. Beat in the eggs, one at a time. Stir in the yogurt, mashed bananas, and chopped orange. Mix well. Sift the flour with the baking soda, salt, and cinnamon. Add the flour mixture to the batter, ½ cup at a time. Mix well after each addition. Stir in the chopped walnuts.

Pour the batter into the baking pan and smooth the surface with a rubber spatula. Bake for 35 to 40 minutes, or until a toothpick inserted in the center comes out clean. Remove from the oven.

Allow the cake to cool completely, then cut it into 2-inch bars. Remove the bars from the pan with a spatula and transfer to a serving plate.

## NO. 364 SUGAR-FREE BLUEBERRY WALNUT OATMEAL BARS

*Makes about 24 bars*

⅓ cup unsalted butter, softened
1 egg
2 teaspoons grated orange zest
2 tablespoons orange juice
1 cup sifted flour
½ teaspoon baking soda

1 teaspoon allspice
½ teaspoon salt
1 cup quick-cooking oatmeal
¾ cup walnuts, coarsely chopped
2 cups fresh or frozen blueberries

Preheat the oven to 350° F. Thoroughly butter the bottom and sides of a 13 × 9 × 2 inch baking pan.

Cream the butter in a large mixing bowl. Beat in the egg and mix well. Stir in the orange zest and orange juice. Sift the flour with the baking soda, allspice, and salt. Add half the flour to the butter mixture and stir until thoroughly blended. Mix in the oatmeal, then lightly stir in the remaining flour. Add the chopped walnuts and blueberries. Mix well.

Pour the batter into the baking pan and smooth the surface with a rubber spatula. Bake for about 30 minutes, or until a toothpick inserted in the center comes out clean. Remove from the oven.

Allow the cake to cool completely, then cut it into 2-inch bars. Remove the bars from the pan with a spatula and transfer to a serving plate.

NO. **365**          **SUGAR-FREE STRAWBERRY**
**BARS**

*Makes about 24 bars*

½ cup unsalted butter,
   softened
2 teaspoons grated lemon zest
2 eggs
1 tablespoon plain yogurt
1½ cups sliced fresh or frozen
   strawberries

3 orange sections, seeded and
   finely chopped
1¾ cups sifted flour
1 teaspoon baking soda
¼ teaspoon salt
2 teaspoons cinnamon
½ cup pecans, coarsely
   chopped

Preheat the oven to 350° F. Thoroughly butter the bottom and sides of a 13 × 9 × 2 inch baking pan.

In a large mixing bowl, cream the butter together with the lemon zest. Beat in the eggs, one at a time. Stir in the yogurt, strawberries, and orange. Mix well. Sift the flour with the baking soda, salt, and cinnamon. Add the flour mixture to the batter, ½ cup at a time. Mix well after each addition. Stir in the chopped pecans.

Pour the batter into the baking pan and smooth the surface with a rubber spatula. Bake for about 35 minutes, or until a toothpick inserted in the center comes out clean. Remove from the oven.

Allow the cake to cool completely, then cut it into 2-inch bars. Remove the bars from the pan with a spatula and transfer to a serving plate.

# INDEX